This study shows how the trinitarian theology of Hans Urs von Balthasar opens up an approach to the controverted question of God's immutability and impassibility which succeeds in respecting both the transcendence and immanence of God. In the course of outlining the distinctiveness of von Balthasar's treatment of this question, Dr O'Hanlon introduces the reader to the Christology, eschatology, and fundamental themes of one of the major Roman Catholic theologians of this century, who is still relatively little known in the English-speaking world.

The immutability of God
in the theology of Hans Urs von Balthasar

The immutability of God in the theology of Hans Urs von Balthasar

GERARD F. O'HANLON, S.J.

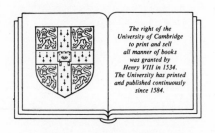

The right of the
University of Cambridge
to print and sell
all manner of books
was granted by
Henry VIII in 1534.
The University has printed
and published continuously
since 1584.

Cambridge University Press

Cambridge

New York   Port Chester

Melbourne   Sydney

Published by the Press Syndicate of the University of Cambridge
The Pitt Building, Trumpington Street, Cambridge CB2 1RP
40 West 20th Street, New York, NY 10011, USA
10 Stamford Road, Oakleigh, Melbourne 3166, Australia

First published 1990

Printed in Great Britain at the University Press, Cambridge

British Library cataloguing in publication data

O'Hanlon, Gerard F. (Gerard Francis), 1947–
The immutability of God in the theology of Hans Urs von
Balthasar.
1. Christian doctrine. God. Immutability. Christian
doctrine of immutability of God. Theories of Balthasar,
Hans Urs von, 1905–
1. Title
231.4

Library of Congress cataloguing in publication data

O'Hanlon, Gerard F.
The immutability of God in the theology of Hans Urs von Balthasar/
Gerard F. O'Hanlon.
Includes bibliographical references.
ISBN 0 521 36649 6
1. Balthasar, Hans Urs von, 1905– – contributions in doctrine of
immutablity of God.   2. God – immutability – history of
doctrines – 20th century.   1. Title.
BT153.I47043   1990
231.4 – dc20   89–78170 CIP

ISBN 0 521 36649 6 hardback

To my mother and father

Contents

Acknowledgements

It is a great pleasure to thank the many people who helped in different ways to make this work possible. Heartfelt thanks in particular to Professor John Thompson; to Werner Löser, S.J.; to Fiona, Eileen, Randal and Brian; to the staff at the libraries in Queen's University and Union Theological in Belfast, Sankt Georgen in Frankfurt and the Milltown Institute in Dublin; to Des O'Grady, Bill Matthews and Hilary Mooney; to Noel, Karen and family; to staff and students at the Milltown Institute of Theology and Philosophy; to the late Professor James Haire and Fr John Hyde, S.J.; to Alex Wright of Cambridge University Press. To these and to so many other friends and colleagues, too numerous to mention by name, in Belfast, Frankfurt, Dublin and elsewhere, I am most sincerely grateful.

Abbreviations

See Bibliography for fuller detail.

A   Abbreviations of works by Hans Urs von Balthasar

Where a translation is listed in the bibliography references in the notes are to the translated version of the particular text, except in the case of H, II/1, II/2 and III/1 where reference is to the original version.

'Allmacht'	'Gottes Allmacht' (1984)
Apokalypse	*Apokalypse der deutschen Seele* (1937–9)
Au Cœur	*Au Cœur du Mystère rédempteur* (1980)
Cordula	*Cordula oder der Ernstfall* (1966)
'Crucifixus'	'Crucifixus etiam pro nobis' (1980)
CS	*Christlicher Stand* (1977)
'Der sich'	'Der sich für mich hingegeben hat' (Gal. 2, 20) (1980)
Die Wahrheit	*Die Wahrheit ist symphonisch* (1972)
'Du Krönst'	'Du Krönst das Jahr mit Deiner Huld', Psalm 65, 12 (1982)
Einfaltungen	*Einfaltungen* (1969)
Einheit	*Die Einheit der theologischen Tugenden* (1984)
Epilog	*Epilog* (1987)
'Geist'	'Geist und Feuer' (1976)
GF	*Das Ganze im Fragment* (1963)
GL	*Glaubhaft ist nur Liebe* (1963)
H, I	*Herrlichkeit*, Bd. I (1969)
H, II/1	*Herrlichkeit*, Bd. II/1 (1969)
H, II/2	*Herrlichkeit*, Bd. II/2 (1969)
HAB	*Herrlichkeit*, Bd. III/2, 1 Teil (1967)
HC	*Homo creatus est* (1986)
HNB	*Herrlichkeit*, Bd. III/2, 2 Teil (1969)
HRM	*Herrlichkeit*, Bd. III/1 (1965)

'Hoffnung'	'Zu einer christlichen Theologie der Hoffnung' (1981)
HW	*Das Herz der Welt* (1945)
Il filo	*Il filo di Arianna attraverso la mia opera* (1980)
In Retrospect	*Rechenschaft 1965* (1965)
K. Barth	*Karl Barth* (1951)
Kennt uns Jesus	*Kennt uns Jesus – Kennen wir ihn?* (1980)
KT	*Katholisch* (1975)
Kosmische	*Kosmische Liturgie* (1961)
M. Buber	*Einsame Zwiesprache. Martin Buber und das Christentum* (1958)
MP	*Mysterium pascale* (1969–70)
NK	*Neue Klarstellungen* (1979)
Parole	*Parole et Mystère chez Origène* (1957)
Pneuma	*Pneuma und Institution* (1974)
Présence	*Présence et Pensée* (1942)
SC	*Spiritus creator* (1967)
SV	*Sponsa verbi* (1960)
TD, I	*Theodramatik*, Bd. I (1973)
TD, II/I	*Theodramatik*, Bd. II/I (1976)
TD, II/2	*Theodramatik*, Bd. II/2 (1978)
TD, III	*Theodramatik*, Bd. III (1980)
TD, IV	*Theodramatik*, Bd. IV (1983)
TG	*Theologie der Geschichte* (1959)
Thérèse	*Thérèse von Lisieux* (1950)
TL, I	*Theologik*, Bd. I (1985)
TL, II	*Theologik*, Bd. II (1985)
TL, III	*Theologik*, Bd. III (1987)
VC[1]	*Verbum caro* (1964 tr)
VC[2]	*Verbum caro* (1985 tr.)
'Warum'	'Warum ich noch ein Christ bin?' (1971)
Weihnacht	*Weihnacht und Anbetung* (1977)
Weizenkorn	*Das Weizenkorn* (1944)

B   Other abbreviations

IKaZ	*Internationale Katholische Zeitschrift – Communio*
ITQ	*Irish Theological Quarterly*
MTZ	*Münchner Theologische Zeitschrift*

NT	New Testament
NRTh	*Nouvelle Revue Théologique*
OT	Old Testament
SJT	*Scottish Journal of Theology*
ST	*Summa Theologica*
TS	*Theological Studies*
ZfKT	*Zeitschrift für Katholische Theologie*

Introduction

The question of God's immutability in theology in general

It has been an axiom almost right from the beginning of Christian theology that God is immutable, unchanging and unchangeable.[1] And neither can God suffer: he is impassible. There was undoubtedly considerable philosophical influence contributing to the process by which this theological axiom was first established and then maintained – to be God is to be absolute and perfect, admitting of neither increase nor diminution in being, and is in contrast to the creaturely characteristic of becoming. However it was neither established nor maintained without embarrassment and difficulty. Did not the OT seem to portray a God of deep feeling, who reacted and responded to men and women, in particular to the specially chosen covenant partner Israel? What of the NT evidence that Jesus is both man and God, that he suffered and died – is God not affected? And – to foreshorten a long list of possible objections which were in fact put to this established position – what of the very deep instinct of the Christian faithful which assured them that they were in relationship with God, were loved deeply by him, and, so, affected him?

Nonetheless, despite the difficulties and the occasional defection down through the centuries, the mainstream of theological opinion has been remarkably consistent in its assertion of the axiom of God's immutability. The present-day theological enquiry into this whole question is a radical attempt to reassess the validity of the classical position. Many tendencies have merged to issue in such a radical enquiry. The notion of history is central to the modern understanding of the human sciences. The assimilation of this notion by Christianity into the manner of interpreting scriptural and other theological texts, and of grasping the developing relationship between God and his people, led quite naturally from talk of the God of history to the more problematic notion of the history of God. Within an evolutionary world framework the notion of change assumed a positive connotation which it did not have in the cyclic world view of Greek philosophy, within which the axiom of divine immutability had become established. Now mutability could more easily be seen as a perfection, and so its application to God seemed less objectionable. In the jargon of our time – which yet expresses, if at times too crudely, a real truth – the context was dynamic and not static, and this seemed to apply not just to the process of obtaining truth but also to the content itself. A related tendency was the anti-metaphysical, or at least de-hellenisation, movement within Christianity in this century, with its insistence on a return to the more basic Biblical origins of Christianity: the immutability axiom was especially vulnerable to this thrust. And even where Christianity retained its dialogue with philosophy the influence of Hegel in the last century and now, especially in North America, of the Process school meant that theologians began to call more into question the old assumption of divine immutability.

Of course the tradition had not been purely monolithic on this matter, and particularly in the new theological climate of today theologians began to notice cracks which had hitherto been missed or glossed over. One knew about Scotus Eriugena, Eckhart and the Kenoticists of the seventeenth and nineteenth centuries, but these had been comparatively easy to dismiss as mavericks. But what of Origen? Luther? It was at the turn of this century that the question really began to surface: spurred on by the late nineteenth-century works of the Reformed theologians Dorner and Cremer, the Christian theological community in this century, and increasingly in the last thirty years or so, has had to rethink its position on the immutability of God. It is too early yet to hail the achievement of a consensus on this issue. Nonetheless enough has been written to make it clear that the attempt to modify the classical axiom is no mere theological fad. The names of Karl Barth, Karl Rahner and Hans Urs von Balthasar, all associated with this attempt, bear eloquent testimony to this, as to the inter-confessional nature of the enterprise. In fact the whole movement is catholic in other senses too, bringing together not just Protestants and Roman Catholics but also those usually seen as progressives, conservatives and moderates, and not confining itself to the European theological world but including contributions from North America, Latin America and Asia as well.[2]

At first blush, it is true, the issue of whether God is immutable or not may appear somewhat recondite. After all, how are we to know such intimate details about the being of God who is a mystery, and, really, would it make any difference if we did know? But on closer examination one begins to appreciate some of the passion and excitement with which theologians discuss this question. If God is our ultimate source of concern it is important that we have an image of him that is as correct as possible, without of course reducing the mystery or exceeding the limits imposed by the divine self-revelation. And one begins to see that more than just our image of God is involved: Christ and his role, creation, the identity, history and end of humankind, including its socio-political dimensions, the Church and its role – all these are part of this issue. The repercussions, then, are vast. They include some possible implications for the nature and development of theological enquiry and truth; if, despite the strong tradition, the axiom of divine immutability need not be considered as part of the Church's solemn teaching as such,[3] nonetheless how can a change in this important teaching be understood as true development and not as contradiction, and thus how can we avoid undermining church teaching in general? Besides, is there not a real danger here of losing something of value, of reducing God to our human image of him – might not the classical Christian position that to be God means to be immutable be the only correct one? The hope is that the tension between this classical position and modern tendencies might be a constructive one and that, in the words of the Roman Catholic International Theological Commission, which reported on this whole area, 'contemporary problems and classical solutions can clarify and enrich each other in productive dialogue'.[4] If this happens then there would be an enrichment both of our image of God and of our understanding of how we should talk about God at all – how we should do theology, in other words.[5]

Hans Urs von Balthasar

Hans Urs von Balthasar is widely recognised as one of the major theological figures of our time, and by now there exists an ample body of literature describing his life and works in general, as well as focusing on central and other specific areas of his thought.[6] Born in Lucerne in 1905, he studied philosophy and German literature in Munich, Vienna, Berlin and Zurich before joining the Society of Jesus in 1929. After studies at Pullach and Fourvière-Lyon, during which he came under the influence of Erich Przywara and Henri de Lubac, he worked as a priest for a brief time in Munich with the *Stimmen der Zeit* periodical, and then as student chaplain in Basle from 1940–8. There he came into contact with Karl Barth, and there too he received Adrienne von Speyr into the Roman Catholic Church. Through his association with von Speyr he became convinced of his vocation to establish a secular institute, and accordingly had to make the difficult decision to leave the Jesuits in 1950. He then lived in Basle as a secular priest, active mainly as a writer, translator, editor (he founded the publishing house Johannes Verlag, Einsiedeln) and guide to the secular institute there. He was not invited to the Second Vatican Council; however, from the second half of the 1960s onwards his major theological stature became more and more widely acknowledged. This was helped by his appointment to the Papal International Theological Commission in 1969, the co-founding of the review *Internationale Katholische Zeitschrift – Communio* in 1972, and by the many honorary degrees and citations which he was awarded by universities and institutes in different parts of the world. It was due mainly, however, to the vast literary output of amazing range and diversity which he produced over the years; the non-availability of much of this in translation has meant that he is still comparatively unknown in the English-speaking world.[7] Von Balthasar died in June 1988, three days before his investiture as a Cardinal by Pope John-Paul II.

These are some of the rather bare facts; behind them lies the life story of a very remarkable person whom de Lubac has described as 'perhaps the most cultivated (person) of his time. If there is a Christian culture, then here it is!'[8] He escapes conventional classification: a theologian who never taught in a university or seminary, who himself regarded his activity as a writer as secondary to his task of helping the renewal of the Church through the formation of new communities, and who in his writing drew on such diverse sources as classical antiquity, the European literary tradition, Western philosophy, the history of religions, music (he was himself an accomplished pianist),[9] biblical and Patristic theology, the medievals, spiritual writers, and the great Christian theologians of all ages. From all these sources he created an overall theological vision which is of a very distinctive kind and within which his particular contribution to the theology of the divine immutability is located.

Balthasar brings impressive credentials to the project of making a contribution to the theology of divine immutability, a theology which demands both knowledge of and respect for the tradition as well as a certain openness to new ways of interpreting it. He was a respected partner in dialogue with Protestant theologians and was always keen to acknowledge his own great debt to Karl Barth.[10] He himself was a Patristic scholar of great learning and originality, and he succeeded in retrieving and reinterpreting some of the great Patristic truths and authors.[11] Concerned with systematic thelogy, in debate with modern thought, and part of the renewal within the Roman Catholic Church which led up to the Second Vatican Council and which rejected the arid neo-Thomism of the day, he nonetheless warned repeatedly, after the Council, of the dangers inherent in a kind of openness to the world and progress which would rob the salt of Christianity of its own unique flavour.[12] This led him to adopt a conservative stance on several issues of church discipline, even though throughout his life and in his overall theological stance he showed himself to be no respecter of labels so that he is difficult to classify in the conventional terms of 'left' or 'right'.[13] He was certainly no slavish proponent of orthodoxy and had a great ability to reinterpret in an original way the tradition he knew so well. He was a member of the International Theological Commission, whose report on this issue we have already cited.

The question of God's immutability in the theology of Balthasar

There is little explicit treatment of the question of God's immutability in Balthasar's work before the 1969 publication of his *Mysterium Pascale (MP)*.[14] It is in this work and in the several volumes of his *Theodramatik (TD)*[15] from the 1970s and 1980s that the issue is tackled most directly. However, as always in Balthasar, one notes the tendency for much important information about any particular topic to be scattered almost at random throughout the entire corpus of his writings and not to be confined to any specific *locus*. This means that while *MP* and *TD* will be the main subjects of our treatment here, we will be drawing on many other places in Balthasar's work (especially from the other two parts, with *TD*, of his major trilogy, *Herrlichkeit* and *Theologik*)[16] to fill out the understanding gained from the central sources.

The specific question of God's immutability, in particular its thematic treatment, is not directly the central concern of Balthasar's theological enterprise. Nonetheless, because it is implied in those areas which *are* central to him, it becomes willy-nilly an important element,[17] so much so that Balthasar himself can characterise the issue of God's immutability and how it is to be resolved as *the* centre of his *TD* (which in itself is clearly at the heart of his other theological writings).[18] It involves the nature of God's engagement with his world and so a discussion of who God is, the person and role of Christ, who we are, and the relationship between us and God mediated by Christ. This means in effect that to get at this issue in Balthasar we will have to consider many of the main areas of theological interest in general.

It will be helpful to indicate in advance the direction in which Balthasar's thought moves. He wishes to retain the term immutability as applied to God. He avoids at all costs the affirmation that God is mutable. Furthermore, while he agrees that some of what immutability involves in God may indeed be understood as the divine fidelity (e.g. to his covenant promise), he is not satisfied simply to reduce immutability to fidelity. What he does point to is a liveliness within God, an 'event', which the more usual understanding of immutability does not convey, and so he attempts to invest the term with new meaning and to call for a new image of God. In doing so he must implicitly at least confront the limits and proper role of theological discourse itself.

Because such is the nature, the process and the direction of his enquiry – unlike one which focuses on a specific, limited area with the intention of treating it in a succinct, comprehensive way – there is no use in asking Balthasar for a definition of the term immutability. The meaning of the term and its nuances will emerge from the cluster of contexts which defines it. For the moment we may use the term heuristically in its common-sense meaning of 'unchanging and unchangeable'. We are asking, then, what Balthasar has to say in answer to the question 'does God change?'

Aim and methodology

Our aim in this study is to establish what Balthasar has to say concerning the immutability of God and to assess the validity of his position. Our approach, then, is issue-centred. This is consistent with the advice given by one of Balthasar's own theological heroes, Maximus the Confessor, that one should attempt to speak the truth and not to list every opinion![19] It means that dialogue-partners who are important for Balthasar (e.g. Rahner, Moltmann, von Speyr, Barth) are treated in order to elucidate the *res*, without claim to comprehensive coverage. This is so even when we initiate a dialogue with English-speaking authors whom Balthasar himself does not address: even though a secondary aim in this is precisely to facilitate the critical reception of Balthasar's thought in an English-speaking world, the primary aim remains that of assessing the validity of his position on the particular issue in question. It means too that there will be no attempt made to trace the internal development of Balthasar's own thought from his earliest works onwards;[20] development will be noted only when it clarifies significantly the issue at hand. These are important observations. Balthasar's vast and labyrinthine body of work is notoriously ill-fitted to the systematising penchant of secondary writers; but by limiting the enquiry as described, we may effectively isolate as our main sources the works to which we have already referred (*MP*, *TD*, with *H* and *TL* since the parts of the trilogy are intrinsically related), in addition to the collections of essays *Pneuma*, *HC* and *SC*, and the works on history *TG* and *GF*.[21] Furthermore, although the issue itself involves such central areas in theology as Trinity, Christology (including soteriology), creation, history of salvation and eschatology, because our particular point of interest is none of these they may all be treated as subsidiary issues. The advantage of this is twofold: first, issues that are subsidiary may be dealt with carefully in a summary rather than comprehensive way, and this will help us to avoid getting lost in the labyrinth or repeating too much material presented in other works on Balthasar; and secondly, due to the fact that these central areas must be included, even if only summarily, we have the opportunity of glimpsing most of the main features of Balthasar's distinctive and splendid theological vision, features which will be outlined thanks to the thread supplied by the insertion of the immutability motif.[22]

We have already noted that Balthasar's treatment of the issue of God's immutability is scattered in form. It is only implicit in his earlier works, and even in the later period when he gives it a more thematic treatment he does so in service of other, larger theological concerns and in a disconcertingly diffuse way.[23] Can the fragments be gathered together to reveal some kind of recognisable and whole form?[24] It will be the aim of our study to achieve this.

There are many possible ways of organising the order of our enquiry. The one chosen here respects Balthasar's own passionately-held conviction that God, and not the human being, is at the centre of theology – and so it seems appropriate to bracket the remaining data between the mysteries of Christ (source of our knowledge of God) and the Trinity (source of our ultimate answers). Chapter 1, on Christ, gives us the most direct entry into the issue. Chapter 4, on the Trinity, both gives us our clearest answer to the question and integrates all the other data. Chapters 2 and 3 deal with the remaining data which forms part of Balthasar's position and argument. Chapter 5 initiates a dialogue with English-speaking contemporaries, while chapter 6 offers a final assessment.

Quotations in the text will, for the most part, be given in English, with my own translation where necessary. The masculine form of the pronoun is used with reference to God for reasons of stylistic simplicity and convenience and in full acknowledgement of the divine transcendence with respect to our distinctions of gender. The introductory remarks in the abbreviations list and bibliography supply other important information concerning style of presentation.

I

Christ and God's immutability

Balthasar's Christology and the question of God's immutability

Balthasar's theology of Christ is one of the contexts in which the question of the immutability of God arises. This is already clear in the 1969 edition of *MP*. In this, on the basis of the text in Philippians 2, 5–11, Balthasar affirms the reality of a kenotic 'event' in God, and asks how we are to maintain this reality in the face of the teaching on God's immutability and without falling away into theopaschism pure and simple.[1] By the time of the new preface to the second French edition of this work in 1981 he goes further in actually relating his own discussion in *MP* to the contemporary theological debate on the whole issue of the immutability and impassability of God.[2] The question is posed in *MP* with reference to the adequacy of the classical teaching in regard to Christ's incarnation and death, and indeed, by implication, in regard to every 'kenosis' of God in salvation history – meaning God's relation to Israel in the OT and, ultimately, to all humankind. These widening implications of *MP* are in fact developed thematically in *TD* and embrace further aspects of Balthasar's Christology. So, in particular, in the soteriological and eschatological dimensions of Christ's work for us, the question arises as to the nature of God: does he too not suffer, is he not affected by sin, can he be simply apathetic to the prospect of any final loss of his creatures to hell?[3]

It is entirely understandable that Christology should be one of the contexts in which Balthasar's treatment of the divine immutability occurs. After all, if Christ is God then the reality of his incarnation, life, death and resurrection, and their saving meaning for us, do spontaneously cause us to ask how God can be considered to be immutable.[4] But in Balthasar the christological context is not just one among others: it is the key one.[5] For Balthasar Christ is the 'figure'[6] who reveals and expresses God in an absolutely unique way. Christ, because he *is* God, is in a certain sense both the source and the content of our knowledge of God. The ontological status of Christ, then, is the

9

reason for his unique gnoseological role. Other figures (e.g. nature, the prophets, even Scripture itself) may point in a direction, be signposts, but are not themselves God. Christ however is God: in his figure we see who and what God is. Christ also, of course, points beyond himself, to the Father – in fact his revelation is trinitarian in character, involving Father, Son and Holy Spirit – but still it is only in the figure of the Son that we know the Father. And Christ is evidently man as well as God, and this means that if his figure both reveals and conceals God then this is not a pure paradox, since the revelation is precisely in the concealment, and the indispensable apophatic dimension is integrated into the positive expression. This position on the humanity of Christ as source, in such a strong sense, of our knowledge of God has clear implications for the issue of divine immutability. So, for example, in *TD*, Balthasar asks whether God is open to being touched by dialogue with creatures. The key to his attempt to answer this question is not simply to state that the man Jesus is capable of being affected thus – and to see this as sufficient in considering the implications for God himself – but rather, grasping the nettle very firmly, to presuppose that in this, as in all matters, the humanity of Jesus reveals what God is like and on the basis of this to consider further what this capacity for dialogue in God might mean.

The Son, then, as Word of the Father reveals and expresses the Father. More specifically, too, it is especially through the obedience of his life and death that the Son carried out this saving revelatory role.[7] This obedience is entirely free, is a sign of the Son's loving unity of will with the Father, and means that the entire existence of Christ is an expression of the Father. But to be more specific still, the high point of this obedience lies in the event of the cross – including its kernel, the descent into hell, and, of course, the resurrection – and so it is this event, at the centre of the revealing and dynamic 'figure' of Christ, which is also at the centre of Balthasar's theology and from which all else is interpreted. The cross is the exposed place in which love appears at its most extreme and as most itself. If this is so, and if one considers in addition the soteriological dimension of the cross, one must ask how this event affects God – and in doing so one is questioning the traditional notion of divine immutability. Does God change in some sense in his attitude towards us because of the cross? Surely at the very least his love for us is something costly, with a dimension that it lacked before, in responding to sin with the event of the cross.

The challenge to the traditional axiom of divine immutability in Process Theology is based on the philosophical principle which affirms the primacy of becoming over being.[8] It is fascinating to note that the issue arises in Balthasar in a very definitely theological context, and moreover within a Christology and theology 'from above' in which the philosophical component is respected and given its due but in which the theological retains a certain priority and normativity.[9]

We have indicated the christological context within which, in the theology of Balthasar, the issue of the immutability of God is raised. Christ expresses a new image of God, and this Christian image is not adequately conveyed within the mainly philosophical framework of divine immutability as commonly – and indeed traditionally – presented.[10] We may now go on to enquire in more detail into specific christological areas and to observe the ways in which they cause Balthasar to modify the notion of immutability. We begin with the mystery of the incarnation.

The incarnation, kenosis and immutability

Does the incarnation change God in any way? At a common-sense level it would seem that the answer must be 'yes'. After all, the Second Person of the Trinity became man at a particular moment in time, and unless this assumption of humanity is regarded in a purely extrinsic sense it is difficult to see how God can be unaffected or not different 'after' this event. Still theologians have consistently maintained that God is unaffected, immutable – how does Balthasar's theology of the incarnation deal with this dilemma? *MP* is the prime source of our discussion here, being Balthasar's first major semi-thematic treatment of the question of divine immutability, dating from 1969.[11]

The incarnation in Balthasar's *Mysterium Pascale*

MP has at its centre a treatment of the Easter Triduum, the 'Mysterium pascale', also frequently alluded to by Balthasar as the 'Triduum mortis'. This theology of the 'three days' includes Christ's death, his descent into hell and his resurrection.[12] It is Balthasar's aim to show the central role of this mystery for the whole of theology. The text is divided into five sections and it is principally the first introductory section which has a direct bearing on the incarnation.

This first section (13–46) clarifies the intimate connection between the incarnation and the Passion by indicating how the two are already related to one another in the original plan of salvation.[13] As part of the Patristic support for this position we meet the view of

Athanasius, shared by all the Fathers, that the Logos was impassible
and could only suffer and die – and so save us – by becoming man
(23). It is also clear from the Patristic context that there is a real
similarity between the incarnation and Passion in what they mean for
God and in particular for the divine Logos. This similarity is contained
in that aspect of 'becoming' which is involved in the incarnation and
which implies a humiliation that is hidden but is as real as that of the
cross. It is this aspect of the incarnation which leads Balthasar to a
discussion of the notion of a kenosis or emptying in God (26–40),
which has of course a direct bearing on the issue of divine
immutability and the possibility of a new image of God.

This discussion opens with a consideration of the text in Philippians
2, 5–11 and is developed by looking at its interpretation by the
Fathers and by examining some modern theories of divine kenosis.[14]
This pre-Pauline hymn, completed by Paul, draws a clear parallel
between the 'emptying' involved in the pre-existent Christ, the divine
Logos, becoming incarnate and the subsequent humiliation on the
cross.[15] The parallel consists not merely in the fact that we are here
dealing with two events which are qualitatively similar: Balthasar
affirms as well that the second kenosis (of the cross) is already
contained in that of the first – and this is an affirmation which we will
meet again and again, in different forms. However it is the significance
of the first kenosis which Balthasar himself now tackles. Without
forcing the text to conform to an interpretation within a two-natures
doctrinal schema, he argues nonetheless that its Christian meaning
can be realised only within a fully christological and hence trinitarian
horizon. And this means that we must allow for some kind of 'event'
within the God whom we know to be above the world and also
'immutable' – an event which consists in the loss of equality with God
in respect of possession of the OT form of divine glory. The inverted
commas are deliberate: Balthasar recognises, on the one hand, the
difficulty of speaking about an intra-divine event, but also, on the
other hand, the difficulty of speaking about God's immutability as if
nothing had occurred in the pre-existent Logos disposing him towards
the incarnation. And so the co-ordinates of his approach are now
fixed – the aim must be to find a way of speaking about the kenotic
event as real, without thereby degenerating into theopaschism pure
and simple.

The interpretation by the Fathers of this same text is now
considered. On the orthodox side in the christological debates
Athanasius, Cyril and Leo all argued against their respective oppo-

nents in favour of a real abasement in the Logos due to the decision to become incarnate and especially in view of the historically sinful condition of humankind. This is a divine renunciation, made out of love, so that there is no 'increase' in God owing to the incarnation but rather an emptying. Once again the inverted commas alert us to a way of speaking about God which Balthasar employs when more straightforward, theological language fails, and again the notion of God increasing or decreasing is one to which we will be returning later. These Fathers, while stressing the reality of this divine humiliation, also insist that somehow this changes nothing in the divine form of the eternal Logos, which remains whole and impassible. Hilary and Augustine make similar affirmations.

But the realities of a divine abasement and a divine immutability are not easily reconcilable. The dogmatic formulations of divine immutability do not really do justice to the text in Philippians in its stammering efforts to express the mystery, and the German, English and Russian Kenoticists of the nineteenth and twentieth centuries perceived this. But already one of the Fathers, Hilary, had made an almost superhuman effort to resolve the issue, and it is in light of his thought that Balthasar develops his own approach. Hilary's starting-point is the sovereign liberty of a God who has the majestic power to empty himself of the divine form and to assume contingently the form of a slave. Hilary maintains that in so doing God remains himself – because the event is produced precisely by his own power – while at the same time really relinquishing the divine glory. But unlike Athanasius, Cyril and Leo, who somehow view the two forms of divine glory and abasement as unproblematically compatible, Hilary is clear that a real change of state or condition is entailed by the transition from one to the other, and accordingly that something does take place in God, a real emptying. As long as the Son is in the form of a slave there is what Hilary calls the *vacuitatis dispensatio*,[16] which does not change the Son himself but which does involve for him in his inmost being a self-concealment which is expressed in his loss of the free divine power.

Before considering the implications of this position we continue with Balthasar's own addition to the thought of Hilary, as he attempts to compensate for the latter's lack of a trinitarian dimension. In this Balthasar contrasts the OT image of God, one of whose fundamental characteristics is to be the God of glory in a divine form shared by no one else, with this new image in Philippians and elsewhere in the NT, where Christ, the divine pre-existent subject, expresses his divinity precisely by renouncing this particular divine form of glory. For God in the OT to be without this form of glory would be a contradiction. But now Christ – and elsewhere in the NT the Father and Holy Spirit as well – reveal that giving away what is proper to self is also a divine characteristic. This is a decisive turn-about in our way of seeing God (32). It means that God is not first and foremost 'absolute power' but rather 'absolute love', and that God's sovereignty is shown primarily not in holding on to what is proper to him but rather in abandoning it in such a way that all inner-wordly opposition between power and weakness is overcome. And God is absolute love as tri-personal self-giving so that the Trinity is the condition of possibility of God's externalisation in a form such as the incarnation. In other words the kind of emptying and self-giving we see in the incarnation is both the image and the effect of the eternal 'externalisation' of God that is involved in the intra-trinitarian life. In this respect too, incidentally, the trinitarian life is itself always 'already' an event – even 'before' the specific kenotic event of the incarnation takes place.

In this context the concepts of poverty and richness are not simply opposites as applied to God, but are dialectical. Balthasar claims this does not mean that God's essence is in itself kenotic in the univocal sense that one concept (kenosis) can embrace both the divine foundation for the possibility of this kenosis and the kenosis itself. In other words, unlike the Kenoticists, he is saying not that kenosis is the central concept in God which subsumes all others in such a way that incarnation and cross are seen as natural and necessary to God, but rather that God's sovereign power is revealed as love and self-giving in such a way that divine kenosis is real, is an expression of this divine power and love, and can and does freely reveal itself in human form in such forms as the incarnation and the cross. We will be examining the validity of this claim in the light of further investigation into the matter. In fact, Balthasar continues, the incarnation and cross, precisely in their affirmation of divine self-giving or 'weakness', now become the high points of the revelation of God's love for us and of God's love in itself – a perception which was not easily attainable as long as the strict anti-heretical position on the immutability of God held sway. All of this, as always in Balthasar, implies a certain analogy between the divine and human natures of Christ which is due to the identity of the person, the pre-existent Logos, and which allows one to see in Christ the revelation of God himself.[17]

From this discussion of Philippians 2, 5–11 then we have seen Balthasar take up a position which rejects the notions both of theopaschism and of divine immutability as traditionally defined. He is arguing that the incarnation and the cross are a real change of condition for God, a real humiliation in fact, not simply compatible with the divine form of glory as usually understood, but pointing to a kenotic event in God which can only be grasped as issuing from the sovereign liberty of the divine trinitarian life of love. The implications of this are considerable. The new image of God in the NT, the God of trinitarian love, does allow us to speak in a real sense of God's immutability even in the incarnation. After all, this is the *sort* God is, always. But this would seem to reduce divine immutability to something like God's fidelity in love. Is this enough? If there is a real change in God's state or condition – even allowing for the fact that such changes lie within the same notion of God as love – does this not imply that God changes, even while remaining faithful? And does Balthasar mean to support Hilary's difficult contention that the incarnation does not change the Son himself but does involve a self-concealment in his innermost being? What about the more actualist viewpoint which, granting the qualitative similarity between the incarnation and the intra-divine processes, nonetheless affirms the new reality of the incarnation itself and asks about its significance for God? Balthasar's further thoughts on the trinitarian 'event' which he posits in God will indicate the lines of his response to these questions. However, some interesting features of this response are already outlined in the account of some modern theories of divine kenosis that now follows.

Balthasar has already referred briefly to the errors of the Kenoticists, while admitting the validity of some of their perceptions. He now (34–40) gives a slightly more detailed account of their thought, which also allows him to make his own position clearer. The incarnation affects the relations between the divine Persons: this is the mystery which human language and thought struggle unavailingly to express. During the human, 'temporal' life of Christ the eternal relationship between the Father and the Son has its centre, in a way that is to be taken seriously, in the relationship between the man Jesus and his heavenly Father – and the Holy Spirit who lives between the two and who proceeds from the Son as well must also be affected by the Son's humanity. The Kenoticists tried to take account of this mysterious reality, so strongly stated by Balthasar. In the course of his treatment of the Lutherans Chemnitz (1522–86: followed by the Giessen school) and Brentz (1499–1570: followed by the Tübingen school) Balthasar rejects the so-called *extra-*

calvinisticum position according to which the Logos even during the human time of Christ does not abandon his government of the world, so that the incarnation and death become, so to speak, just one occupation among others. Such is the logic of the positions of Augustine and Aquinas – and this negative interpretation of their thought reveals the extent to which Balthasar feels compelled to revise the tradition and to posit some real kenosis within God which has ontological status and is not merely functional, soteriological, or a simple addition which does not affect God.[18].

Balthasar maintains that the position of the nineteenth-century German Kenoticists, writing under the influence of Hegel, is also inadequate. His main opponent here is of course Hegel himself, to whom he attributes the view that the absolute Subject, in order to become concrete and himself, must make himself finite in the nature and history of the world. In different ways theologians such as Thomasius, Frank and Gess think within this perspective of speculative idealism in which the Logos ultimately loses himself within the processes of world history in order that the Trinity becomes itself. This is unacceptable.[19] Although also influenced by Hegel, the Anglican form of Kenoticism at the turn of the century (in particular between 1890 and 1910) was essentially an independent attempt to reconcile Patristic theology with the realism of the human Jesus newly brought to light at the time by biblical studies.[20] This school tried to locate the key to this whole discussion in the empirical aspect of the self-consciousness of Jesus, and in so doing, in different ways, both Gore and Weston speak openly of God's self-limitation. But, Balthasar maintains, God is not limited – somehow one must retain the paradox that *in* Jesus' full humanity the *full* power and glory of God are present to us. And this is made clear by a quotation from P. Althaus in which the point is made that in the utter weakness and distress of the crucified Christ – which one may not view in separation from the 'divine nature' – is found the fullness of God's divinity. Althaus continues: 'La reconaissance de cette vérité fait disparaître, il est vrai, la vieille conception de l'immutabilité divine. La christologie doit prendre au sérieux le fait que Dieu lui-même, dans le Fils, entre réelment dans la souffrance, mais par là même est et reste tout entier Dieu.'[21]

Balthasar goes on to develop his own thought in the light of these positions. It is clear that if the divine kenosis is to be regarded as a renouncement by God, a self-limitation, then not only must it be associated with the divine liberty (and so it is neither natural, as in a Gnostic framework, nor logical, as in an Hegelian one) but also, as some of the Fathers saw, it must be seen in terms of the almighty power of God now present in the weakness of the incarnate Son. It is precisely a sign of God's power that he can freely descend to such depths. Balthasar had earlier described this power in terms of absolute love. He now proposes a theological truth to bring together the two seemingly irreconcilable aspects that are involved in this issue. On the one side there is the divine immutability, understood in such a way that the incarnation appears as an external 'addition'. But Philippians 2, 5–11 makes it clear that the divine kenosis is not an addition; and its location in God makes it difficult to grasp in the Patristic and Conciliar ontic categories of nature and person. But on the other side there is suggested a divine mutability, within the consciousness categories of German Idealism or Anglican Kenoticism, in which the divine consciousness of the Son is alienated within a human consciousness for the time of the incarnation – so that God really does become less than God, does not remain God, and the divine is confused with the human. The Lamb slain since the beginning of the world (Rev. 13, 8; also Rev. chapters 5,6,9 and 12) is the theologoumena with which Balthasar seeks to unite these two extremes.

The Slain Lamb of the Apocalypse lies at the intersection of eternity and time. The slaughter is not understood gnostically as if there were some heavenly sacrifice independent of the earthly, historic, bloody one offered at Golgotha on the cross – rather, the former is the eternal aspect of the latter (Rev. 5, 12), which is in line with Pauline thought as well. This points to a supra-temporal state of the Lamb which is not just the continuation of the sacrificial state of the resurrected Christ but which is, rather, co-extensive with all of creation and which, accordingly, in some way affects the divine being. Balthasar appeals to recent Russian theology, purified of its Gnostic and Hegelian tendencies, to support this position. Thus Bulgakov,[22] freed of his sophiological presuppositions, would echo Balthasar's own intuition that the ultimate foundation for the kenosis is the disinterestedness of the divine Persons as pure relations within the intra-trinitarian life of love. This disinterestedness takes the form of the kenosis of incarn-ation and cross in view of the responsibility which God eternally takes for the success of his creation in the contexts of human freedom and sin. In this sense the cross is written into the world from the beginning and is an indivisibly trinitarian design so that the Father and Holy Spirit are both involved in it with the Son – the Father as the one who sends and abandons, the Holy Spirit as the one who unites through-out separation and absence.

This theology of the Slain Lamb is also to be found in the

Congregationalist P. T. Forsyth.[23] According to Forsyth this heavenly sacrifice is the crucial act which unites God and the world. He sees in it the supreme obedience of the Son, of which the earthly life and cross of Christ are but an aspect. Similarly Temple[24] observes that the cross opens up the mystery of the divine life itself so that it becomes clear that without himself being the subject of our suffering there is nonetheless nothing that goes on in creation that is strange and external to God's own life. Indeed, Balthasar goes on, had not Origen already transcended the dogma of God's utter impassability in believing himself forced to ask whether even the Father himself was not without suffering?[25] And does not the *subline altare tuum* of the Roman Eucharistic canon not refer to the same reality as that indicated by the Slain Lamb, *viz* the eternal aspect of the sacrifice at Golgotha? Therefore, as Barth[26] maintains, the humiliation and exaltation of Jesus Christ are the two aspects of one and the same action, so that God does not lose his divinity in abasing himself like this but rather confirms it.

We may now draw together the main lines of Balthasar's treatment of the incarnation in MP in so far as they affect the issue of God's immutability. First, there is no claim in Balthasar to have definitively solved the problem. Rather, he rejects the notion of a definitive solution altogether, stressing the intrinsically mysterious nature of the issue and acknowledging this in part by his linguistic usage. But secondly, it is clear that he does see the need to point in a direction other than that indicated by the two extremes of the traditional axiom of immutability and the less traditionally acceptable one of pure mutability. So although the view of Athanasius and the other Fathers that God is impassible is accepted in some sense, still the Patristic and Conciliar ontological framework in which this is traditionally understood is judged to be inadequate to the scriptural data. This will mean, *inter alia*, that it will not do simply to describe the divine nature as immutable and treat this as the decisive point without reference to what goes on in and between the divine persons.[27] Equally unacceptable is any Hegelian solution in which God has to change in order to become truly himself. Thirdly, Balthasar's position, based here mainly on the text in Philippians 2, 5–11 but seeking support too in the general sense of Scripture, and in Hilary among the Fathers, is to affirm the existence of an event of self-giving in God which is due to the nature of God as inner-trinitarian love. This event, given certain realities – creation, human free will, sin – will lead to the kenotic incarnation and cross of Christ. Because the event is already grounded in God's nature, and because its temporal form is due to God's free decision and not to any necessity, we may correctly retain the notion of divine immutability. However the event is real – as are its temporal forms – and this implies that God is free and powerful enough to remain God in this self-giving and in allowing himself to be affected by what is not divine. This is difficult to grasp. At its most comprehensible we may say that it opens up for us a new image of God as absolute love, not absolute power – but it also points to God's freedom and power to be God in ways which our human reason cannot understand but nonetheless, on the basis of the scriptural evidence, is forced to affirm as being so. And it calls into question the nature of the divine immutability – is it not simply a description of an unfailingly habitual state of divine love within which there can be many different modalities and expressions, and thus change? Such might seem to be the logic of Balthasar's position at this point. However another possible perspective is opened up by the Slain Lamb motif which he uses to connect the temporal and eternal aspects of the divine event. Within this perspective, it seems that here is suggested at least the possibility that the temporal is contained in the eternal in such a way that God is always so and the divine immutability is maintained. But this needs further investigation, in particular to obviate a Gnostic downgrading of temporal reality that might seem to be implied.

In 1981, twelve years after the first publication of *MP*, Balthasar wrote a preface to the second French edition of the work.[28] In this he addresses the contemporary debate on the immutability and impassibility of God. First, in a rather unsympathetic tone, he notes that Kitamori, American Process Theology, various polemics against the divine impassibility, and the Hegelian theology of Moltmann have combined to suggest to Christians that the axiom of divine immutability does not correspond adequately to the biblical revelation. But secondly, while restating the intrinsically mysterious nature of the divine kenosis, which he here likens to that of the mystery of the Trinity itself, Balthasar himself warns of the danger of interpreting the kenosis in terms of the human nature of Christ only. If one holds to the position that the divine nature is incapable of any becoming or change, of any real relation to the world, then one risks underestimating the weight of the biblical assertions and one verges on Nestorianism and monophysitism. And thirdly Balthasar once again sketches his own approach to reconciling the two extremes, which is to relate the event of the Son's kenosis to what by analogy we may call the eternal 'event' of the divine processions. This event is supra-temporal but real and reveals the divine 'essence' as one of gift – the self-giving of the Father 'returned' in the free act of the Son and 'represented' in its character of absolute love by the Holy Spirit. So the deep self-giving of the Father may already be called a 'supra-kenosis'; and in it are constituted simultaneously the persons of Father, Son and Holy Spirit. In this God is the abyss, the bottomless ground (Eckhart's *Un-Grund*) of absolute love, and so it contains eternally all the modalities of love, including compassion and that 'separation' which is motivated by love and based on the infinite distinction of the divine hypostases. And so these modalities are contained in advance of their appearance throughout the course of the history of the salvation of sinful humanity. Within this scenario God has no need to 'change' when he shows his love for us with all – including the incarnation – that it involves. All the contingent 'abasements' of God are already eternally included and indeed exceeded within the eternal event of love. And so the very real sufferings of the cross are a manifestation of the Son's grateful giving to the Father, the Son who is always the Slain Lamb.

In this short preface Balthasar has clarified his position. The term event as applied to God is an analogous one. It allows one to describe God in terms of a liveliness which is mysteriously supra-temporal. And perhaps also the comparison between this mystery of the divine kenosis and the early Church's grappling with the mystery of the triune God is a helpful pointer to an orthodox precedent for our own need to develop the axiom of divine immutability in a way more compatible with Scripture.

However, difficulties remain, and we may conclude by mentioning two of the main ones. It is not clear in what sense all is contained in God: once again this raises the difficulty that contingent, created, historic reality seems to be downgraded. Secondly, however, if created reality is given its due and some provision is made for its effect on God, then one must ask further about the nature of the divine event, in particular about the possibility of limiting the divine immutability to some kind of divine fidelity in love while allowing for a mutability that is supra-temporal. Both these questions have to do ultimately with the relationship between eternity and time. And they raise the over-riding difficulty of describing this analogous event in God at all, in particular of coming to terms with a love which contains all the modalities whose created expressions include change, suffering, compassion and so on, but which is present in God in a different kind of way. Balthasar speaks of a 'supra-kenosis' in God;[29] may one also begin to talk about supra-suffering and the like in God, and – more importantly – begin to indicate the differences and similarities between this and the created forms? Certainly Balthasar rules out any purely creaturely change or suffering in God.[30] We are already beginning to see the nuanced way in which he proceeds and his refusal to be trapped into any blatantly extreme positions. Nonetheless we will continue to question whether the internal logic of this nuanced approach is in fact coherent. A particularly pointed illustration of this is the claim that in speaking about an event in God he is not maintaining that God's essence is in itself univocally kenotic. Is this claim, in the text of *MP*, sustainable in the light of the description in the preface which outlines the way in which the event constitutes the Trinity? We move now beyond *MP* to different if related aspects of his theology of the incarnation in its bearing on the issue of divine immutability.

The incarnation and myth

The incarnate Logos Jesus Christ who dies and is raised from the dead is no mythological figure.[31] Time and again Balthasar contrasts the gods of myth with the Christian God[32]. The reality of the Christian God's incarnate, historical, material existence as Jesus Christ is stressed – this sober affirmation of what is human and worldly is seen as distinctive in contrast to the imaginary, symbolic, inconsistent, often Gnostic and docetic characteristics of mythology. In mythology, when the gods do get involved in our world-process they become so entangled that the transcendent element is lost.[33] Such a god – present again in today's post-Christian Process Theology version[34] – would mean that the ultimate outcome of the drama of world history would be uncertain, and could even be tragic. The incarnation points to a way in which God can remain really God and yet get involved intimately with our world. Balthasar, then, warns us against any mythological reduction of the divinity to human proportions only, and accordingly against any merely human attribution of mutability to God.

But of course if, as Balthasar maintains, the incarnation does not mean any 'mythical' change in God and is simply one of the infinite possibilities which lie in God's eternal life, surely when the particular possibility of incarnation is actualised then a new reality does emerge and change of some kind occurs in God? Balthasar's own formulations in the discussion are, at this point, so careful as to be almost opaque. On the one hand he speaks of the immutable God through the incarnation becoming related to creation in a way which gives his inner relations *a new appearance*.[35] This would seem to imply that whatever change occurs is external only. But he goes on to qualify this by saying that it is not something merely external, as though this relationship to outside reality did not really touch God. And this would seem to echo his statement elsewhere that while God is not mythically 'mutable', neither is he philosophically 'immutable'.[36] This whole question concerns the relationship between the eternal God and his created temporal effects. The section that follows will help us to clarify our position.

The incarnation already in heaven?

We are here once again touching on the question of the relationship between the historical incarnation and that eternal kenosis in God of which Balthasar spoke in *MP*. Basic to all Balthasar's discussion of this issue is his insistence that the incarnation is a free act of God's love and not first of all a means whereby God seeks to supplement his own being.[37]

Within this horizon his thought now reaches out in two directions. First, there is a real sense in which the whole temporal order unfolds itself within the eternal.[38] The incarnation, and every other aspect of the human life of Christ, and our lives too, are part of God's design for the world from the beginning and are already accomplished within this design. Since God is eternal and it is God who becomes incarnate there is a very real sense in which, from the timeless view of eternity, the plan to become incarnate and the incarnation itself are not primarily temporal events at all. 'The Incarnation is not an episode in the life of God', as C.S. Lewis remarks, quoted by Balthasar.[39] There is then no temporal change in God due to the incarnation, and if we are to speak at all of a potency being actualised in the event of Christ becoming incarnate then clearly we may do so only in an analogous sense which would take account of the non-temporal nature of the reality in question.

However the second direction in which Balthasar's thought moves is more positive in its evaluation of the temporal order. The incarnation – as indeed the entire life and death of Christ – is also really in time. In fact the temporal reality of Christ's life is peculiarly suited to expressing his intra-divine relationship. As Son he is constituted by receptivity to the Father, and this is expressed very well by his experience of temporality in the world, an experience of continual receiving and offering back again.[40] This temporality is real, not just an appearance. The earthly existence of Christ is not merely a repetition of something that has already taken place in heaven. In fact, of course, pre-existence as applied to the eternal Logos is not properly a temporal term at all: eternity is not measured in 'before' and 'after'. Rather, in the reality of his temporal life, guided by the Holy Spirit, one might compare Christ to an actor playing a part for the first time, receiving it by inspiration, scene by scene, word by word. The play does not exist in advance, but is conceived, produced and acted all in one. The incarnation is not the nth performance of a tragedy already lying in the archives of eternity. It is an event of total originality, as unique and untarnished as the eternally here-and-now birth of the Son from the Father.[41]

Clearly, within this perspective it will not do simply to say that the incarnation occurs already in heaven and leave it at that. Rather, it must be true that in some way with Christ's incarnation God enters time, the eternal breaks into the temporal, and that this affects God in such a way that the notion of absolute divine immutability as taught philosophically is no longer tenable.[42]

There is no easy synthesis of these two directions in Balthasar's thought. Time and, more so, eternity are mysterious realities, and whether one says that time is contained in eternity or that eternity 'for a time' enters time there is still no clear grasp of how this process is possible. The crux of the matter is to begin to see how Balthasar can give a certain primacy to the eternal, while insisting on the reality and integrity of the temporal process.[43] Within this perspective it would seem that we must answer the difficulty raised in the previous section by saying that the incarnation does indeed change God but not in a temporal, mythological kind of way. And it is in this perspective too that we can grasp how the Trinity as 'event' must include that liveliness and movement which we associate with time, without, however, being subject to time as such. In other words it would seem that although up to now we have tended to use the terms 'eternity' and 'time' in a mutually exclusive way, in fact it may be that timelessness is not the best way to characterise that divine way of being which is capable of entering time and being affected by it, albeit non-temporally. In this respect we will need to pursue Balthasar's own hint, in his discussion of the Slain Lamb motif and elsewhere, that there is a supra-time in God.[44]

Does the incarnation change God?

The discussion of this one aspect of the immutability issue has opened up a vast area, and indeed introduced us to most of the themes which we will meet in the course of our study. Accordingly it will be helpful to summarise some of our main findings.

The incarnation has as its presupposition what may be called an event in God, and so it reveals to us that God is not rigidly immutable. Moreover the incarnation itself does affect God; its reality is present and effective within the divine event. In both of these senses it may be said that the incarnation does change God. Accordingly a philosophical concept of divine immutability deriving from an anti-heretical context and usual in theology is no longer admissible. This conclusion Balthasar bases on the evidence of Scripture, Fathers such as Origen and Hilary, and his own trinitarian clarifications.

However, the incarnation is a free act of God and is consonant with the nature of God as self-giving trinitarian love. Moreover its effect on God is not to be measured in temporal, spatial or other univocally created categories which would imply some kind of mythological change. Kenosis is a proper theological term to describe the reality of the incarnation, but it is only used properly if one recognises that it has a decidedly anthropomorphic aspect. This resides in the attribution of temporal and spatial change to God. In fact God remains eternal and united throughout whatever change is due to the incarnation.[45] And in the light of these clarifications it may be said that the incarnation does not change God. Accordingly a concept of mythological, temporal mutability, involving theopaschism or some kind of self-alienation in God, is rejected.

It is vital to be aware of the fact that Balthasar can in this way legitimately answer 'yes' and 'no' to the question about change in God. With this awareness we are less likely to dismiss what seem to be mutually contradictory sets of statements – for example, that God wins nothing for himself through the incarnation and, elsewhere, that the Trinity is 'enriched' by the same incarnation.[46] The former statement is in the context of maintaining God's freedom to become incarnate – he does not do so to supply something that is missing in the divine life. And the latter statement is to be understood within the context of a description of the divine eternal life as event. Ultimately both sets of statements derive their validity from different meanings of the term change or mutability. So is change something that is due to external cause or internal deficiency, and is it measured in temporal and spatial categories; or is it something that may, in God, be seen as a perfection which allows for life and variety, and even for an immersion in time without itself becoming temporal? Our future enquiry will be guided by the attempt to become more precise on these two notions of change and their inter-relationship. Can God in the incarnation really, temporally become what he already eternally is, and can this temporal becoming be understood in some way to point to an intrinsic characteristic of the divine eternal fullness of life? Only a more detailed examination of Balthasar's theology of the trinitarian event will help us here. And can one really allow for a divine immersion in the temporal, and, maintaining the primacy of eternity over time, still hold that this immersion really affects the divinity but not in a temporal way?[47] A more detailed discussion on the relationship between eternity and time will tackle this question. There have already been hints of Balthasar's approach to these two related areas in his use of terms such as supra-kenosis and supra-temporal, terms which in themselves raise the whole issue concerning the nature of theological discourse itself.

At this point, then, we may put forward as an hypothesis the notion that a trinitarian event in God, of the kind described briefly and provisionally above, is Balthasar's way of tackling the issue of God's immutability. Our main task now will be to verify the hypothesis as well as to investigate the intelligibility of this event and to assess its explanatory adequacy, within Balthasar's own constantly reaffirmed assertion that it is intrinsically mysterious. This will lead us further into the area of the relationship between time and eternity and also into the question of theological discourse. The scriptural image of which Balthasar most frequently avails himself to focus the christ-ological aspect of the discussion concerning God's immutability is that of the Slain Lamb. By it we are reminded that the kenosis of the incarnation is always directed towards that of the cross – which is the central point of Balthasar's theology, and to which we now turn.

The cross, kenosis, soteriology and immutability

We have already seen that in Balthasar's theology there is a very close connection between the incarnation and the cross. Does the cross, understood as the central point of God's *revelation*, add anything to what we already know, from our discussion of the incarnation, about the divine immutability? The cross is also very much the revelation of a God who saves. Does this *soteriological* dimension of Christology have something special to say to us about the way in which God might change? With these two inter-related questions we have indicated the main areas of Balthasar's theology of the cross which are of interest for our theme.[48]

The cross as kenotic revelation of God

(1) We may begin with a fairly bald account of Balthasar's description of the event of the cross, drawing once again on *MP* as our principal source.[49] Chapter 3 of *MP* describes Good Friday (81–137). The distance between Father and Son begins already in the Garden of Olives, where the solitude of Jesus is apparent, as in a very real and personal way, himself without sin, he assumes the sin of the world. This means that he suffers – freely and out of a love that is expressed as obedience to the will of his Father – what sinners suffer when they fear the eternal loss of God. This distance and solitude take the form of a struggle to say 'yes' to the Father's will, to the shameful death of a sinner abandoned by God, handed over by the Father because of the need, rooted in love, to judge sin. There is a great mystery here, one aspect of which is the fact that because of the need to judge human sin the love of all three Persons of the Blessed Trinity now expresses itself in an obedience of the Son which involves bitterness and blindness, while still remaining free. The centre of the abandonment which Christ experiences is revealed with his cry on the cross and his subsequent death. The entire Trinity is involved in this event of the cross – the Father wants the reconciliation with us which is effected through Christ's death, and whose fruit is the Holy Spirit in us.

The full implications of the way in which Christ dies this 'second death' of the sinner, and in the unique way – possible only because of his inner-trinitarian relation to the Father – in which he takes upon himself all the sin of the world are brought out in Balthasar's very distinctive and original theology of Holy Saturday (*MP*, 139–77).[50] Balthasar attempts to describe this 'hiatus' between the cross and resurrection, where 'God is dead', with a mixture of both realism and reserve, drawing on the OT, the NT and the experience of the Church down through the ages, including that of the great saints and mystics of the cross.[51] Christ is now in solidarity with the essential passivity and solitariness of the dead, and the expression 'descent into hell', a later interpretation of the NT affirmations on this theme, ought not to take away from this central notion of passivity.[52] Because of his ability to substitute for our sins Christ's experience in Hades, the OT Sheol, is absolutely unique.[53] He alone experiences the full consequences of the 'second death' – that is the definitive, timeless abandonment by God that is the NT hell and that consists in the vision of sin itself, detached from its adherence to individual people.[54] This is the ultimate point in the Son's obedience to the Father – the supreme cadaver-obedience which takes the measure of all that is opposed to God, and is willed by the Father in his responsible love for his creation, and is only possible because God is trinity.[55] It is the resurrection (*MP*, 179–264), involving the Ascension and Pentecost as well, which reveals the full significance and justification of this event of the cross. Finally Balthasar argues that it is the difference between the Father and Son, who are however related and one, that makes possible the cross as the high point of God's love for us. If God were simply one he would become ensnared in the world-process through the incarnation and cross. But because God is triune, with both poles of difference and unity guaranteed by the Holy Spirit, the difference between Father and Son can accomodate all created differences including that extreme distance shown on the cross which becomes a revelation of the closest togetherness of Father and Son.[56] In this way the ever-greater trinitarian love of God is the presupposition of the cross.[57]

These trinitarian presuppositions will be clarified further in our treatment of the divine event. In particular we will need to look at the spatial metaphors which Balthasar often uses to describe this event, the precise role of negative opposition within the Father/Son relationship, and the seemingly pervasively kenotic[58] character of the event (to which we have already alluded). What is clear, however, is that this event involves the eternal give and take of trinitarian love, which can contain the most extreme and various modalities within it, so that the eternal circulation of life that this implies is not adequately conveyed by the traditional axiom of divine immutability.

(2) We need at this stage to comment on some of the gnoseological aspects of this description of Balthasar's theology of the cross. From the way in which he uses the names Jesus, Christ, the Son, the Word almost interchangeably for the Second Person of the Trinity, it is clear that for Balthasar it is this person who is both the grammatical and the ontic subject of the events of the cross, and of the affirmation that the 'Word of God is dead'.[59] We have already referred in our discussion on the incarnation to his refusal to limit the effects of Christ's created properties to his human nature – and it is even clearer with respect to the cross that this has very considerable implications for the thesis of God's immutability. We will deal in more detail with this whole matter of the nature/person aspect of Balthasar's Christology in a later section (see p. 42). It is related to the objection that in pursuing such a line Balthasar lays himself open to the charge, which he himself would want to refute, of lapsing into a pure and static paradox or dialectic.[60] How can the Word who is eternal life be

also dead? And many such paradoxical-sounding formulations
abound in Balthasar's theology of the cross. The trinitarian presuppositions already referred to in the section on the incarnation, taken in
conjunction with a consideration of the nature of theological
discourse itself, are his ultimate answer to these charges. This answer
will be outlined at a later state of our study. Finally we note that the
kenotic existence of Jesus with its divine implications is already
sufficiently established by Balthasar's account of Good Friday.[61]
Therefore a refusal to accept his controverted Holy Saturday theology
would not significantly alter his general position on divine immutability, whatever real diminution it would involve in respect of
Balthasar's overall theological vision.

(3) We have already outlined the trinitarian presuppositions of the
cross, what it is in God that allows the cross to happen. But what
about looking at the process from the other end – does the cross affect
God, or is it simply and purely a revelation of what would be the same
without the cross? Prescinding from the final soteriological aspects of
this question for the moment, we may still ask to what extent Christ's
death goes beyond its function as revelation of God actually in some
way to influence the God who is being revealed.

The cross is an 'emptying' in God. As such it is the extreme point of
that emptying which occurs already at the incarnation. This emptying is real even if throughout it God still remains God. This means that
an historical event affects God.[62] This is so even though the temporal
cross is present eternally in God so that it is real in God 'before',
'during' and 'after' its earthly occurrence and, in particular, even
after the resurrection, the cross of Jesus is an abiding reality in
heaven, the eternal God being capable of containing all these different
modalities.[63] There is a great mystery here, in the way a temporal
event can be present to God eternally, and can affect God albeit in a
non-temporal way. We will return to this matter, already raised in the
course of our discussion on the incarnation, and especially under the
Slain Lamb motif, in a later chapter. What is important to grasp here is
that however one approaches the relationship between eternity and
time it is clear that for Balthasar the cross cannot be reduced to some
Gnostic heavenly cross – nor to an instance of some more universal
metaphysics of being.[64] This means that, with all its divine presuppositions and eternal dimensions, still it remains true in some sense that
through the historical cross God's emptying reaches a definitive stage,
and that this is in some way something new and an enrichment of the
Trinity.[65]

Does this emptying involve suffering in God? Clearly the cross is not an instance of a more general philosophical law which would require the divine being to suffer in a human way.[66] But perhaps God chooses freely to suffer like this? Balthasar will refuse, as we have seen before, to take this way out. There is no creaturely change, or suffering, or indeed obedience within God.[67] Yet we must allow that the Logos is somehow affected[68] – and indeed we have already seen Origen raise the possibility at least of the Father's suffering, in the context of the Son's cross. Once again we must wait to see if a term like 'supra-suffering' can be used to describe something in God analogous to suffering in us but present in him in a very different way.

The soteriological aspect of the cross

Does Christ through his obedience merely reveal the fact that the Father, and thus God, is 'already' reconciled with us sinners (Rahner),[69] or does he (as Balthasar maintains) in some way effect this reconciliation? If the latter is true then there is implied a change in the Father's attitude to us due to the cross of Christ. From what we have learned already we may anticipate how Balthasar will go about describing this 'change'. It will not be a temporal, created alteration in God. It will be real. Its reality will be grounded in the trinitarian event which makes it possible for God to contain within himself all the modalities of love – including, in this instance, anger at that refusal of love which is sin. What will be of interest to us then is not so much the details of Balthasar's soteriology as such, but rather how what is said there clarifies the way in which these modalities are present within the event and so helps us to grasp in what the divine immutability consists.

We will proceed by outlining briefly the main points of Balthasar's soteriology. Our principal source will be the almost catechetical-like exposé *Au Cœur du Mystère Rédempteur*.[70] This is a simple précis of what appears in greater depth and detail in Balthasar's main soteriological work, *TD* III, to which we will then turn.

Soteriological outline

As we have already seen in *MP*, Christ, himself without sin, freely and in obedience to his Father assumes the sin of the world and experiences in a unique way the 'second death' of the sinner. In this solidarity with us, abandoned by God, he is in fact most united to the

Father and unites the Father to us. What are the logic and implications of these statements?

We are dealing with a mystery and hence the different factors that are involved cannot be forcibly integrated into a totally coherent system.[71] Accordingly the four concepts traditionally used to throw light on this mystery all have deficiencies; they need to be taken together to complement one another and even then will not be entirely adequate. These concepts[72] are:

(1) *Sacrifice*. Christ as both priest and victim surpasses all other instances of sacrifice.

(2) *Redemption*. But from whom has Christ ransomed us? Not from the devil, asserts Balthasar: but – significantly – neither from God the Father's justice or anger, since it is precisely the Father who, out of love for the world, handed over his Son.

(3) *Satisfaction*. Here Balthasar confronts our own problematic directly. It is indeed true to Scripture that Christ effected our reconciliation with God and that the cross is not merely a symbol to express the fact that God is already reconciled with us. But this would seem to imply that an event in the world was able to change God's attitude, and surely this is metaphysically impossible?

(4) *Merit*. As Son of God, and yet related to us in being man, it is certainly true that the concept of merit has a place in any explanatory account of the cross. But does it sufficiently indicate how Christ can substitute for us?

This is Balthasar's initial sketch of the terrain in *Au Cœur*. The Pauline *pro nobis, pro me* (Gal. 2, 20; Cor. 5, 14; 1 Cor. 15, 3) cannot just be a matter of solidarity[73] – it must somehow be an effective substitution. And if this is so, what is being said about the relationship between anger and love in God, as well as the effect on this relationship of the historical event of the cross?

After a section in which he deals with the identity of the Jesus of history and the Christ of faith Balthasar goes on to present a scriptural interpretation of the relationship between God's anger and his mercy.[74] Both the OT and the NT (Rom. 5, 9; Thess. 1, 10; 1 Thess. 2, 16) speak of God's anger in relation to sin. Did Christ have to pacify this anger, and does this explain why his mission of reconciliation took such a terrible form? But this does not accord well with the fact that the NT also states that the Father takes the initiative, out of love for the world, in handing over his beloved Son to this work of reconciliation (Jn. 3, 16; Rom. 8, 32; 2 Cor. 5, 19); and right through his life, as for example in the parable of the prodigal son, Christ reveals this loving disposition of the Father. Balthasar attempts to resolve this apparent contradiction with the help of a double distinction. First, God's anger is not a passion but is rather a total reprobation of sin. Secondly, this means that God can continue to love the sinner while hating and condemning his sin. Within this scenario reconciliation will be effected when a way is found to separate the sinner from his sin – and this is precisely what Balthasar believes is the correct interpretation of Christ's saving work as proclaimed by Paul. God's justice (*Gerechtigkeit*) – and this both in the OT and in Paul is the divine saving justice, not something vindictive – is accomplished by the concentration of universal sin in Christ (2 Cor. 5, 21; Gal. 3, 13), which is only possible because of Christ's loving obedience and hence sinlessness. And it is Christ who then takes our place and who suffers in himself, for and instead of us, the effects of sin (Rom. 8, 3; Eph. 2; 2 Cor. 4, 14–15). This representative substitution of Christ for us, the *sacrum et admirabile commercium*[75] of the liturgy – including but going beyond the notion of his solidarity with us[76] – is successful, so that we are really, ontologically, and not just in an external, juridical way, transferred into a state of reconciliation with God. It is a substitution which makes of the event of the cross, in both Paul and John,[77] more than just a pure symbol of God's intense love for us or of the absence of any anger in God. This event is what God uses to reconcile the world to himself.

Balthasar goes on to discuss some of the different theological accounts of the scriptural data.[78] In particular he argues that to treat Christ's salvific work as if it were accomplished merely by a privileged man is an inadequate counter-position.[79] In different ways this is the position of theologians such as Küng, Schillebeeckx, Galot and Rahner. Rahner's position is of direct interest to us.[80] One of the premises of his argument is that it is impossible that a secondary cause could influence God and make him change his opinion. Therefore there can be no question of a sacrifice which would appease an angry God. Rahner goes on to consider Jesus in terms of the incarnate sign of God's initiative and engagement in our favour. Balthasar's objection to this view is that Jesus need not be God to accomplish such a mission; his human death and resurrection by God are sufficient to indicate God's saving love for us. What is implied – but not stated – in his rejection of this position is that, within the parameters laid down earlier in our treatment of the incarnation, there is indeed some sense in which a change must occur in God, and for this to happen Jesus must be both God and man. The further implication of this is that while secondary causes *per se* cannot influence God, still in so far as they are rooted in the Trinity itself – as Christ obviously is, and as we shall have to investigate concerning purely created reality – they may do so.

Balthasar now attempts to focus the matter in his own way.[81] One must take serious account of what the Bible, both OT and NT, has to say about God's inexorable judgement (*Gericht*) in what concerns anything contrary to the divine sanctity and love. This judgement, the divine anger at sin, the devouring fire of God (Hebr. 12, 29; 1 Cor. 3, 12; 1 Pt. 1, 7) ultimately must be one with God's love and justice (the technical term in Scripture for his mercy, hence for the saving aspect of judgement). This judgement of sin (Jn. 12, 31; 16, 10–11) is what Christ experiences on the cross. This may not mean that the innocent Christ is punished[82] instead of us who are guilty. Nor is the notion of sacrifice best suited to describe Christ's act of filial obedience.[83] Rather, the idea of substitution (not *penal* substitution), as expressed in the apostolic and credal *pro nobis*, conveys best what is meant. This substitution, a representation in the strong sense, which must be on the ontological and not merely social or psychological level, involves mysteriously a willing and loving concentration in Jesus of all the opposition to God which is found in us, his brothers and sisters. This opposition, the sin of the world, is handed over to God's saving justice which must reject it – and this accounts for the experience of abandonment by God which was Christ's on the cross. How does this approach square with the Anselmian idea of satisfaction, the classical soteriological explanation up to about thirty years ago and now almost unanimously abandoned?[84] The medieval image of the reparation of God's injured honour must be set aside, but we must substitute instead the idea of the divine love scoffed at by sin. This means of course that there is a vulnerability in God arising from his free creation of beings who are capable of sin. It means that Anselm's basic concern is correct: God's justice is both gracious and exigent, so that it will not do to consider the divine love without reference to judgement or exigency, as if it were heedless of human response. Such indifference would be unworthy of God and – it is implied – a downgrading of creation as well. Still, is it not cruel, inhuman for the Father to send his Son to such a death? Balthasar returns to the trinitarian aspect of the cross to answer this objection, and indeed to point to the ultimate source of a soteriological explanation. The cross is a trinitarian drama in a way which necessarily rules out any notion that an Arian-like, subordinate

Christ might be sufficient. In this drama the divine Son and Holy Spirit not only approve of and execute the plan of the Father; in fact they conceive of this plan in perfect unity with him. The plan involves the suffering of the Son in order that this world might in the end be judged to be 'very good'. This suffering is not the Son's simple acquiescence in the Father's proposal – it is the Son's proposal too, and the Son offers himself to accomplish it.[85] And this proposal by the Son, *humanly speaking*, touches the heart of the Father more deeply than the sin of the world does. In this way one may speak of a wound of love in God from before creation, unless indeed (and Balthasar leaves this in the air) one says that this is the sign and expression of that wound which is always open in the heart of the Trinity, and which is identical to the procession and circumincession of the divine Persons in their perfect beatitude. This wound would precede the wound that Anselm refers to in speaking of the offence given to God by sin.[86] And it would explain how the Father's will that the Son should suffer on the cross would show both his infinite love for us and his infinite respect for the offer of his Son. This offer, realised through the Holy Spirit to the point of that extreme diastasis between Father and Son, on the cross and in the descent into hell, becomes, as we have seen, the ultimate revelation of the tri-personality and love of God. Balthasar believes that this interpretation of Christ's saving death, shared by Moltmann, is not Gnostic or otherwise rash in character, but is rather in harmony with the full weight of the biblical assertions.

One final clarification of this outline is readily accessible in the article 'Über Stellvertretung' in *Pneuma und Institution*.[87] Here Balthasar offers a brief anthropological sketch of human freedom by way of showing how an individual's freedom is affected by being part of the whole human race. In particular, dying for another may affect the beloved in a deep way that is human and is not an external, magical abuse of the beloved's freedom. This is a remote pre-understanding of how Christ's death effects a real ontological change in us without being a manipulative abuse of our human freedom. Similarly – and more controversially, certainly – Balthasar considers the possibility that Christ's descent into hell on Holy Saturday can provide a way of seeing how even the seemingly definitive choice of the damned against God may be respected and yet changed through this extreme solidarity out of love with those who have chosen to be solitary. The ultimate logic, then, of the efficacy of Christ's saving death for us is that of love, the love of the Trinity for us. It is within this logic that the other ways of looking at this death – juridical theories of the imputation of Christ's merits to us, or those which stress Christ's representative powers due to his physical solidarity with us – find their subordinate but true place.[88] Finally, of course it is clear that in Balthasar the ontological change that occurs in us through being reconciled with God in this way, without exercising our own freedom, is intended to be the prelude to the process of justification in which our active free choice is required – Christ's substitution for us has its *inclusive* as well as exclusive aspect.

We may conclude by making some comments on how this soteriological outline affects our understanding of the divine immutability. The attempt is made to take the realities of human freedom and sin seriously in such a way that they affect God without making him dependent on them to the extent of losing his divine sovereignty. This combination of divine sovereignty and vulnerability can be reconciled only within the trinitarian context. The lively and dramatic image of a trinitarian God allows sin to affect God without in any sense forcing or dominating him. This is so because within the inner trinitarian life of love there is present that ultimate in self-giving which surpasses and contains all other modalities of love, and so is able to take account of the effects of the refusal of love (the 'risk' God takes in creating us). The trinitarian 'drama' or 'event' is such that God's justice and love are 'finally' identical, but only in the course of a lively interaction during which they remain differentiated, albeit related.[89] The question remains open as to whether this trinitarian drama involves a 'wound' in God which is identical to the trinitarian processions themselves, or is merely 'consequent' on the decision to create – the question already raised as to whether or not God is essentially kenotic (see pp. 14, 21 above).

In speaking then of the efficacious aspect of Christ's cross Balthasar is careful not to say that the Father's attitude is changed in any univocal sense. His position has to be understood within the framework already described, which includes the different possible meanings of change and the mysterious relationship between eternity and time. Within this framework he is asserting that while secondary, created causes cannot *per se* change God, they can, when taken into the trinitarian life, become part of that eternal drama of love which allows opposites to exist and reconciles them. So, through the trinitarian love, the Father's anger at sin is indeed deflected by the cross so that God loves us eternally. The cross then becomes not just the sign of an ever-loving immutable God, but rather both the sign of a God whose love is costly and dramatic as well as an intrinsic, if temporal, effect and 'cause' of that eternal love. God then changes in a non-temporal way while being able to use a temporal 'cause' (the cross) as instrument of that change. This means that the possibility that God's love can contain modalities such as anger and reprobation is grounded ultimately and exclusively in the trinitarian reality of God.

Some further details of Balthasar's soteriology with reference to the divine immutability: TD III

Balthasar's main soteriological treatment, a major concern of which is the exact presentation of the concept of representation (*Stell-vertretung*), is contained in his *Theodramatik*, Bd. III.[90] We limit ourselves here to those aspects of this work which are of direct interest to our theme and are an advance on what has already been outlined.

(1) First, then, early on in *TD* III,[91] Balthasar deals with the question already adverted to of the trinitarian basis for the realities of God's love and anger. When the Father gives everything to the Son this inner-trinitarian *traditio*, although itself above risk, contains within itself all the costly dangers which are inherent for God in creating the world he does. There is a continuity, then, between the trinitarian processions and missions which allows the unity of God's love and anger to appear. The power of the world, of sin, touches God's 'outer', if not 'inner', honour and so calls forth his anger.[92] This anger is then a divine 'suffering' due to God's engagement in our world. Once again here Balthasar allows us to speak of some reality of suffering that is present in God in a divine way, and is due to the world. However we will have to question further the nature of this suffering and of the distinction he makes here between God's 'outer' and 'inner' honour, which would seem to be connected with the notion that the original divine *traditio*, while it contains within itself all other modalities, is nonetheless itself without risk.

(2) Next, in a section which deals with the world's need of the cross,[93] Balthasar notes how the reality of sin, whose seriousness is measured ultimately only by the cross of Christ, means that God's justice and anger must be essential components of his mercy and love. However, even though it is because of our sin that God is revealed in this way to us, still the essence of the divine drama (the *Theodramatik*) does not lie in the opposition between sin and holiness. This is shown by the fact that in heaven there is still drama, the beatific vision is in fact a life of movement and event. The essence of this life consists in

the richness of dialogue between God and us, of which the this-worldly reality of sin is but an aspect. The thought remains undeveloped here, but Balthasar has said enough to indicate his belief that the inherently dramatic nature of divine life – and our participation in it – can embrace negativity without itself being constituted by it. This would suggest an important counter-balance at least to any tendency to conceive of the divine essence in essentially kenotic terms.

(3) There follows an historical account of soteriology,[94] beginning with the NT and continuing up to present times, which repeats much of the information already to hand in our soteriological outline. However it also includes some clarifications, and it is to these that we now address ourselves.

First, in a discussion of the soteriology of St Thomas Aquinas,[95] Balthasar notes with approval the way in which Thomas understands the cross as mysteriously effecting, and not just expressing, God's reconciliation with sinners. Balthasar speaks of a mysterious circle in Aquinas' thought which appears also in his theology of the prayer of petition. In this God has always reckoned with our free requests within his eternal and immutable plan of salvation, but this means as well that he lets himself be 'moved' to something through these prayers. Inner-worldly events, then (sin, the cross), touch God, and yet they do not (since all is already contained within the eternal divine plan). Aquinas brings the two poles of this paradox closer together by saying that it is God's eternal love which determines the loving event of reconciliation accomplished in time. Once again, from a somewhat surprising source, since Aquinas is so clearly in favour of the divine immutability, there is support for the view that this love allows itself to be affected, and by inner-worldly causes.

Next, in an excursus on the soteriology of Karl Rahner,[96] Balthasar's own position becomes clearer by contrast to that of Rahner. Central for Rahner, as we have already seen, is the assertion that the absolutely immutable God cannot be changed from an angry to a reconciled God through the inner-worldly event of Christ's cross. Balthasar points out that both the Scriptures and Anselm (whom Rahner opposes) knew this in the sense that they asserted that the whole economy of salvation derived from the love of the Father. Nonetheless Balthasar insists that the reality of God's anger and justice must be preserved within the over-riding divine love.[97] This will mean allowing some kind of willed mutability within God's eternal love – as indeed Aquinas seems to do in his theology of petitionary prayer. In fact Rahner himself has formulated the theologoumenon that God who is immutable in himself can himself change in what is other than himself, and has spoken of the self-emptying, the kenosis and genesis of God – does this not affect God? It is quite clear here that Balthasar's criticism of Rahner's soteriology does indeed ultimately lead back to their respective positions on the divine immutability. And while in several works[98] Balthasar expresses himself in agreement with Rahner's formulation on this issue, it is clear that his own understanding of the Rahnerian formulation, in allowing for change within God, goes further than Rahner would wish to go.

(4) Balthasar now presents his own position[99] – again we will advert only to clarifications or new elements. In order to integrate the various scriptural motifs used to describe Christ's saving work on the cross, we are directed towards an image of a God who is neither an immutable spectator nor a patient being operated on in a passive way to remove the cancer of sin. And so Balthasar, as before, focuses on the central trinitarian dimension of the cross. On the cross (with the descent into hell of Christ) the full distance between the Father and Son is visible as never before. The Holy Spirit who continues to unite them does so in a way which appears precisely as this distance. In this we are given an insight into the full seriousness of the inner-divine drama. This drama of the immanent Trinity, revealed in the economic, can be appreciated properly only if one avoids an incorrect notion of the relationship between the immanent and economic Trinity.[100] It will not do, like Rahner, to identify too closely the two, emphasising the economic Trinity excessively and formalising the immanent.[101] Nor may one, like Moltmann,[102] propose a Hegelian-type identification in which the cross is seen as the fulfilment of the Trinity in a Process Theology-like way which has no difficulty in directly ascribing change and suffering to God, and which ends up with a mythological, tragic image of God. Balthasar relies once more on Bulgakov to help him strike the correct balance in this matter. The Father's generation of the Son within the Trinity can be characterised as the first divine 'kenosis' which underpins everything else. In it is seen the utter self-giving of the Father to the Son, a renunciation of being divine by himself, a letting go of the divinity and, in that sense, a divine 'godlessness', prompted by love. To it corresponds the eternal thanksgiving of the Son, as total and uncalculating as the giving of the Father, and so absolutely complete that the Son's mission to the point of the cross is already contained within his procession from the

Father and what it involves, and is a modality of that procession. The absolute, infinite distance between Father and Son, product of this divine kenosis, the infinite otherness of the Son from the Father, is eternally held open and yet united and bridged by their common Spirit, their subsistent 'we'. This inner-divine distance is then what freely allows and contains all other inner-worldly distances: it can embrace and overcome even the reality and consequences of sin. Within this context there is no simple identification, as in Process Theology, between the world process (including the cross) and the eternal, timeless 'process' of the divine hypostases. The economic does not constitute the immanent Trinity. Rather, we must tentatively approach the mystery of the inner-trinitarian event by means of a negative theology which rules out any inner-worldly experience and suffering in God, and yet which establishes that the conditions for the possibility of such realities outside God are in fact to be found within God. But these realities of pain outside God have christological and trinitarian implications, so that one is then forced to conclude that the trinitarian event must also allow God to participate in suffering, must justify in fact the full soteriological reality that we have described.

But does this mean that there is suffering in God? Balthasar gives no simple answer to this. He speaks of a razor's edge type of theological approach which rejects all fashionable talk of 'God's pain', and which yet must take into account that the economic revelation of the Trinity in Christ seems to demand the very thing which negative ('philosophical') theology forbids – the participation of God in suffering.[103] Thus while Balthasar distances himself from Moltmann's direct talk about suffering in God, nonetheless he vindicates the thrust of Moltmann, and Protestant theology in general, in taking serious account of the Biblical 'pathos' of God in a way which is lacking in an image of God based on the classically understood divine '*apatheia*'.[104] There is in God, in the careless[105] self-forgetfulness of the divine event, the starting-point for that which can become suffering when it comes into contact with our careful selfishness. And yet Balthasar does not actually say that God suffers. He refrains from doing so because he believes that the demands of negative theology are just and that one may not reduce God to a mythological figure necessarily involved in the world process. But if one accepts all these just demands may one not still, in response to the requirements of the revelation in Christ, speak of God's suffering? It is clear that Balthasar wants to posit some reality in God that at least corresponds to suffering. We will return to this point. Balthasar does go on to contend that the philosophical rejection of all emotions in God has only a limited justification, and he draws on the treatise by Lactantius *De Ira Dei* to show this.[106] Lactantius is attacking the attribution to God by many of the Church Fathers of the notion of impassability, *apatheia*. He maintains that a God who is happy and involved in our world, but who only loves and does not also hate what is evil, would be self-contradictory and deserving of no respect. Anger is an integral aspect of the grace of God in dealing with human beings who reject the divine law. God's anger is intimately connected with the OT notions of God's zeal for the covenant, his jealousy with regard to Israel, his chosen one. This divine anger – mentioned about 1,000 times in the OT[107] – is real and yet always contained within God's love and mercy, and this is true of the NT as well. The anger of Jesus in the NT is not just something human but is rather an expression of the divine attitude. And ultimately of course it is Jesus himself who, on the cross, bears the burden of this divine anger at sin and disarms it in his representation of us.[108]

In this context Balthasar goes even further in describing how all this affects God, and so, by implication, how one must speak of suffering, or emotion of some kind, in God. He refers to the credible presentation by A. Heschel of God's passionate engagement in our world, God's 'pathos'.[109] The divine pathos, according to Heschel, is not an essential attribute or immutable quality of God. Rather it is an aspect of God's involvement in our world which expresses his 'constant care and concern', so that God is 'moved and affected' by the process of our world; he is 'involved, even stirred by the conduct of men' to joy or sorrow, agreement or indignation, to communicate love or anger as a form of 'suspended love'. This loving and just divine pathos is distinguished from the anthropomorphic representation of emotion in mythological deities. Balthasar's approving references to Heschel on this theme are extremely significant. He rejects Moltmann's attempt to integrate Heschel into a system which would insist on the absolute identity of immanent and economic Trinity and thus tend towards a mythological notion of a suffering God. Heschel's divine pathos is not simply a passive affection: it is an ethical response to human action which passionately summons us to a more appropriate response. His way of insinuating that while God is affected by us, still he is so in a way which clearly demonstrates his own mastery of the situation, harmonises well with Balthasar's own attempt to locate the capacity of God to respond in this way to us totally within the Trinity itself.[110] In other words, all the modalities of responsible love are already contained at least *virtualiter* within God – we are needed not to make God *responsive* as such, but only to enable him to respond *to us*. However, within this carefully determined perspective it is clear that Balthasar is indeed arguing for some kind of suffering and feeling within God. But what kind? Certainly not the kind which would attribute suffering to God as one of his essential qualities – Balthasar makes this clear in refusing Moltmann's use of Heschel and in drawing attention to the latter's own rejection of any attempt within the Western metaphysical perspective to interpret what he means. But would it satisfy these criteria, and the rejection of theopaschism, to state that God freely decides out of love to suffer? Or must we say that what freely takes place in God out of love is analogous to what we call suffering, a supra-suffering?[111] Or, finally, might not one of the differentiating qualities in God's analogous suffering – in so far as these may properly be identified – be precisely the freedom of divine suffering? We await further clarification to establish more clearly the truth of the reality Balthasar intends to convey.

The assessment of Balthasar's soteriology: a methodological note

The main concern of our enquiry is the issue of the divine immutability; the methodological question now arises as to the bearing of an assessment of subsidiary issues (in this case Balthasar's controverted soteriology) on this main concern.

We note first that a definitive assessment of Balthasar's soteriology lies beyond the brief of the present enquiry.[112] What we have tried to present is the inherent plausibility of the main lines of his approach, which has affinities with Anselm and Barth. This approach indicates why the loving God's forgiveness of our sins is such a costly business, and why atonement is appropriate to respond to the divine anger, which in turn is a mark of the divine respect for our freedom. Of course this position on atonement is challenged by many contemporary theologians: Schillebeeckx,[113] for example, plays down the salvific value of the cross altogether, while Rahner,[114] as we have seen, is critical of the Anselmian approach. O'Collins in particular maintains that Balthasar's approach presents a monstrous view of God, influenced by 'dogmatic preconceptions' and misinterpreting the New Testament.[115] However, this is too sweeping – it does seem to me that Balthasar's position has the great advantage of pointing up the intrinsically costly dimension of God's forgiveness of sin. This advantage would be better maintained against his critics if Balthasar.

as Schwager suggests,[116] related the anger of the Father more to the divine permissive than to direct will, and if it were also made clear that in expressing this anger the Father is in solidarity with all the victims of unjust oppression throughout human history.[117]

Secondly, a provisional plausible position on soteriology satisfies the methodological requirements of our study. This is so because first of all Balthasar's position on the divine immutability will be the result of considerations derived from several different areas of theology, and so will not be dependent on the correctness of any one of these areas.[118] And secondly it will be possible to assess the validity of the position on immutability on its own merits, and from its viewpoint, if necessary and desirable, to return to question and assess some of the subsidiary issues which led to this position, including the soteriological issue that we have just been addressing. To a certain extent, then, there is a reciprocal relationship in our study between the several subsidiary issues and the main theme of divine immutability, with the latter holding primacy both in terms of ultimate interest and in terms of evaluative function. This relationship does not constitute a vicious circle, despite the fact that it is only through the subsidiary issues that we can arrive at a position on our central issue, provided that our position on the subsidiary issues cannot be shown to be inherently contradictory, and provided that our position on the central issue is open to an independent assessment. This kind of independent assessment would base itself on the intrinsic intelligibility of Balthasar's final position on the divine immutability, prescinding from its derivation from the several subsidiary topics we will have treated. If this intelligibility can be established, then, to an extent that needs to be specified, the judgement on the subsidiary issues will be more definitely favourable. If this intelligibility is lacking it may still be possible to distinguish strong and weak points, and so to trace back and identify the required modifications of the issues in question. But in any case enough has been said to justify the procedure that is adopted here, and throughout the foundational part of our enquiry, as we move towards Balthasar's position on the divine immutability in our fourth chapter.

Thirdly, having clarified the general lines of our procedure it may still be useful at this point in our enquiry to anticipate a little how a particular assessment of Balthasar's soteriology might influence his position on the divine immutability. The fact that Christ suffers on the cross and that this implies something about God which requires some modification of the traditional teaching on the divine immutability is a generally accepted theological position nowadays.[119] Such is not the case when it comes to his explanation of the manner of Christ's substitutionary representation of us on the cross, and the way in which God's anger at sin is resolved through the loving but painful dialogue to the point of abandonment between Father and Son. Balthasar's controverted[120] position here means that a certain negativity is inserted into the inner-trinitarian relationships – is this possible? Our judgement on this will have to await the fuller presentation of his theology of the trinitarian event in chapter 4.

The status quaestionis: does the cross change God?

Through the two related aspects of Balthasar's theology of the cross we have verified the hypothesis, advanced in our discussion of the incarnation, that the key to his understanding of the divine immutability is to be found in his notion of the trinitarian event. We have also confirmed the main lines of our previous description of this event. We have filled out this description by adverting to how that which is most opposed to God may, in Balthasar's view, be contained within the relationship between the Father and the Son, as it is maintained by the Holy Spirit. This has led to a most dramatic image of God, and to some further unanswered queries about its kenotic character and the place of negativity within God. Furthermore the question about God's suffering has been raised and developed in a very explicit way – Balthasar's final position on this issue will become clear only after a consideration of his views on the nature and person of Christ (to which we turn next), and of his definitive treatment of this whole question in the eschatological context of *TD*, iv (to which we address ourselves in chapter 2). Other outstanding issues (the use of paradoxical and imaginative language in interpreting the cross which raises difficulties about theological discourse, the relationship between time and eternity) have been noted and will be treated where appropriate later on in our study. In a methodological note we have indicated as well the way in which our final position on the divine immutability may be assessed, without the need to offer a definitive judgement on particular issues which form part of the approach towards that central topic.

The person and nature of Christ

Traditionally theologians have spoken of the immutability and impassibility of the divine nature, while allowing that Christ could change and suffer in his human nature.[121] Balthasar goes beyond this Chalcedonian framework in his Christology. We need now to investigate this matter of the constitution of Christ (as distinct from our account of the incarnation as event on p. 11 above) precisely because of its relevance in the tradition to the question of divine immutability.

First, by way of establishing the parameters of his thought, it should be made clear that Balthasar's attitude to the Chalcedonian dogma 'itself is much closer to that of Barth than to that of Moltmann.[122] Far from dismissing the two-natures distinction, Balthasar sees this dogma as protecting the mystery which Scripture proposes to us. [123] In going beyond Chalcedon, then, he is not claiming that its teaching is incorrect. Rather he sees himself as being faithful to the scriptural witness in retaining the truth of Chalcedon and yet going beyond that Council's particular, historically limited content and function in order to come to a more adequate presentation of the mystery for our times. Thus from his discussion in *MP* of the text in Philippians 2, 5–11, in which he arrives at the necessity of positing a real kenosis in God, and from his repeated emphasis on the ontological, personal identity of the Logos as the subject who unites the two distinct natures in Christ, he will refuse to limit the change and suffering which Christ experiences to his human nature alone.[124] This is the advance on Chalcedon and its traditional interpretation which Balthasar proposes. The tendency to consider the human nature of Christ as an *instrumentum conjunctum*[125] which does not affect the divine person he sees as Nestorian in character. And so he is anxious to insist on a more than merely logical *communicatio idiomatum*,[126] to accept that the formula 'one of the Trinity has suffered' does indeed mean that God has 'suffered', albeit mysteriously. But why 'mysteriously'; why not say univocally that God suffers? Because – and here we find Balthasar's respect for Chalcedon – there *is* an enduring and incommensurable difference between God and the world, between the divine and human 'unmixed' natures of Christ. Any facile attribution of change and suffering to God, based on the fact that the person of Christ is affected by his human nature, represents a failure to maintain the distinction between the natures; it is a relapse into monophysitism and results in a mythical notion of God.

Secondly, we must attempt to indicate how Balthasar develops further this razor's edge approach.[127] By refusing to limit the human experience of Christ to his human nature alone, is he not in fact abandoning what Rahner describes as the 'pure Chalcedonian' position to take on a 'neo-Chalcedonian' one which is incompatible with Balthasar's own insistence on the enduring distinction between the two natures?[128] There is no clear-cut answer to this dilemma, but the approaches towards an answer are instructive. One such approach is by way of going beyond a philosophically-derived notion of the divine nature, with its attempt to specify essential divine attributes, to a consideration of the data of revelation which show us that God's nature is in fact intrinsically inter-personal, is the structured trinitarian event to which we have so often referred.[129] *The* divine attribute or prerogative now is love, so that the real kenosis in God, invovled in Christ's incarnation and cross and the way in which Christ 'deposits' (*Hinterlegung*) all he has and is with the Father during his earthly existence, is entirely consonant with this notion of God as personal trinitarian event.[130] In other words there is the basis in God for what can become suffering. Within this perspective, while the philosophically-based notion of the divine nature is retained – and so it is not said that God suffers in his divine nature – nonetheless more emphasis is placed on the freedom of the divine persons to be as they, in love, decide to be, and hence to be affected personally in their mutual relations by the suffering of Christ.[131]

But all this still leaves us with a certain disassociation between the human and divine natures of Christ that would seem difficult to sustain. It seems strange that the kind of influence which the earthly life of Jesus has on the *persons* of the Trinity should have no foundation at all in their own *nature*. A second approach in Balthasar is more promising in this regard. In it, while maintaining the real distinction between the divine and human natures, he time and again refers to the way in which Christ's humanity is an appropriate expression of the divinity.[132] Within this perspective he will speak of a 'christological analogy of Being' within which it becomes possible, without identifying the two natures, to speak of a certain likeness within the ever-greater dissimilarity between the human and divine.[133] This way of speaking may be illustrated by what he has to say on the obedience of Christ as being the supreme manifestation of the divine being.[134] When speaking thus Balthasar makes it crystal clear that there is no creaturely obedience in any univocal sense within God. Yet because Christ is obedient, and is the Son of God and expression of God, there must be some mysterious way in which obedience is not foreign to God, or in which human obedience points to something real in the nature of God. Can this 'something real', analogous to human obedience, be specified any further? It seems it can be. Balthasar claims that while the use of the concept of obedience to describe the Son's relationship to the Father in the Trinity is an anthropomorphism, nonetheless, since all speech about God is in some sense anthropomorphic and since this particular concept has a basis in scriptural texts such as Philippians 2, 7, it does point to a reality which one may not simply think away.[135] This reality is different from that of human obedience, which is based ultimately on our ontological status as creatures who come from nothing and are radically dependent. However, one may identify a positive aspect of human obedience which can serve as an image of what is in God, as a revelation of the divine being. This aspect may be described as a filial attitude. When applied to God it points to the way in which the whole being of the Son is there to express and represent the Father, without any trace of subordination. Furthermore it points to the perfect selflessness and self-sacrificing nature of love in God, in all its trinitarian dimensions. In other words, whereas human obedience, even when freely rendered, is rooted in the natural necessity which binds the creature to his creator, there is an essential freedom in this reality when it is applied to God, a freedom which is proper to that love which is inherent in the divine nature. This type of specification of the way human realities of Christ may be applied to God involves a rejection of those aspects of the realities which are proper to the dependent, contingent nature of creatures. It involves instead an acceptance of those aspects which point to a mode of love that embraces a self-giving to the point of being freely affected by the other, and a divine enrichment that is neither necessary, nor temporal, nor caused by anything external to God (since the whole of creation, as we shall see in the next section and more fully in chapter 2, is 'in' Christ and God).

It is within this second approach, and within a contemporary context which can evaluate suffering and receptivity in a more positive light than was possible within a cosmologically-grounded natural theology lacking in developed personalist categories,[136] that Balthasar moves to posit an analogous suffering in the divine nature. It is this tendency in his thought which explains why he draws on writers like Lactantius and Heschel to support the contention that there is something like suffering in God, a supra-kenosis or supra-suffering. And the use of the analogy between human suffering and the reality which corresponds to it in God will be regulated along the lines already described with reference to the notion of obedience. However, in all such cases it is useful to recall that the small progress

in specifying how the analogy works does not by any means dissolve
the mystery. In particular it is worth noting that analogous attribution cannot simply be divided up into aspects that are identically
similar between God and us and others which are totally different,[137]
rather as if one were to describe a centaur as being similar and
dissimilar to a man and were able then to go on to identify in a precise
way the similarity and dissimilarity. The gap between creator and
creature is so great that even after one has eliminated those aspects of
the created analogue which quite simply do not apply to God – for
example the ontological necessity inherent in human obedience – one
must still respect the fact that the positive aspects – for example the
filial attitude expressing the selflessness of love – are present in God in
a way that is very different from its presence in us. Nonetheless,
granted some similarity – without which all talk about God is
equivocal – can one from scriptural, theological considerations posit
an analogous suffering, anger, pathos and so on in the divine nature,
just as traditionally one spoke in philosophical terms of God's
analogous love, knowledge, power and so on?

There is no direct answer to this question in Balthasar. He does not
explicitly say that there is an analogous suffering in God's divine
nature. The two approaches presented here are not related in such a
way that the tendency to posit an analogous suffering in the divine
nature is actually realised and affirmed in those terms.[138] The
language is altered slightly, and many careful formulations – for
example, that the obedience of Christ is a human revelation both of his
divine person and of his *divine being (seines göttlichen Wesens)*[139] – are
used which avoid a direct statement about an analogous suffering in
the divine nature. Perhaps these two approaches can and ought to be
further related and, while remaining respectful of the mystery, we
should give a more definitive answer to our question in the terms it is
posed here; this is something we will return to later. Certainly the
refusal to go this far has probably obviated the need for a more
systematic philosophical engagement with both Process thinkers and
traditional Thomists. What we get instead is a transposition of the
discussion into the terminology of the divine trinitarian event, with its
focus on the nature of God as inter-personal and on an analogy
between human and divine nature which is regulated by the
difference between divine and human love. We may expect further
enlightenment in this particular area from our discussion of the divine
attributes in chapter 2.

The God/Christ relationship as model for the God/us relationship

The relationship between God and Christ is one of *expression* and of *dialogue*. First, then, as expression of God, Christ tells us about the Father, himself, the Spirit, and the one trinitarian divine being of God.[140] As word of the Father he is the archetype of every self-expression of God *ad extra*.[141] By 'expression', a term developed in some detail by Balthasar in his treatment of Bonaventure,[142] he does not mean that Christ is a mere reduplication of the Father.[143] Rather – and this takes us on to the second aspect of the relationship – Christ is personally other than the Father, so that God is revealed as a trinitarian event in which there is mutual interaction and dialogue between the personal poles.[144] In being so clear about the tri-personal nature of the mysteriously one, identical, absolute, divine being, Balthasar is affirming the reality of a real I/Thou[145] exchange within God who is love.

This trinitarian relationship between God and Christ is the model for the relationship between God and us. In particular the reality of Christ as personal expression and dialogue partner of the Father becomes the exemplar of our relationship with God.[146] Thus, while creation in general is an expression of God, and is taken into the inner-trinitarian relationship by existing 'in' Christ, this is particularly true of the human being, made in God's image and likeness, and sharing the same nature as Christ himself.[147] Of course this is not to say that created being ever sheds its creaturely status; created being in its various hierarchial grades, including humankind, is a deficient, analogical expression of God, whereas Christ, who uniquely *is* God, is the perfect divine expression *ad extra*.[148] Nonetheless this general framework indicates the likelihood that, within the careful parameters already outlined, Balthasar's theology of creation and its history will allow for some interaction with God of a kind which will support the positions noted so far on the issues of God's immutability and impassibility. This framework will have to accomodate in its detail the objection that nothing can be added to God – that, in the words of the old Scholastic adage, while creation means that there are more beings, it does not mean that there is more of being (*plus entia, non plus entis*).[149] These details will emerge in our second chapter; for now it is enough to have indicated how the notion of Christ as expression and dialogue partner of God is used by Balthasar to suggest an analogous relationship between us and God.

Summing up

This christological account has shown us how Balthasar, blending different themes together in an internally consistent and complementary way, can answer both 'yes' and 'no' to the question about change in God. His careful approach firmly rejects any direct speech about the mutability of God, just as it also insists on the need to qualify the traditional understanding of divine immutability. A middle way is sought by appealing to the trinitarian presuppositions of Christology, and in particular to an understanding of the Trinity in terms of what may be referred to analogously as an event of inter-personal divine love. A more precise description and explanation of this event, along with its significance for the issue at hand, will be presented in chapter 4. It will involve, as has become obvious on many occasions in the course of our christological discussion, some account of the relationship between time and eternity (chapter 3) and of the whole nature of theological discourse (chapter 4). In the meantime, in order to present an adequate descriptive account of the data used by Balthasar as a source of his explanatory theology of the divine immutability, we need in chapter 2 to examine the bearing which created reality and its history have on our issue.

Within this formal framework it is worth highlighting some particular aspects which have emerged and are crucial for our continuing enquiry. One such aspect is the identification, in varying degrees of detail, of the divine freedom as being an important regulatory principle in differentiating the analogous attribution to God of created properties such as suffering. Balthasar's thought in this area, presented most fully in our section on the *person and nature of Christ*, needs the further development it will receive in chapter 2 in the section on the attributes of God in order to become at least descriptively clear, although its ultimate grounding must lie in his theology of the trinitarian event. Related to this aspect are several questions which are inter-related and also demand a trinitarian answer. These concern the precise description of negativity within God, the extent to which God is pan-kenotic, the varying suggestions which imply that there is a 'wound' in God always, or that in fact God is touched only in his 'outer' and not in his 'inner' being. In these Balthasar's concern seems to be to preserve the divine freedom and sovereignty while allowing for the power of love to be vulnerable – but once again we need to develop his thought further before we can assess the validity of his attempt. A final aspect worth highlighting is the way in which our methodological note (see p. 40 above) spelled out in some detail the relationship between subsidiary and main issues and thus facilitated our procedure throughout the enquiry.

2

Creation and God's immutability

God created our world and entered into a covenant with men and women. This covenant involves the gradual, free, historical insertion of humankind into the life of God, a process that culminates definitively at some end-point. It is not our concern to offer a theology of creation, the history of salvation and eschatology *simpliciter*, but rather to present Balthasar's thought on how these areas affect our theology of God. In other words, do the act of creation, the historical interaction with creatures and the end result of that interaction affect God, matter to him, change him? This relational way of putting the question indicates that, within the rich multiplicity and variety of created kind, our focus will be mainly on humankind, so that along with the metaphysical question concerning the possibility of the very existence of created reality we will be addressing the more existential point, so important to Christian spirituality, concerning the significance of men and women for God, the sense in which their relationship with him is one of reciprocity. Can such a non-Deistic relationship be conceived without lapsing into the other extreme of a mythological God?[1] It is one thing to concede the possibility, within the framework outlined in chapter 1 of Christ (who is God) affecting God; it is quite another matter, worthy of distinct and more detailed consideration, to ask whether we (who are not God, and not Christ) can also in some way affect God.

The act of creation: its presuppositions and effects

(1) We may begin by laying down the parameters of the discussion with a set of basic statements.

First, the act of creation does not change God.[2] Nor does the creation of human freedom, with all that this involves, change God.[3] These bald assertions are intended to convey Balthasar's rejection of any mythological change in God which might so easily be suggested by a common-sense, picture-thinking approach to this question

which immerses God in our spatio-temporal world. The decision to
create is not taken in time, and the space occupied by creation is not
outside God but is rather within the divine, eternal life.[4] And so if
Balthasar goes beyond Aquinas and is willing to speak of a real
relationship between God and creation,[5] he does so within a context
which – as in the case of our discussion of the incarnation – sees
creation as one of the infinite possibilities which lie within God's
eternal life.[6] This means that, once again, it is the divine, trinitarian
'event' itself which, in its eternal liveliness, is the locus for anything
which may remotely resemble change in God.

Secondly, this divine event is the presupposition of creation.[7] This
statement is meant in two different ways. First it is intended to identify
the actual roles, and their appropriateness, of the three Persons of the
Trinity in the act of creation and its subsequent history. While all
three Persons are responsible for creating, it is possible to specify
further their proper contribution.[8] The role of the Son is of particular
importance and we have already indicated some of its significance (see
p. 47 above); the Son as word and expression of the Father is not just
the efficient but also the exemplary and final cause of creation. By this
it is meant that the world, and especially men and women, participate
in a limited way in the Son's role and being as expression and idea of
God, and are thus 'in' the Son.[9] However the second meaning of the
statement concerning the divine presupposition of creation is more
important for present purposes. This meaning relates to what we have
already hinted at about the importance of establishing that God is love
in himself, independently of any creation. The mystery of the Trinity
does establish this, and in so doing clears the way for the specifically
Christian notion of a free creation, beyond all Gnostic-type theories of
an impersonal emanationist and natural creation, or the more
modern, idealistic, Hegelian-type attempts to see creation as a way in
which God becomes himself (thus confusing the realms of creator and
creation in a way which can lead either to pantheism or to atheism
according to the way the basic thought is developed).[10] If God is love
'already' as Trinity, if this love is natural only in the sense that,
beyond our notions of freedom and necessity, it constitutes the being
of God, without any hint of external exigency, then we can see the
sense in which creation can derive from and be an expression of this
same divine love without at all losing its character as a free act of God.
God is necessary, creation is not; and yet creation is due to what most
centrally makes God divine – *viz.* his being as love, now expressed
freely *ad extra*. Balthasar speaks of a caesura[11] between God's eternal

'yes' within the Trinity and the 'yes' which seals the free decision to create – the function of this caesura is not to introduce a temporal factor into God's being, but rather to point out that, while God's eternal inner-divine liveliness does not naturally issue in creation, nonetheless the freedom with which he creates is in accordance with his nature as love in the self-giving way that is revealed in the Trinity. Within this framework creation is affirmed as good in its own, dependent reality: it is not God, but neither is it a mere accident or appearance.

Thirdly, then, the statement that the world is real and distinct from, if dependent on, God leads to a series of assertions which touch directly on the issue of the divine immutability and, furthermore, point to the need to deepen our present discussion. Thus Balthasar can speak of the real and mutual relationship between God and the world (in particular the world of human beings), which God freely enters into but by which he is then in a certain sense bound and limited.[12] The language of kenosis is used to describe this situation, as it was to describe the original event within God, and realities such as the incarnation and cross.[13] By it Balthasar means to assert that this kind of limitation is not something foreign to God, making him less than divine[14] – rather, as indicated in our first chapter, it is precisely here that we find the central NT revelation of the power of God's love which can remain itself while taking on the very real modality of weakness. In other words, once again we are referred to the trinitarian event for an explanation of the kind of effect which creation may have on God. But this will only work if we can find some way to allow creation its distinctive reality while rooting it firmly in the trinitarian life of God. How can this be done? If creation is simply distinct from God, then it limits him in a way not adequately explained by the divine event alone, while if creation exists simply within the divine event then one must question whether it is really distinct from God and, in particular, from Christ. What is required then is a further reflection on the formal identity of the partners in the God/world relationship before we go on to consider the dynamics of the relationship itself.

(2) Christian revelation and spirituality are so imbued with the notion of a mutual relationship between God and the world that it can take something of an effort to appreciate the philoso-phical–theological problem that this involves.[15] The denial by Aquinas of the existence of any real relation between God and the world is but one form of the way in which ancient and modern

thinkers have come to conclusions on this issue which are apparently at variance with the simple scriptural 'given'. Why does one speak of the riddle of the participation of things in the divine ideas of them?[16] The problem becomes apparent when one takes into account the reality of God's 'otherness', which is equally well grounded in Christian revelation and spirituality and also has philosophical roots.[17] God as creator is so totally other from us his creatures that he does not simply stand against us as the other in an I/Thou relationship, but, in being superior to us, is in fact closer to us than we are to ourselves (*St Augustine's interior intimo meo et superior summo meo*), is in fact the 'not-other'. The creator is unique in existing simply, absolutely; we exist by participation in him, our very definition as creatures implying a constant relation of dependency on our creator.[18] This means that God is not constituted by any relation he may have to the world, whereas we are constituted by our relation to God.[19] It is this basic truth, of course, which Aquinas intends to express by his rejection of the technically-understood notion of a real relation between God and the world. And this 'otherness' of God, with its strange mixture of transcendence and immanence, means that the relationship between us and God is no ordinary one of mutuality and reciprocity as between two human equals.[20] An equal relationship like this would make God mythological. In particular because God *is* fully, and we exist only 'in' him, (*viz.* by participation in his being according to an image and likeness of him that develops through history), then it is we and not God who are changed in this relationship as we become more fully like him. But before we can develop this aspect of the relationship, and qualify this latter assertion in the way Balthasar does, we must first tackle the more basic problem concerning this 'otherness' of God. This may be formulated by asking how, if God is the fullness of Being, is everything (Sir. 43, 27; 1 Cor 15, 28), there can exist anything else at all?[21] We have already identified this problem in terms of how creation can be both distinct from God and yet 'in' God. Its philosophical form is that of the question concerning the one and the many. One may ask how, if one equates the Absolute with Being, and outside Being there is nothing, there can be room for the many relative realities which are not God, not the Absolute. The answer will be important of course, but so too is the question, for without the latter one fails to appreciate the problem and thus the careful language and distinctions which are required when one speaks of the mutual relationship between God and the world.

We must now look more closely at Balthasar's trinitarian answer to this problem. The key insight here is that it is of the essence of God, who is absolute and thus dependent on nothing outside himself, to be triune, which means to be internally related in love as Father, Son and Holy Spirit. This positive reality of distinction and difference within the one, absolute God is what makes possible the existence, through free creation, of the many distinct beings which are other than God and intrinsically related to him in dependence.[22] It makes it possible because difference – the Father is *not* the Son – is seen as something central to the divine omnipotence understood as love, and so the fact that creatures are different, are *not* God, in no way limits this omnipotence. Of course this creaturely 'not' (the creature is not God) is not identical with the trinitarian 'not' (the Father is not the Son), otherwise once again we would be forced into saying that creation is necessary. But given that creation is a free act of God's love, its true if analogous reality must be understood to be grounded in the trinitarian 'not' – the infinite distance between the world and God has its foundation in that original distance between God and God, within God.[23] In particular, of course, the created world as expression and gift of God is to be understood according to the trinitarian reality of the Son's existence as expression and gift of the Father. As image and likeness of God creation participates in a limited and multiple way in the unique, singular and full expression of the Father by the Son. Its goodness can be seen in the way in which creaturely becoming can both express the inner liveliness of the eternal relationship between the Father and the Son and be a sign of increasing faithfulness to the Idea of creation present in the Son as expression of the Father.[24]

What is being said here is that it is the fact that God is relational that allows the world to exist, taken up as it is into that relation between the Father and Son which is the Holy Spirit. A relational trinitarian God is one in whom distinction does not abolish unity. It is according to this model that the Hypostatic Union is correctly interpreted by Chalcedon in its so-called two-natures teaching, which states that the divine and human natures of Christ are unmixed and yet inseparable, while both the Trinity and the Hypostatic Union are models for a correct understanding of the relationship between the world and God in which the world's distinction is maintained within its intrinsic and necessary ordering to God. That the distinct reality of the world is in fact constituted by this relation to God – while the reality of God, as we have seen, is in no way constituted by the existence of the world – means that one may speak of a real and mutual relationship of God to the world only within the real relationship between God and God, that is between the Father and the Son in the Holy Spirit.[25]

Formulations like the above owe much to a relational ontology which goes beyond but includes the categories of substance metaphysics more familiar to ancient philosophy. Balthasar himself also uses a more explicitly pictorial approach to get the same points across.[26] The life of God involves an eternal, mutual exchange of love between persons who are different – and this is only possible if there is something like an infinite space and duration within God. The Trinitarian event, then, means that the Father's 'womb' is 'empty' once he has generated the Son, that the Son who is God in receiving rather than taking is 'poor' in all his richness, that the Holy Spirit as mere 'breath' of the Father and Son is in some sense also 'without being' – in other words the self-giving of the persons within the trinitarian life of love, which includes the way in which each person allows the other two to be, involves this kind of freedom of space, without any implication that God is less than God because of this. And it is within this space that we find our home, so that just as in God the Father never absorbs the Son but all three Persons remain distinct, so too we are allowed to be and remain ourselves and free within the room which God gives us in his own home.

It will be useful now to summarise how what has been said establishes the formal framework of the God/world relationship in a way which addressed the objections we have made and opens up an approach to considering how the dynamics of this relationship may affect God. The trinitarian event means that there is difference within the unity of God and a personal exchange which involves an eternal liveliness and increase.[27] The more exact details of this event, whether in pictorial or in more technical form, will be presented in chapter 4; for now, the important assertion is that the world is itself, and distinct, only as related to God, and hence that it adds to God not in any quantitive sense but only as a further expression of the relationship between the Father and the Son. In other words, the world in itself is 'from nothing'; its reality in itself, which is true and distinct, is from God, in particular from the free expression of the Father in the Son, and so any 'adding' that is involved is to be understood only within the 'adding' that is part of the eternal event of Father, Son and Holy Spirit.[28] This means that the existence of God and the world together is not greater than the existence of God alone,[29] except in the sense that God himself as trinitarian event of love is always 'ever-greater'. What it is vital to grasp here is that any effect of the world on God does not emanate from a reality external to God; the world on its own is nothing – its power to be, to be distinct and to affect God comes from God. One might object that it is one thing to accept that differences exist within God of a personal kind which are shown in the 'ever-greater' of the trinitarian event, but that the widening of the term 'difference' to embrace distinct beings who are not God brings with it precisely the unacceptable corollary that God is affected by external, created reality. However the brunt of Balthasar's argument is that it is the trinitarian difference that makes possible the one between creator and creature; that within the infinite distance between Father and Son, and the infinite possibilities this contains, there lies the intelligibility of the free creation of our finite world. To put it crudely, then, that God can posit the world as real and distinct from himself, albeit united in dependent relationship to him, is less miraculous than that within God himself there should exist Father, Son and Holy Spirit, really distinct and yet one.[30] The paradoxical fact that creation possesses its 'of itselfness' from God and not apart from him is made possible by the trinitarian mystery in which identity of nature and being is within personal opposition.[31] And this means that when God freely actuates one of the infinite possibilities inherent in the divine event by creating our world, what the world, which is not-God, gives to God is in fact its own but is so from God – it is, then, God's own gift to me but also to himself within the life of the Trinity.[32] Which means in turn, of course, that any change that occurs in God due to us does so from and within the trinitarian event.

It is worth stressing again that Balthasar is clear that the world is not just some sort of appearance, lacking in a reality of its own, nor is its reality, distinct from God, provisional as if it were its ultimate fate to be absorbed in God. The world exists really, participating in the existence of God; and human freedom in particular, analogous to God's infinite freedom, is genuine even when it goes against its character as image of God in issuing in a creaturely 'no' to God. This means that there is a real sense in which – as was true of Christ – the world is both the expression and the dialogue partner of God, so that we may indeed speak, with care, of a covenant and a mutual relationship between God and the world.[33] This needs to be stressed because phrases which speak of the world as 'taken up into' the divine relationship between Father and Son, as 'within' the trinitarian event, as 'in' the Son, or of time and history as being 'contained' in eternity, and so on, convey linguistically the impression that the reality of the world is downgraded. It should be clear by now that with the use of such language Balthasar in fact intends to convey the exact opposite: in his view the only way to guarantee the distinct reality of the world is to see it in dependent relation to God. It is intrinsic to God's power as trinitarian love to be able freely to create beings that are not-God, and which yet are such precisely as part of the relationship between Father and Son.

(3) We have been establishing in a formal way the identity of creation in order to prepare the ground for an understanding of how God might be affected in the dynamics of his relationship with the world. The absolutely dependent being of the world has been presented, according to the christological and trinitarian models and causes, as distinct precisely in its relation to God, particularly in its participation in the trinitarian relationship of the Son to the Father which involves the Holy Spirit. This is a different understanding from positions which would say that the world is necessary, or a mere appearance, or is God, or is distinct from God in the sense of being independent or separate. Rather, the world is really but relatively independent. Creation is most itself and most free when it realises its dependence on God, by analogy with the Son's utter receptivity and gratitude towards the Father. This means that Balthasar has indeed established a framework within which we, who are not God and not Christ, may in some way affect God. We may do so as one of the modalities of the eternally enriching relationship between the Father and the Son: the mutuality of the I/Thou relationship between God and the world is real, with a proper contribution from the side of the world, but all within the relationship between God and God in the Trinity. And in this way of course God is no more limited – in the sense of being made less than God – by his relationship with the world than he is by the intra-divine relational life.

The historical aspect of the relationship between creation and God

Having established who the 'partners' are in the God/world relationship we now go on to investigate the sense in which this relationship may be said to develop or change through time. It is clear, of course, that human beings undergo change in their relationship with God over time. However, given that Balthasar has established the possiblity that creatures may affect God as one of the modalities of the relationship between the Father and the Son, we will now examine how this possibility is actualised in the course of human history. We will consider three themes through which Balthasar develops his approach to this issue.

God's immutable providence and our free history

What does human temporal freedom imply for our understanding of the eternal immutability of the divine plan and of God himself? This question is addressed by Balthasar in a section of *TD*, II/I.[34] Here he notes that the exercise of human freedom is made possible because the omnipresent God assumes a certain latency (*Latenz*) or incognito vis-à-vis creation, in such a way that the human will is not forced by the one choice of the overwhelming and absolute good that is God himself but is faced with many choices about various partial goods. Of course in these different choices there is implied a decision about God too; and in this sense God accompanies us as well as being hidden from us, and his hidden revelation of himself makes it *possible* for us to choose him without making this *necessary*. This introductory framework is followed by an account of God's accompaniment of us in which our question concerning the divine providence and immutability is tackled more directly.

God's plan for the world (Rom. 8, 28–39; Eph. I, 3–10) is one and it is universal. It involves the eternal presence of God in every possible and actual created time. As such it always contains God's 'answer' to every exercise of human freedom, including of course that part of the answer which is forgiveness of sin won through the blood of Christ. In this plan, then, it is in the Son that we are both chosen and saved: he is the immutable image and idea of all creation, of all individuals and groups, of whatever era. He is so, however, in a way that allows for genuinely free human activity, that does not impose a pre-determined fate. Unlike the Stoic cosmic version of the Logos as idea of the world, the Christian revelation proposes in this role the eternal Son of God whose eternal freedom as readiness towards the Father is always the same, whatever particular modality (e.g. the incarnation, the cross) it assumes. In other words, because God's plan covers all – and in particular because, as trinitarian and soteriological, in the Son it allows for the extremes of human freedom – then it can really allow us to be free and to change, without this involving new decisions for God. This means that there are no grounds, in considering the relationship between God's providence and the exercise of our human freedom in time, to polemicise against the immutability of God. To predicate immutability of God is not to falsify the lively and personal God of the Bible by attributing to him a 'sub-personal' attribute borrowed from the 'geometrical' thought of antiquity. Nor is it sufficient to interpret immutability and the text in Exodus 3, 14 as simply a promise of God's eternal fidelity to his people without foundation in his being – immutability very correctly has an ontological basis, and it will not do to set up a false opposition between the scriptural revelation concerning divine immutability and philosophical pre-understandings, however insufficient in themselves. This assertion of an ontological divine immutability means at the very least that there can be no creaturely change in God's being. However at this point Balthasar does distance himself from the way immutability was understood philosophically within the classical ontological horizon of understanding – such an understanding misleads in its attempt to explain the immutability of the plan and being of the God of the Bible, which must include realities like the incarnation and the cross.[35] Instead we must, once again, look to the trinitarian life for a revelation of what divine immutability involves. In that God's life and plan show a maximum of content – which eternally allows and responds to our every temporal exercise of human freedom – they can be rightly called immutable. But neither the life itself, nor this 'maximum', can be pinned down by a full stop; eternal life is not the negation of time or space but rather the unimaginable supra-fullness (*Überfülle*) of time and space for freedom, which expresses the fullness of life that happens eternally in God. God's eternal plan, then, has 'space' and 'time' for all created space and time. Once again we have here in Balthasar a reference to that 'ever-greater' aspect of the trinitarian event, to which we must return in more detail in chapter 4.

With this understanding in mind Balthasar goes on to explain the impression that can derive from the Bible of a mutable God. No human insight can grasp how the two sides of the cross, the justice and mercy of God, are finally resolved in the last judgement: but what is clear to faith is that this resolution is eternally present in God. This means that the Bible, especially the OT, can speak many times of God changing his attitude, of his regret (*Reue*), where it should be clear that what is referred to is the confrontation between the partial, changing situation of the human being and the totality of the divine plan. In this context it is indeed suitable to speak of God's punishment of us in response to sin, followed by his forgiveness. But the OT also says that God does not change his attitude – and this refers to the fact that in some mysterious way the real confrontation between our historical exercise of freedom and God's will is always resolved within God's eternal plan and does not require any change on God's part, as if he had to respond to some unforeseen eventuality. This treatment of the apparent mutability of God in the Bible is a restatement by

Balthasar, in the context of this discussion on providence, of the basic
position we saw him adopting about the realities of God's anger and
mercy in his soteriology. He concludes this account of the universality
of God's plan by stating that talk in theology of the 'mutability of God'
is to be avoided precisely because of God's absolute freedom. This
freedom, expressed in the ever-greater love of God which the Father
reveals through the Holy Spirit in the obedient, self-sacrificing love of
the Son, is the most constant thing there is, and also, viewed from the
world, the most moving and flexible (*Beweglichste*).

Balthasar's basic position may now be stated in a number of brief
points. First, our lives are truly in time but are present to God all at
once, eternally. We will be examining the relationship between time
and eternity at greater length in chapter 3; for now it suffices to note
how such an eternal divine presence in what is genuinely temporal
can mean that God's plan of us is indeed immutable. It is so because
the eternal God can take into account all at once what in us goes on
consecutively, and thus can plan comprehensively and without need
to adjust to unforeseen elements. Secondly, our changing lives
through time are patterned after the relationship of the Son to the
Father, not according to some impersonal Idea which would lead to a
life that was totally imposed on us. Because of this there is room in
God's plan for us to be genuinely free; this personal aspect, with all its
attendant risks, is possible because of the different modalities (many of
which were indicated in our first chapter) which the relationship
between the Father and the Son can assume eternally. Thirdly, our
free, changing, temporal lives affect God in so far as they are taken up
into this relationship between Father and Son in the Trinity (see
p. 52 above) and so, from within this relationship itself, 'introduce'
different modalities into the divine life. Of course the 'introduction' in
question cannot be temporal, nor is its eternal nature to be equated
simply with the nature of God himself – we must still distinguish
between God's necessary being and his free decision to create. But God
is present eternally to his free creation and time, and this presence
does entail various modalities within the trinitarian event which
would not otherwise be there.

God's immutability and the prayer of petition

The same basic pattern is evident in Balthasar's treatment of the
prayer of petition.[36] With this topic we are dealing with an instance of
the interaction between the concrete historical situation of the

creature and his/her immutable God, an instance of great importance for the lives of Christian men and women.

The order of divine–human interaction is a personal one. This means that freedom is respected, the relationship is dialogical and not simply automatic or 'natural'.[37] It means that there can be such a thing as divine anger in response to my sin, and that I may ask for forgiveness of that sin. In particular this personal order is one between creator and creature in which all that the creature has and is depends on the creator. It is the existence of this kind of order between God and us which makes petitionary prayer intelligible. But does this then involve a mutability of God in response to the concrete exigencies of our historical situations? No, because God in his eternity can take all secondary causes into account in his plan for us, and because he has at his disposal an infinity of ways in which to lead all to what is best, so that, no matter what kind of free decisions we take, there is no need for God to improvise, as if he had to change his world plan in a way unexpected to him 'after' and as a result of our activities. The omnipotence of God, which includes his omniscience and the universality of his plan, is at the heart of this explanation – but so too is the mysterious relationship between time and eternity which allows God to be always present to what in us is experienced consecutively, in time, and thus to be always the same while permitting and responding to our real, temporal freedom.

But once again, this time from the perspective of the prayer of petition, this 'sameness' of being in God has to be opened out beyond the confines of the traditional notion of divine immutability. While it would be incorrect to say that God is loving only in response to our prayers, it would be equally wrong to suggest that he is loving in a way which is indifferent to them. Instead we must find a way of showing how God really does deal with us in a personal mode so that he allows himself to be influenced by our prayers. And so – analogous to his soteriological account of Christ's cross[38] – Balthasar proposes the paradoxical position that our prayers are both the effects and the 'causes' of God's love, that God is both unmovable and movable by worldly events. By the latter he means to insist on the real secondary causation of petitionary prayer.[39] This occurs, of course, within the framework already outlined in which God freely wills that this should be so, and in which we and our activity are 'in Christ' so that – once again as in the soteriological aspect of the relationship between the Father and the Son – we become part of the inner-divine event. This means that the primacy lies with the freedom of God's love, yet in such a way that the value of the created contribution is preserved. This contribution becomes part of the 'process' by which, within the divine event and its inner liveliness, different modalities or aspects of God's love (e.g. anger and mercy in response to sin) are allowed to co-exist and yet be eternally reconciled. We, then, are joined to the prayer of Jesus through the Holy Spirit, so that our prayer is, in a real sense, part of God's prayer to God[40] – something which can only make sense within a trinitarian context. Similarly not just our prayers but also our lives are 'co-redemptive' when understood within this same context which maintains the unique, primary role of Christ in reconciling us to the Father while graciously offering us a secondary, participatory role.[41]

Our dialogue with God in freedom and through time and history

This theme, concerning the dialogue and often opposition between the eternal, infinite freedom of God and the finite, temporal freedom of human beings, is clearly crucial to Balthasar's notion of *Theodramatik*.[42] In line with the framework set out on p. 57 above concerning the identity of the 'partners' in the God/world relationship, Balthasar sees a real mutuality existing between infinite and finite freedom. This mutuality does not threaten the transcendence, sovereignty or initiative of God. The human creature, although altogether unequal to God and thus 'in' God in the way described (p. 54 above), is nonetheless truly free and does not merge with God in a way which would destroy the reciprocity of the relationship. Indeed, as already indicated, far from overwhelming or forcing us God gives us a freedom that is our own to the point of permitting us to sin. Yet true inner freedom is not to be had in a titanic exercise independent of God, but rather we are most free, and most ourselves, when we are most intimately inserted into the divine life. Thus the analogy of Being is developed by Balthasar into an analogy of freedom, or inter-personal love, in which the derived, dependent, graced freedom of the creature must be real and the creature's own precisely if it is to be an expression of the divine freedom.[43] If this expression – whose dissimilarity will be greater than a nonetheless enduring similarity – is lacking then the analogy fails. By establishing freely this kind of reciprocal relationship between himself and the world God has chosen to be affected by our finite freedom. He has in this sense given us rights over himself, and this divine vulnerability is seen most dramatically in God's relationship to the sinner. In this context Balthasar speaks, with St Francis and Tauler, about 'one of the tenderest of God's qualities, which one may describe as "divine poverty" '.[44] And elsewhere, in an attempt to convey the same reality, he notes that God relates to the world not only in a masculine way as *Deus faber* but also in a receptive, feminine way, suffering the salvation of the entire universe.[45]

God's sovereignty is not threatened by this drama, in which he chooses to make himself vulnerable, because God is triune. Once again, then, it is the trinitarian event which grounds the possibility of this kind of dialogical relationship between God and us. Already as triune God is dialogical, and we are created in the Word and given a participation in the inner-trinitarian exchange. We are given this truly, if dependently, and thus without any diminution of the divine power as occurs in mythological accounts of God's relationship to the world: 'However immeasurably the power of God is above all creaturely power in its sovereign independence, God still seeks to preserve in the working of his grace the covenant mystery of mutualness, as he laid down in his creation and as he reveals as his inner trinitarian secret.'[46] This inner trinitarian secret, this kenotic love, with its inner liveliness, is what makes possible that kind of 'mutability' in God in response to the influence of creatures.

The drama between infinite and finite freedom, then, shows that there is a real mutuality, that God is affected, and that all this is possible because of the nature of the trinitarian event. A final comment is in order about the historico-temporal character of human freedom in its relationship to the eternal freedom of God (see p. 58 above). In his concern to remove any impression that God out-manoeuvres us in a way which destroys our human freedom, Balthasar reminds us that God's eternal omniscience and providence contain a differentiated awareness of human time with its past, present and future.[47] Because of this it is more correct to speak of God creatively (through the Holy Spirit) responding to each human decision and situation as they arise, than to imagine that God's response is 'already' always decided.[48] We may express this by using the image of drama which Balthasar so favours: not only does the drama conceived by God require us to be actors in it, not only does it retain its own dramatic sense even when related to the interior drama of God himself (like the play within the play in *Hamlet*),[49] but also – as was said of Christ's incarnation – it is a drama conceived, produced and acted all in one, 'not the nth performance of a tragedy already lying in the archives of eternity', but 'an event of total originality, as unique and untarnished as the eternally here-and-now birth of the

Son from the Father'.[50] We will take up this notion of the creative originality involved in the mysterious relationship between time and eternity in chapter 3 (see also pp. 69–75 below).

Conclusion

The temporal, historical life of humankind, because of its character as expression of God, already tells us something about the liveliness and difference that are within the Trinity and that cause us to qualify the traditional meaning of divine immutability. But men and women, through time and history, not only express God, they also interact with him. Balthasar is clear that in this interaction history as history has meaning for God.[51] It has it within the trinitarian event, as described; but we must be careful to insist once more that its own character as history, as created, and thus as different from God, is maintained. It will not do, then, to reduce the mystery in an undifferentiated way to that of the inner divine life alone.[52] We make our own contribution to God within that life and because of it.

Critics[53] have suggested that in fact (if not in principle) Balthasar gives too little room in his theology to the material aspects of human history, that the 'vertical' integration of what is created into God leads him to ignore a more evolutionary view of history which would attend more to the positive role of human development in a 'horizontal' sense. I have argued elsewhere that there is validity in this criticism.[54] However it would still seem that Balthasar's framework - regardless of some of the details of his own use of it – does in principle allow human beings a true identity, history and role in their relationship with each other and with God. And it is this framework, with its consequences for God himself, which is of interest to us here. It implies, as we have indicated, qualifications to the traditional way that the divine transcendence as immutability was understood. But of course the framework itself depends for its ultimate intelligibility precisely on Balthasar's position on the trinitarian event, as on the relationship between eternity and time. Should his position on these two issues prove to be satisfactory – a matter for our third and fourth chapters – it would seem that in this very mysterious relationship between God and us, which is without an exact human analogy,[55] Balthasar has found a way to respect the human, historical contribution without threat to the divine transcendence.

Eschatology and God's immutability

Introduction: the question

We focus now on the end-point of the historical relationship between creation and God; how does this eschatological point of view affect the issue of the divine immutability? A major source for our account will be Balthasar's *Theodramatik, Bd* IV, *Das Endspiel* (1983),[56] in which is presented the author's trinitarian–christological eschatology.

Our treatment, then, will be shaped by the question concerning the ultimate fate of humankind and the effect of this on God.[57] Is this end-point of human history tragic for God, or an enrichment of him, or a mixture of both, or does it not matter to him at all? If some people are condemned to hell, does this mean that God as creator is tragic, that in some way his will that all be saved is so thwarted that he is defeated, a failure? In other words, in this theocentric eschatological approach Balthasar, instead of posing the traditional question about what man would lose if he lost God, is daring to ask what he knows is the far from unproblematic question about what God would lose if he lost man. Rejecting an older approach, which with a certain amazingly cool indifference could assert that God's glory was served equally well by either our eternal happiness or our eternal punishment, Balthasar nonetheless wishes to respect the NT texts concerning the twofold issue of divine judgement, the increasing opposition to the love of God after the event of Christ, and also the freedom of man to make a definitive choice with his life without being forced or overwhelmed by God.[58] In doing so he must reject any simple apocatastasis solution.[59] Obviously, in presenting the matter thus the question about universal salvation is of key concern to us. But it is so because implicit in Balthasar's rejection of the older approach is an acknowledgement that in some way the world does affect God: this certainly is consistent with all we have said so far in chapter 2, but the eschatological issue, as we will see, is the real testing-ground to see if statements about our effect on God, the way Christ saves us, and our continuing freedom to say 'no' to God can really hold together. We are, then, brought face to face in the ultimate way with the meaning of creation and salvation for God: can the world really 'contribute' something to God, within the trinitarian event, can we be sure that this contribution is positive, and, if not, what does this imply about our image of God?[60]

Steps towards a solution: the theology of hope and of the pain of God

The theology of hope

The contemporary theological interest in hope – and, in particular, for our purposes, the theology of Moltmann in this area, inspired by Bloch – may be used as a first step towards establishing Balthasar's position.[61] The issue may be stated thus: if the mission of Jesus is in some sense incomplete until the last of us is saved, is there a sense in which not only we hope for this salvation but God hopes for it too? And what are the implications of this hope in God – for God?

The question is approached in the context of an attempt to state what is proper to Christian hope, in distinction from pagan or Jewish hope. In particular the enquiry focuses on the problem at the centre of modern eschatology as to whether the primarily 'vertical' thrust of Christian hope can include a genuinely 'horizontal' dimension. The discussion with Moltmann addresses this problem;[62] we are less interested in the detail of this discussion than in the position on the theology of God which we see Balthasar adopting throughout it.

He is critical of a position which ascribes relevance to the future, 'horizontal' history of the world after the Christ-event as an object of theological hope.[63] He argues that this position implies that God becomes himself through the world's becoming. Balthasar sees at its root an excessive and confusing identity in what is admittedly that most mysterious, central and difficult matter of the relationship between the immanent and economic Trinity. It is simply not true – *pace* Hegel – that because love must have the other as beloved, the world is necessary to God (and thus that there *must* be an economic Trinity). The abandonment of the Chalcedonian two-natures teaching – and with it of the abiding distinction between creator and creature in all realms – leads to a mythological God into whom worldly becoming, time, pain, death, negativity of all kinds are inserted. But there can be no ontological negativity within God. This notion of a coming, becoming God is very close to the position of Process Theology, in which, ironically, a 'two-natures' teaching is retrieved – but now in such a way that God himself is spoken of as having a double nature, an (ideal) 'primordial nature' and a (real) 'consequent nature' with which he has bound himself to inner-worldly becoming. This is a false way to do justice to the scriptural teaching on God's compassion and to the admitted need to interpret it in a way that goes beyond the Greek notions of impassibility and immutability.

Balthasar's own stress is on the present, 'vertical' thrust of eschatology in the NT and, within this, on the significance of future 'horizontal' world history as the object of Christian mission rather than hope.[64] Christ's historical mission is successfully complete: what we do now after Christ is our contribution within the eternity of the trinitarian event as described. Within this scenario, however, Christian history and hope, with their temporal aspect, are seen as a reflection of something which is really in God, but which manifests itself differently in him from in us. They are in God eternally; thus one can speak about an 'eternal history' in God, (and of God with the world), and an eternal 'original image' or 'supra-idea' (*Urbild, Über-Idee*) of hope in God. In other words there is in God, mysteriously, something like a capacity to receive (thus allowing for the 'not yet' of hope and for a 'supra-time') which is compatible with the divine eternity. This capacity – entirely positive in God – is the original image (*Urbild*) of everything in the realm of creation that is composed of act and potency. A passive potency is active in the sense that it has the power to receive; within the Trinity the positive nature of receptivity or passivity is seen by the way in which the Son receives his being from the Father, the Holy Spirit from Father and Son, without any suggestion that this receptivity betrays a lack of being as in the case with potency in the realm of creation whose origins are *ex nihilo*. Similarly in the Father, while there is of course no loss of his divinity, there is in the 'generation' of the Son a surrendering (always, eternally in God – this is not a way of suggesting God was first Father and then decided to be Trinity) of being God on his own, a certain renunciation and then communication of all that he is and has. One stammers[65] in the attempt to speak of these mysterious passivities – already referred to also as modalities – within the divine *actus purus*. Their existence – which allows for something like hope, and, indeed, faith and prayer within God[66] – is due to the infinite differences (and their interaction) that are within the identity in love of Father, Son and Holy Spirit. These trinitarian differences are, as we have already seen, enabling presuppositions of a creation which is free even to the point of sinning. Thus while Balthasar does not speak of the 'original image' (*Urbild*) of sin as being in God he does maintain that that experience of separation from God, which is the effect of sin, must be capable of being integrated into the trinitarian differences. There it is positive, because again it is one of the possible expressions of that love between Father and Son in the Holy Spirit which has freely created finite freedom and now bears the consequences of that freedom's entirely negative act of sin.[67]

In refusing to attribute hope – or any other inner-worldly attribute, including pain – in any univocal sense to God Balthasar maintains the distinction between creator and creature. Similarly the related, but different, distinction between immanent and economic Trinity is held open. The world is not necessary to God: the beloved other (who is also equal, the same God) is within the Trinity, thus enabling God to exist without the world.

Finally, Balthasar, with reference to the issue of salvation raised at the beginning of this section, says that as Christians we hope that by God's mercy we may come successfully through his judgement.[68] Our salvation is also a 'hope' of God, an economic side of that supra-hope (*Über-Hoffnung*) which already exists within the trinitarian event and without any necessary reference to the world. This divine hope is described in the terms used by the French poet Péguy in his interpretation of the NT on this theme.[69] Péguy, inspired by the three parables in Luke 15 concerning the lost sheep, the lost coin and the prodigal son, speaks of the hope of Jesus that each individual will be saved. This hope reveals the heart of God to us in this matter: despite the divine anxiety and worry in the face of our sins and the possibility of our ultimate loss of eternal life God continues to respect our freedom because of the hope he has in the wonder of his grace. God's anxiety and hope are a consequence of his love for each one of us, a love which makes him dependent on us. The unguarded, poetic language of Péguy must be transposed within the framework already described: Balthasar would agree with him that there is something like hope in God, a hope which contains all the seriousness of created hope but still is very different from the latter. In particular it is present eternally in God, even while having as its object in this case a truly temporal order of being and events. This supra-hope makes it more difficult to be triumphalist about our salvation. It also breaks through an overly rigid notion of the divine pre-knowledge and providence: Balthasar wishes to leave room within God for the newness, the wonder, the vitality and youthfulness that are associated with hope.[70] These are part of the inner-trinitarian event, due to the interaction between the divine Persons. We will need at a later stage to examine more thoroughly the relationship between the divine omniscience and this eternal 'supra-hope' with its temporal referrent (see also pp. 63–4 above).

The theology of God's pain

The question remains: do we say an ultimate 'no' to God? No answer is given yet, but Balthasar first considers the implications for God of this possibility in us of saying 'no'. The thematic treatment of divine impassibility that ensues is of major importance for the issue of divine immutability.[71]

Many contemporary theologians who are well aware of the axiom of divine immutability, and of the need to guard against a notion of a mythological God, still speak about the pain of God. They do so in the context of a general movement away from a Greek ontological consideration of God as 'absolute Being' towards a Johannine notion of God as love. This movement has created a new sensibility for the effect on God of sin, the cross, and the possibility of eternal damnation for some of his creatures. As one example among many others Balthasar cites the approach of G. Martelet in speaking of the infinite pain of the God of love in response to the existence of hell.[72]

Balthasar makes it clear from the start that he will not accept any such univocal attribution of pain to God. Created suffering is not simply the same as that inner-divine receptivity for which he has already argued. Nonetheless Balthasar is clearly sympathetic to the underlying concern of contemporary theology in this whole area, and believes that the history of this concern may be traced back to the biblical and Patristic witness.

A brief analysis of the biblical and rabbinic data leads Balthasar to conclude that it supports the notion that in some way God is influenced in a painful way by what we do. He goes on to speak of the Patristic attribution of immutability and impassibility to God. He maintains that the Fathers were correct to reject the notion of a mythological God who changes or suffers in the same way that we do. However in general, with some exceptions, when they used the term *apatheia*, borrowed from Greek philosophy, they did so in a way which allowed God that liveliness, freedom and emotional response to human beings which are characteristically biblical. The term *apatheia* was stressed so strongly because for the Greeks the opposite term, *pathos*, had so many connotations which made it utterly unsuitable for application to God. It implied an external experience that was not freely willed, and was understood in connection with sin.[73] Nonetheless Origen ascribed pathos to the eternal Son and even to the Father; and in doing so he was not as isolated a figure as modern commentators, overlooking the differentiated and qualified use of *apatheia* in the other Fathers, have asserted.

Balthasar concludes by establishing the following parameters: pathos in God cannot mean an unwilled determination from outside. In other words God can only be touched passively if there is a corresponding active, free choice in him to be so affected. Furthermore, one must understand the forms of divine liveliness (such as mercy, patience etc.) after the analogy of human emotions but without thereby ascribing temporal mutability to God. Immutability is not just an 'economic' attribute of God vis-à-vis the covenant with us: it must be a property of God himself. It seems that what Balthasar is proposing here is a liveliness in God analogous to human emotions, which is such that the divine freedom and eternity may be specified as features which distinguish God's suffering from the human analogate. He notes finally that the more rigid interpretation of divine impassibility in the post-Patristic era led to the modern reaction.

We may briefly indicate Balthasar's response to some modern theologies of God's pain. His main criticism of three Hegel-inspired theologies on this issue (Moltmann, Gerard Koch and the Japanese Kazoh Kitamori) is that in different ways they betray their reliance on the basic position which Balthasar attributes to Hegel, that God needs the world to become himself, and that in particular the inner divine life of love is an insipid and unreal game until the introduction of inner-worldly negativity, such as suffering and death, brings it into the seriousness of real life.[74] The Scottish Episcopalian Bertrand Brasnett, although not Hegelian, also has an unwelcome tendency to suggest that creation is necessary for God's greater joy, which leads him to the unacceptable conclusion that dependency and suffering (in response to our sin) are inner elements of God's being.[75] Balthasar will argue that it is only within the Trinity that we can find an adequate foundation to posit something like suffering in God in a way which maintains the 'greater dissimilarity' of the reality as it exists in God. It is a more developed notion of this trinitarian foundation which Balthasar finds lacking in his generally very sympathetic account of Barth's theology of divine suffering.[76]

Finally Balthasar reports the position of the Roman Catholic theologian Jean Galot, who, with the help of the Thomist Jacques Maritain, argues for some kind of passibility in God.[77] Galot's enquiry proceeds through three stages: first, God is immutable in his being (not just in his fidelity to the covenant), so that one must distinguish between a necessary trinitarian life of God which no suffering can affect, and the free decision of the divine persons to create which results in their being affected by pain. Secondly, this mysterious suffering of the divine Persons is not just metaphorical;[78] rather, there is a real analogy between created and divine suffering, albeit the latter, as a *modus* of the divine love, is a perfection which exists within God's joy. Thirdly – and very hesitantly, because here he is going against his own basic first stage above – Galot suggests that perhaps within the Trinity itself there is the basis for a connection between love and pain. He finds this in the ecstatic nature of inner-trinitarian love, which is productive through 'loss of self', and which although itself without pain has in it an inner self-renunciation and sacrifice which can be considered as the source of that renunciation which lies in God's love for us and which contains an aspect of pain. Balthasar wants to accept some form of the trinitarian basis for suffering in God as advocated by Galot, but rejects the latter's abrupt and almost Palamite distinction between an untouchable divine inner life and a relationship of God to the world that is affective.[79]

Balthasar concludes by indicating his own position in the light of the preceding discussion. There is in God something which is somewhat analogous to worldly suffering and which is the foundation for the latter. Philosophically, with Maritain, Balthasar is prepared to accept that we have no proper name for this divine attribute – it is however an integral part of the divine perfection and happiness and allows God to be freely affected by such aspects as the suffering of Christ and our sins. With Maritain again it may be described loosely as a victorious seizing or acceptance or overcoming of pain by God.[80]

This philosophical description is anchored in the trinitarian framework with which we are already familiar. There is something ultimately unsatisfactory in Rahner's formulation that God is immutable in himself but mutable in another: with Varillon[81] Balthasar believes one must go further and at least begin to suspect that in God becoming is a perfection of being, movement a perfection of immobility and mutability a perfection of immutability, that, to speak poetically, the eternally active life of God is like an ever-newly bubbling fountain. Martelet, Schürmann and Hofmann are cited[82] in support of Balthasar's own contention that this life is rooted in the trinitarian life of self-giving. This self-giving is absolute, without built-in assurances or reservations:[83] humanly speaking it would imply an absolute 'risk' for the giver were it not that this gift is eternally received with a thanks that is willing to express its love in the most extreme way. This dynamic of self-giving and thanks applies to all three persons of the Trinity and is not, again *pace* Hegel, a game of love that is without ultimate seriousness. Rather the selfless love which unites the infinite distances between the Persons in the Trinity is so real that it can contain within it all inner-worldly distances, events, and pain. It does so, of course (as we have already shown in pp. 50–7 above), while respecting the relative independence of inner-worldly events. It is this totally 'in earnest' trinitarian love, this divine 'bleeding to death', which is in fact the life-circulation of God, that is the foundation both for inner-worldly suffering and indeed for that death in God which lies beyond worldly life and death and is represented biblically by the motifs of the risen Christ and the Slain Lamb. It is within this framework that Balthasar accepts Ulrich's[84] remarks that pain and death are interior to God, flowing forms of the divine love and eternal language of the divine glory, utterly compatible with the divine beatitude and so capable of victory over the extremes of worldly suffering and death.

It remains to comment briefly on Balthasar's position on the theology of God's pain. While, as before, he rejects all merely fashionable talk about pain in God, it is clear that he is sympathetic to the concern which underlies this kind of talk. Moreover, again as before, Rahner's formulation (God immutable in self, mutable in the other) which attempts to do justice to this concern is implicitly rejected as inadequate to describe the inner liveliness of the trinitarian event. This rejection is related to the acceptance by Balthasar that while the distinction between the immanent and economic Trinity is valid and must be retained, it must not be pushed in the direction of a dualistic separation between God's 'inner' and 'outer' nature. There is in God the basis for what in us is suffering, and furthermore the free power to allow himself to be touched innerly by our suffering. This basis and this 'being touched' by our suffering may not be described simply as divine suffering; rather they exist as that anonymous divine property which Maritain speaks about and which itself is rooted in the eventful nature of the trinitarian life. It is within this context too that we may best understand Balthasar's own previous remarks on the fact that sin affects God's 'outer' but not 'inner' honour: these remarks may now be interpreted as meaning that God's necessary economic response to sin (and hence the effect on his 'outer' honour) is rooted in his own freedom to create and in that anonymous divine perfection which is the triumphant acceptance in God of what corresponds to suffering in us (which perfection being, of course, entirely positive means that God's 'inner' honour is untouched). In other words God is capable of being freely affected but not of being overcome by the effects of our sin.

The more precise formulation and implications of Balthasar's position will emerge in our section on the attributes of God (p. 79 below). Now, however, we must return to the central eschatological issue which we are addressing: would God be affected by the eternal damnation of individual creatures, and, in the light of what we have just reported concerning the pain of God, does the presence of something like infinite pain in God permit such a loss of the damned or does the victorious nature of this 'pain' prevent this loss?

Overview of Balthasar's solution

We have encountered Balthasar's own basic confidence that some-how Christ's saving work will be completely effective (p. 23 above) and yet, respecting the power of created freedom, his refusal to accept the thesis of an apocatastasis, a universal salvation (p. 65 above). Is it possible to combine these disparate aspects satisfactorily? The follow-ing summary review of the pertinent features of Balthasar's escha-tology addresses this question.[85]

The scriptural evidence points to two different sets of data with regard to the final outcome of the relationship in history between humankind and God. The first set states that all are saved. Apart from the individual NT texts which support this, there is the more general evidence of an asymmetry between God's grace and his judgement of our sins, shown clearly by the way in which Christ substitutes himself for those who deserve damnation. This is so despite the fact that it is also clear from the NT that evil and sin become more serious as a refusal of the love of God that is revealed in Christ, that this evil can be expected to increase, and that in this sense hell is a properly NT state. Nonetheless Balthasar argues that Christ's unique experience of hell (see p. 26 above) shows us the extent of God's involvement on our side, and suggests a way of grasping how this trinitarian concern is efficiacious and underpins anything we could do to thwart it.

But there is a second set of data, one which prevents the pilgrim Christian from adopting an exclusively triumphalist strain. The NT is clear about our need to accept freely in this life the salvation won for us by Christ, and many texts indicate that the twofold outcome of God's judgement on us, resulting in heaven or hell, corresponds to our response. Although these NT texts are nuanced – one must take into account their paranetic function, the way OT 'judgement' imagery is borrowed without necessarily implying the same content, and the fact that the sayings of Jesus concerning hell are all attributed to him before the saving event of the cross – and although they may not be taken as a prediction or statement of what actually occurs, they do establish the *possibility* at least that some will be lost in hell.[86] This possibility is rooted in God's respect for our freedom – the saving God will not force the freedom which the creator God has given – and our tendency to sin. This tendency, whose increasing seriousness and incidence are noted in the NT, is also something which we ourselves can experience in the existential way which led Kierkegaard to say that while he could easily believe that everyone else would be saved, he still remained in fear and trembling concerning his own fate.[87]

Is there any way of seeing how these two polar positions might converge, if not harmonise? Balthasar moves cautiously in this area, clearly sympathetic to the modern tendency towards something like an apocatastasis teaching, and yet firmly committed to retaining the reality for us of the second possibility mentioned above. The scriptural evidence of a God who comes not to judge but to save indicates that God would only condemn us if there were no good at all in our lives to relativise what we might judge to be our definitive rejection of God. However, one must still grant the possibility of such a condemnation, or, rather, of God's respect for our definitive rejection of him. Would this not be tragic for God? Balthasar goes further in the attempt to answer this question, and in doing so is clear that he is proceeding hypothetically and not categorically.[88] In a series of approximations to what the reality of hell may consist of he suggests a difference between the eternities of heaven, hell and the state of Jesus on the cross, such that the condemned sinner may experience the definitive timelessness, the isolated *nunc stans*, of being forsaken by God and yet – because hell is a NT, christological place also in the sense that Christ's cross is raised at the far side of it – still be separated from his sin and transferred into the quite different, inclusive supra-time of the eternity of heaven. Such a notion would indicate the way in which the trinitarian event, and in particular the infinite distance between the Father and Son which is bridged by the Holy Spirit, assumes a modality in the paschal mystery of Christ which enables it responsibly to take into account every eventuality (including hell) of a free creation. However, since Balthasar wants to retain the traditional position that there can be no repentance of a definitive choice after death,[89] it is not clear (unless one supposes some experience of hell in this life) how and when the sinner condemned to hell may with his or her own free consent be saved by the cross of Christ.

The hypothetical nature of these approximations, and the difficulties that surround them, are clearly recognised by Balthasar. He is aware that a *theologia viatorum* is different from a *theologia compre-hensorum*: there is no way to systematise in a complete synthesis the two positions mentioned here.[90] We are affected by the seriousness of the possibility of hell for ourselves and it is beyond our competence to remove its threat with any kind of knowledge that is certain. Because of this it is correct that there should be no *a priori* watering down of the scriptural texts which reveal this possibility. Nonetheless – and this is Balthasar's position – it is also correct on the scriptural evidence to hope that all will in fact be saved. This is already a step beyond the Augustine-inspired theologies of a double predestination. It is the attitude personified by someone like St Thérèse of Lisieux.[91] It is a sure hope[92] which takes into account the NT imbalance in favour of the efficacy of God's grace.[93] It is a hope which leaves open the NT tension between the two positions mentioned, and, which, because it is not knowledge, must be accompanied by fear. But equally it is a hope which does not deceive, and we should not retreat behind the daring which it expresses.

This position is an incomplete solution to the question about universal salvation, and good reasons have been given for such incompleteness. However we must now take a further step: what is the significance of Balthasar's solution for the issue of divine immutability? This will be our final attempt to establish within this eschatological perspective the meaning for God of the relationship he has with creation, and in particular with humankind.

What does the world mean for God?

(1) By investigating the meaning of the world for God we also come closer to finding out what kind of being God is. Throughout this chapter we have seen Balthasar construct a theology of creation, its history and end, which maintains the divine transcendence while allowing God to be affected by humankind. From the many aspects of this theology that have been discussed we may, in summary form, point to the key conclusion that creation is an additional gift from God to God within the trinitarian life.[94] This means that there is an eternal enrichment of God through creation, an enrichment which must be understood to include that positive, joyous and victorious acceptance of something like suffering in God (due to his free decision to create and be affected by us).

The mystery of the trinitarian event, then, is clearly at the heart of this theology. Within this event there is a gratuity of self-giving which admits of creativity, wonder, surprise, receptivity and increase, even within the fullness of being that is God. This ever-greater, ever-new quality of the divine life is different from the needy 'becoming' which is characteristic of created beings: it is rather the confirmation of the supra-fullness of the divine being (pp. 59–60 above), whose immutability is not something rigid and without movement but is an eternal duration within whose perfection of stillness there is room for flowing life and increase (pp. 55–6, 71 above). Equally the perfection that is inherent in the self-giving of the inner-divine conversation has a renunciatory character which is real and entirely positive in God and is the original image whose expression can issue in such forms as the cross and abandonment of Christ. It is within this understanding of the trinitarian event that Balthasar can speak of the relatively independent good that is created reality (p.52 above) as providing a real enrichment to God. In this way he highlights the non-necessary but important, real and uniquely precious contribution of the world and each individual in it to God. God is eternally different, other, enriched due to creation and all it contains. And of course it is this understanding, with its paradoxical assertions and its underlying problematic concerning the relationship between time and eternity, which we must investigate more closely and assess in the following chapters.

(2) But even allowing for the clarifications which we may hope for later, it might seem that even such a provisionally positive position on the world's contribution to God is not entirely unproblematic. If we have described the eschatological issue as the real testing-ground of hypotheses concerning the importance of the world to God (with the implications this has for the divine immutability), and if, as we have seen, there is no complete solution to this issue, then might it not seem that even this provisional position is unwarranted?

The incompleteness of the eschatological solution lay in the NT tension between the assertion of the efficacy, through Christs' cross, of God's will that all be saved and the continuing possibility of our damnation. In our present state of knowledge it was found impossible to resolve this tension fully, although a doctrinal and theological convergence was established which prevented us from retreating behind the hope that all in fact would be saved. The significance of this incomplete solution, issuing in this kind of hope, is manifold. First, it cannot be the case that God is merely indifferent to our ultimate fate, that his glory is proclaimed equally by either our salvation or our damnation. Secondly, it is clear that with whatever pain and suffering there is in God, with whatever distinction one makes between its immanent and economic characteristics, God remains eternally happy and omnipotent.[95] God is not ultimately tragic, mythological (pp. 21–2 above). Thirdly, it would seem that the concurrence of these two points must favour the salvation of all. And so it does. Nonetheless this conclusion, as we have seen, cannot be drawn with certainty. Balthasar does not speculate as to whether the compatibility of something like infinite pain with God's eternal joy and victory might allow for the existence of some creatures in hell. He nowhere espouses this speculation; apart from its intrinsic logical difficulties it runs counter to the scriptural evidence and to his own theological understanding, and represents a retreat behind that hope for the salvation of all which Scripture ordains. However, if one were pursuing a strictly human enquiry then the logical sequence of the argument would demand that this possibility be at least considered. Balthasar's decision not to take this road, to take his stance beside, and not behind, the Christian hope for the salvation of all, is an indication of his understanding that the enquiry lies under God's word,[96] and that the element of mystery is at the heart of the manifold significance of the incompleteness of the solution.

It is part of the task of the theologian not to take away mystery, but to focus it more, make it less diffuse. This is what God's revelation of himself does – it increases the mystery of his own being, but now in a more positive sense.[97] With regard to the mystery in question here several points may be made. First, when one has recourse to the notion of mystery as a theological explanation one is not simply bypassing the logic of human enquiry.[98] One may assert that the matter in question transcends the level of finite logic and still attempt to show that this logic is not abused. It would be logically absurd, and unworthy of human acceptance, if the mystery of the Trinity were proposed in such a way that we were asked to accept that God was one and three in exactly the same way.[99] The theological elaboration of the distinction between the categories of substance and relation was one attempt in the history of theology to show how the mystery could be affirmed without violating human reason. Similarly it is clear that in the mystery under present discussion we are not dealing with an absolute contradiction: the two sets of data (pp. 73–4 above) are not on the same level, with one proclaimed as fact and the other as possibility, and it is their irreconcilability in any certain sense which constitutes the mystery. Secondly,[100] this irreconcilability is grounded in the general norm of the subordination of reason to God's word in theological methodology, and in this particular instance in the function that God's word takes on in instructing us about our present situation rather than giving us either certain knowledge about our own future or indulging in speculation about the effect on God of this future. Given the situation that we simply do not have all the data available now to reach a certain conclusion about our future, we are justified in accepting the human limitations of our knowledge and in standing by that hope which the Scriptures proclaim as the Christian stance vis-à-vis universal salvation. The possibility of our damnation, that 'if' which prevents a situation of complete knowledge, is clearly a teaching directed at our existential lives of freedom and decision – the possibility is proclaimed to be ours, not God's, the teaching is about us, not God, and within this context Balthasar is surely correct to refrain both from trying to rationalise the mystery that is involved and from any improper speculation concerning the implications for God. In doing so he is simply allowing the scriptural data to set the agenda and the limits of theological enquiry, while respecting the human questions that arise.[101] Thus there is no question of a 'weighing up of the odds' in this whole matter – rather, one remains soberly with what one is given by God, one distinguishes carefully within and between the domains of knowledge and those of hope, and with such a foundation one speaks about the implications for God. Thirdly, just as, in the way described, our belief in the victorious omnipotence of God is not threatened by our uncertain knowledge of universal salvation, neither is it threatened by the suggestion that in some sense this universal salvation may be described as a mystery to God as well. We refer to the way in which Péguy could speak of the economic side of God's supra-hope as having for its object the salvation of all (p. 68 above). It is part of a whole context which describes mystery, wonder and a supra-hope as modalities of the interpersonal relations within the Trinity itself and without prejudice to the divine omnipotence or omniscience – a context which we must investigate more thoroughly later on. We have argued, then, that Balthasar's positive position on the contribution of creation to God – provisional on the further enquiry into the nature of the trinitarian God and of the relationship between time and eternity – is justified even on the testing-ground which the necessary incompleteness of his solution to the eschatological issue represents.

The attributes of God

Our focus has been on God; in this concluding section our aim is first to set out in a broadly comprehensive way the results of our findings so far and then to offer as indicated a more precise account of the particular issue of divine 'suffering'.

(1) From the many themes that have been treated under the general headings 'Christ and God's immutability' (chapter 1) and 'Creation and God's immutability' (chapter 2), a consistent pattern has emerged. God is both ethically and ontologically immutable. Although this immutability requires to be understood in a wider horizon than that of Greek metaphysics, nonetheless such an understanding cannot violate the requirements of philosophy in insisting that there can be no created, temporal change in God – for the worse or for the better. Nonetheless the traditional notion of immutability must be opened out to take account of the scriptural revelation of the trinitarian liveliness of God.

This liveliness, referred to often in terms of the 'ever-greater' of the trinitarian event, is eternal. The remaining chapters will deal more precisely with the notion of an eternal trinitarian event, its interaction with the realm of time, and the problems to which this gives rise. What we offer now is a descriptive account based on the extent to which this event has emerged as already giving an intelligibility to the many different questions arising from the relationship between Christ, creation and God. The liveliness in question is one of an interpersonal exchange of love within the triune God: its 'ever-greater' nature consists in the richness and freedom of that exchange which can admit of an infinite variety of modalities which, because eternal, do not imply any mutability of God in the strict sense.

Within this pattern many attributes and activities of an unusual nature are ascribed to God:[102] surprise, wonder, faith and hope as well as prayer, nostalgia, expectation, joy, newness, trust, obedience, increase and becoming. These are modalities of that inter-personal event of self-giving within the triune God, a self-giving whose kenosis or 'death'[103] reveals the weakness of God to be the living power of his love, a power which unites the infinite otherness of the Persons as the one being of God. In addition, of course, God's power is revealed in the free creation of the world and all that this entailed, including the role of Christ. This economic side of God means that additional attributes are ascribed to him in recognition of the effect that creation has on him, within the trinitarian relationships as described. These attributes include anger, jealousy, fear, anxiety, patience, hope and a suffering that is ascribed to God not just in the person of the Son but in which very mysteriously the Father[104] and Holy Spirit[105] are also involved. It is said that God learns.[106] And there is that joy and enrichment which God receives from the gift that is creation.

Several comments on this list are in order. First, it should be noted that Balthasar also maintains those attributes which are traditionally ascribed to God: omnipotence, infinity, perfection, holiness, eternity, oneness, happiness, truth, goodness, love, knowledge and so on, including immutability. It is his move from a philosophically-dominated approach to the tract *De Deo Uno* to a consideration of the triune God of revelation which has prompted him to modify some of those attributes, to add new ones, and in general to focus more on the intrinsically inter-personal nature of trinitarian love rather than on a philosophically-limited nature of God.[107] Secondly, the unity of these attributes is affirmed, also in line with traditional Christian thought on this matter. Our multiple assertions are due to the limitations of discursive, created understanding when confronted with what is also a divine attribute, *viz.* the mystery of God.[108] Thirdly, it is clear that one of the key principles underpinning the unusual nature of Balthasar's list of divine attributes and activities is that which asserts that receptivity in God is a divine perfection.[109] If this can be accepted, if divine receptivity is not grounded in need or deficiency, and if it is eternal (and thus immutable), then the way is indeed open to what the list proposes. Fourthly, there is a distinction, but not a separation, between the immanent and economic attributes of God. So, for example, that supra-hope within the Trinity which is due to the way in which inter-personal love, even within the one omniscient being of God, respects the personal freedom of the other[110] is not the same as the supra-hope which is attributed to God in respect of our salvation. The latter is a modality of the former;[111] to say otherwise, to assert an identity, would be to assert that the world is necessary to God. Fifthly, both immanent and economic attributes in God are the original images of what corresponds to them in created beings.[112] In speaking thus Balthasar is affirming that none of these attributes can be ascribed univocally to God – hence his frequent use of inverted commas or the prefix 'supra-'.[113] As found in God, these attributes exhibit that difference in similarity which is the hallmark of analogical discourse; in particular they exhibit in God a perfection, happiness, freedom and non-temporality which they lack in us. Sixthly, there are distinctions to be made in considering what we might refer to spontaneously as the 'positive' and 'negative' attributes attributed to God on this list. There is no ontological negativity within God; no evil, no sin, no defeat. The 'death' that is the trinitarian event of utter self-giving is an entirely positive reality of divine beatitude. This means that there is no original image of sin in God. There is, however, that which gives rise to and can contain what in us, due to our use of freedom, issues in sin. In a somewhat similar way it may be understood how something like God's anger, which we might spontaneously think of as a negative attribute, is in fact positive. This is so because it is an economic side of God's love, which exists due to our sin and so has a positive original image within the immanent nature of God, even though the economic appearance of the attribute tends to conceal its origin in a way that is not true of more positive-sounding attributes (e.g. surprise, joy).[114] Finally, the list is not inclusive of all the attributes assigned to God by Balthasar; sufficient numbers have been included, however, to indicate the way in which the traditional nature of immutability has been opened out, and this was the purpose of our exercise.

(2) Our aim now is to gather together what has already been said concerning the notion of divine impassibility in such a way that more precise answers may be given to the questions which have already arisen in our discussion due to Balthasar's modification of this notion. Is there an analogous supra-suffering in God? If so, is it attributable to the divine nature? And what implications does all this have for the inter-related issues of kenosis and negativity within God?

It is clear that Balthasar does want to affirm that something which corresponds to created suffering does exist in God. It does so of course in a non-univocal way, with all the modifications which have been noted; but does this mean, then, that one may attribute suffering to God in the proper, if analogous, way that traditionally one could attribute love, knowledge, power and so on to him? We must carefully note the many strands which coalesce to form Balthasar's answer, an answer which, in turn, opens out to the other questions posed above.

First, then, there is his position on analogy in general.[115] Because we are created in God's image and because God has chosen to reveal and communicate himself to us in human ways there is a similarity between us and God which means that our speech about him is not simply equivocal. Nonetheless this similarity obtains within an even greater dissimilarity, that *major dissimilitudo* to which the Fourth Lateran Council refers. Within such a framework there is of course no room for a definition of being or attributes that would be common to both God and us. However God's self-revelation and the expressive similarity of creatures to God are sufficient to allow us to use our knowledge of Christ and of created reality to come to a dim knowledge of God. This knowledge, based on the attribution to God (by way of the traditional steps of negation, affirmation and excess or eminence) of what is best in creation, will be expressed in language which will serve as a pointer to, rather than an adequate description of, the divine being. Within this general framework Balthasar is concerned to move beyond the contribution that creation of human beings as a whole can make to our knowledge of God to consider that particular contribution of the concrete personal encounter between God and individuals (Christ and all others). This concern means that for him the analogy of Being (whether of attribution or of proportionality) is widened beyond a merely logical or even ontological framework to issue in an analogy of personality or freedom: while the analogy of faith must be extended in such a way that spirituality and prayer become sources for our knowledge of God in systematic theology.[116] The highlighting of the personal in this concrete way is already a move beyond the boundaries of a more traditional analogical discourse.[117] It implies not just the modification of some traditional categories (e.g. how can one grasp the perfection that is receptivity in inter-personal encounter within the traditional categories of potency and act?), but also a certain appropriate imprecision (in cognisance of the uniqueness involved in such encounters). This imprecision is appropriate to the mystery of God's incomprehensibility of which theology affords a positive grasp; and in addition, as we shall see, Balthasar is aware of degrees of precision within language about God, even allowing for our essential incapacity to measure the distance between our most precise utterances about God and the divine reality itself.[118]

This awareness becomes evident in Balthasar's speech about suffering in God. While in one sense all talk about God is necessarily anthropomorphic, within the very general framework of analogy that has been described it is possible to distinguish between affirmations which are more properly anthropomorphic (metaphorical, poetic) and those which are more properly analogous. Thus it is acknowledged that speech about God's heart, his wound, that bleeding to death which is the life of the trinitarian event, is metaphorical in nature and is different from the proper attribution, within an analogical framework, of something such as love to God.[119] Traditional theology understood this; it is one thing to say that God is a rock, quite another to say that God is love.[120] Both, of course, are perfectly valid ways of speaking about God, but they are different and it was generally accepted that the more literal nature of analogical discourse was something to be sought after in theology. Balthasar's speech about divine suffering implies that these differences are real and important but are part of an overall spectrum or continuum[121] of human speech about God, the status of individual instances of which it may be difficult to determine precisely. So while he insists that the divine kenosis is real, that something corresponding to suffering does exist in God, that in a general sense this 'something' may be said to be analogous to suffering, still in his most thematic treatment of the issue he takes the position that because suffering, as it is in God, is so different from how we experience it then it is better, with Maritain, to refer to it as an anonymous divine perfection. It is as if there existed no word in English to describe what the experience of love is, and the only words available were lust or desire: clearly these words could not be applied properly to God.[122] Similarly in the case of suffering – the term has to be transposed doubly, first to convey a quite different experience from what our term conveys, and then (as is usual in analogical discourse) to transfer that reality to its quite different existence in God. In recognition, then, of the peculiar difficulty surrounding this term as applied to God, Balthasar uses it in a way which situates it somewhere on that continuum between metaphor and analogy strictly so called. If we go on in what follows to refer to an analogous, supra-suffering in God then we must also bear in mind this intrinsic imprecision of the designation, while being equally convinced of its non-anthropomorphic status.[123]

This imprecision does not prevent us from knowing a certain amount about the reality referred to in God. 'He who formed the eye does He not see?' (Ps. 84, 9): there is the original image, the supra-idea, the foundation in God for what is suffering in us.[124] This foundation is found first of all in the immanent Trinity, in that renunciatory mode of self-giving which exists in God independently of any created world. Its economic form is made possible by this immanent foundation, is in response to our sins, and is revealed in the incarnation and death of Christ. These latter events are, of course, the human expressions of what goes on in God. As before, the distinction between immanent and economic suffering in God does not coincide with that between an 'inner' and 'outer' effect; God is affected innerly by the suffering he undergoes in his economy even if his inner honour remains intact. What one can say however is that the divine economic suffering is not an essential attribute of God in the same way as its immanent archetype; it is a mode of divine love which – like anger and jealousy – comes to resolution within the supra-time that is God's eternity and so is always subordinate to the divine beatitude. Furthermore it is different in being a suffering that is in response to evil, which obviously immanent suffering is not. But again this immanent suffering by the divine Persons of one another, which is also a modality of the utter joy and happiness of trinitarian love, is totally real and in earnest. In its readiness to perform the utmost for the other out of love it contains already within it, *virtualiter*,[125] those modalities of suffering love which become, eternally, economically active in God in response to sin and its overcoming. Does this mean that there really is something like pain in God's immanent being, and is it more or less than what is present economically? One is left stammering here: Balthasar would seem to be suggesting that this mysterious reality is indeed within the immanent God, that it is the anonymous perfection which is part of God's happiness, and that while in its own modality it does not take the form of a response to evil it does include and resolve such a possibility and so, in that sense, somehow goes beyond the reach of economic pain.

The reason for Balthasar's reluctance to attribute suffering to the divine nature are now more apparent (see pp. 45–6 above). Although his christological analogy of Being (pp. 44–5) gives grounds for such an attribution, there are counter-arguments to persuade otherwise. These include the intrinsic difficulty of the notion of suffering as applied to God, the fact that suffering as a category of perfection derives from the discourse of receptive personal encounter rather than that of nature, the shortcomings of the term 'nature' in distinguishing between God's immanent and economic suffering, and, as indicated earlier (pp. 43–4 above),[126] the greater emphasis in Balthasar's theology on the freedom of the divine Persons to reveal the nature of God to us in a way which respects but transcends the boundaries of philosophical enquiry. It would seem that in the light of these arguments, and perhaps also in deference to a venerable tradition, Balthasar concluded that to attribute suffering to the divine nature would be to invite misunderstanding. This conclusion would then, in turn, be based primarily on grounds of linguistic convention: within the framework described it would be quite conceivable that Balthasar, if he so desired, could construct a different understanding of the divine nature and attribute suffering to it. This linguistic screen should not conceal the reality that is being asserted, which is that there is indeed something corresponding to suffering in God in the way described.

This discussion also throws light on the inter-related issues of kenosis and negativity within God. God's supra-suffering is intrinsic and subordinate to his joy and happiness.[127] This may be grasped in a remote way from the nobility which human suffering can sometimes impart, and also from its co-existence with joy (e.g. the experience of the mystics, but also phases of human love). It confirms the assertion that the supra-kenosis within God, that renunciatory character of the love of the Persons within the Trinity, is entirely positive and due to the fullness and perfection of the divine being rather than to any deficiency. This remains the case even when this renunciatory character takes up that modality of opposition between Father and Son in overcoming the effects of sin. This modality, and its correlated economic modes such as divine jealousy, are what may be referred to pictorially as the dark side which is contained and overcome within the light of God's love. In more prosaic terms, these modalities are ontologically positive despite their negative appearance. This means that even though sin has its existence only within the trinitarian life in the sense that its possibility (in an inverse way) and the overcoming of its effects (in a direct way) are rooted there, nonetheless there can be no ontological negativity attributed to the fullness of being that is God. As before, then (see pp. 80–1 above), we need to distinguish two meanings of the term 'negative': one is that ontological negativity which is sin and is contradictory to the notion of God, while the other is that renunciatory reality with its many apparently negative modalities which is utterly consistent with the victorious perfection of God.

Finally, while poetry and spirituality may have been quicker to perceive the liveliness of God in all the ways mentioned in this discussion on the divine immutability, Balthasar is clearly attempting to introduce this scriptural legacy into theological discourse. In doing so he is shaking off the tyranny of an overly narrow philosophical approach and seeking to replace it with a language whose greater imprecision means more faithfulness to the Scriptures, without sacrificing the rigorous demands of a more broadly conceived philosophy and the challenge to speak about God in a way which includes, but transcends, the level of symbolic consciousness which is proper to poetry.[128]

(3) We have outlined the framework within which Balthasar maintains the reality of the effect of creation on God; when one

combines this with the evidence from the way in which Christ reveals God (see chapter 1) there emerges a way of speaking about the divine immutability and impassibility which is quite untraditional (see pp. 79–81). Greater clarity has been achieved in understanding the world's relative independence of God, the nature of divine supra-suffering and its relation to supra-kenosis and negativity. This clarity has not resulted in a uniformly precise and systematic form of technical linguistic expression; we may suppose that at least part of the reason for this lies in the exploratory nature of Balthasar's whole enterprise, his attempt to break new ground in a careful, nuanced way which is faithful to the truths enshrined by the tradition.

But it is also due partly to the intrinsically mysterious nature of God himself, in response to which there is a corresponding and appropriate inadequacy of human language and thought. There is no 'solution' to the 'problem' of God; the only solution that is available is in response to the problem of how one speaks most correctly about the mystery that is God. Such a solution will recognise the rightness of not being able to say 'what God is'.[129] God's being is his own secret, not to be seen through by any rationalistic system – a temptation that constantly besets theology.[130] And even when this secret is revealed, the mystery is heightened, albeit now in a more positive sense (as, for example, in the revelation of God's love on the cross). In seeking to express this in human language our principal means is by way of negation, excluding ways of alluding to God which reduce the mystery to created proportions. This task is also accomplished when we more tentatively – and with due imprecision – try to understand the mystery in a positive way within an analogous framework. Paradoxically, then, this 'due imprecision' itself becomes part of the correct way to make the mystery more precise – with the help of the ability to determine different degrees of this positive understanding in the way described (see pp. 81–5 above).

It is in the service of this task to make the mystery more precise that we must continue to put those questions which we have noted in the course of our enquiry and which have not yet been adequately answered. What is the relationship between time and eternity which is such that one may speak of a supra-time and space within God in a way which makes accessible the notion of an 'ever-greater' God who, within his immutability, can 'become' eternally? May one go any further in grasping how receptivity can be a perfection in such a way that one might go beyond the position of an Aquinas, who, while admitting that the perfection of everything was in God, denied that anything corresponding to pain could be in him on the grounds that pain, or receptivity or passive potency of any kind was an imperfection?[131] Finally is there point any longer in trying to defend the immutability of God when already one has conceded a willed mutability within God – akin to Barth's 'holy mutability'[132] – so that the retention of the term 'immutability' can assume the appearance of mere deference to linguistic convention? The chapters which follow attempt to come to terms with the explanatory issues which these questions raise.

3

Time, eternity and God's immutability

The relationship between time and eternity has emerged as a key explanatory principle in the description of divine immutability. Our aim here is to present a thematic account of this relationship in order to provide us with a means of assessing both Balthasar's overall position on the immutability of God as well as his related positions on the various problematic aspects of the issue which have arisen in the previous two chapters. This thematic account will be limited to those features of the relationship which are pertinent to the immutability issue; we are not presenting Balthasar's comprehensive theology of the relationship between time and eternity.

Two preliminary remarks will help to indicate the nature of the task at hand. First, our mode of being, our categories of thought and expression are so intrinsically temporal that it is notoriously difficult for us to approach this whole matter. Of course in another sense this is but one aspect of the difficulty already referred to concerning any created 'solution' to the 'problem' of God (see pp. 85–7 above) – the basic thrust of all such solutions must lie in the elimination of false ways of speaking about God, and in the choice of less inadequate positive ways of expressing the mysterious relationship between creature and creator. Our aim, then, is to speak correctly about this issue in a way which yields truth that is respectful of mystery and yet wary of semantic mystification. A second introductory comment may prevent one such possible instance of mystification. God is the being who is eternal, we the beings who are temporal – eternity and temporality are not in themselves beings, and in particular are not subjects who have a life and personal freedom of their own.[1] Linguistic usage may lead to an unconscious reification of time and eternity.

Time

For everything there is a season, and a time for every matter under heaven (Ecclesiastes, 3, 1)

Following St Augustine, Balthasar is very much aware of the mysterious and fragmentary nature of time.[2] As creatures we do not possess our being in the all-at-once, gathered way in which God exists. Our incompleteness is evidenced by our multiplicity and variety and by the changes which occur in us, which are made possible by our consecutive existence in time. Under this aspect time is the principle of differentiation between us and God; it is a characteristic of creaturehood, of the creature's ontological nature of coming-to-be which, in turn, is based on the real distinction between essence and existence in created being.[3]

But within concrete consciousness created time is also sinful time.[4] Time for the sinner is experienced not just as the medium of change expressing incompleteness but more threateningly as a wandering away from God in the direction of the non-divine and of non-being. It is 'lost time' in which the fleeting, transitory nature of created time is experienced as a moving towards death in a wearying, fearful way. Within this perspective time is connected with change and dispersal in a negative sense which contrasts with the perfection of God's eternity and immutability.

This distinction between created and sinful time alerts us to a further significant feature. Time is not something merely objective in the physical sense of a phenomenon that can be measured by the movement of the planets. Rather, as human creatures we possess a sense of time, a feeling for it, which in the account of Augustine is due to the soul's experience of a duration which is a form of extension, albeit not of a physical kind. This stress on the personal, interior nature of our experience of time allows full weight to be given to the very real qualitative differences in human awareness of time, without thereby reducing our knowledge to a subjective level.[5] Time is, then, objectively real – in this wider sense which includes our personal experience of it. This means that while Balthasar approves in some sense of the Platonic notion of time as the image of eternity, as expressing eternity, this is not to be interpreted along lines which would assert that as expressive image time is unreal, a mere appearance. In particular the process of the creature's integration into God is a really temporal one involving the full seriousness of his/her acts of freedom.[6]

It is clear that for Balthasar, as for Augustine, time is by no means an exclusively negative reality. It is positive, first of all, precisely in being the principle of total differentiation between us and God: this distance is itself a good creation of God. Next, it is part of the good purpose of our good creator in that it allows beings to move in the sense of becoming closer to God, and it facilitates as well all the other lovely changes which contribute to the beauty of the universe. In fact time is the medium of the good and beautiful deeds of God himself; history is the medium of all the events between God and the world, in particular, of course, of the Christ-event itself.[7]

Jesus is our principal source of knowledge concerning the reality and meaning of time. This can only be so if his own existence was a truly temporal one: the incarnation is not a matter of play-acting; the different stages of Christ's life (infancy, youth, adolescence, adulthood) are real temporal progressions, and his knowledge of his 'hour' is clouded in its detail by the limitations inherent in our existence as temporal beings with respect to knowledge of what is future.[8] The time of Jesus shows us how the totally negative time of sin and the partially positive time of creation find their true meaning and fulfilment beyond themselves in God's eternity; and furthermore it reveals how eternity is already breaking into time.[9] We will return shortly to these connections between time and eternity as revealed in the life of Jesus.

Eternity

The truly temporal Jesus is the same person who is the eternal Christ. Just as, within 'the christological analogy of Being', the humanity of Jesus Christ is the appropriate expression of God's divinity, so too his 'time' expresses (without being identical to) the eternity of God.[10] This is the general principle guiding Balthasar's enquiry into the meaning of eternity.

The differentiated liveliness of eternity is brought to light from several different points of view with the help of this principle. First, the temporality of Jesus is seen as a very appropriate expression of the way in which the Son receives his being from the Father within the Trinity – the temporal mode of the receptivity of being, bit by bit, over an extended period, is in Christ the created expression of that eternal relationship of receptivity to the Father which in turn indicates that give and take which is characteristic of the whole Trinity. This temporality expresses, clearly and precisely, the fact that the Son in eternity makes nothing his own in any way which contradicts its being given to him, continually, ceaselessly, by the Father: and so his possession and experience in this world of that which is his own is going to be, not all in one flash, but something received from the Father, possessed only in him and through him, and hence continually offered up to him, given back to him and again received as yet another new gift of love.[11]

Eternity, then, is such as to allow this very real interchange of love within the Trinity.

This is borne out by a second viewpoint on eternity which focuses on the way in which the temporal becoming of Jesus reveals the liveliness of God's own being.[12] What is being maintained here is that the temporality of Christ's life, the way in which it may be broken up into different periods, is not simply the created antithesis of an eternity which may only be described in terms of an immutable state. Rather, even when one allows for the real difference between created and divine being, acknowledging the limitations of the former, still it is also true that created being (principally in the unique case of that being which the Son assumes in the incarnation) tells us something positive about the being of God. In this instance Balthasar argues that the becoming which is intrinsic to temporality points to an analogous becoming intrinsic to eternity. He is careful to obviate any gross misunderstandings: there is no creaturely becoming in God, we may not revert to an Arian notion of Christ and may not speak of a process in God if by doing so one implies consecutive temporality. Eternity is thus not measurable by temporal categories; the perfection of God does not allow of any development from potency to act. But, ultimately indescribable though it is, God's eternity may be spoken of in a way which allows for the category of *event* as well as that of *state*, an event which is characterised not simply by a fixed order of trinitarian relations but rather by a liveliness of interaction which may, however inadequately, be described as a movement from act to act, from fullness to fullness.[13] It is this aspect of eternity, reflected also in the way in which Christ's time (waiting for his 'hour') has particular regard for the future, which allows Balthasar to acknowledge in passing the validity of the concerns of the Process theologians, of speech about God's historicity, and to speak constantly about God in terms of the 'open' comparative rather than the 'closed' superlative – the God who is 'ever-greater'.[14] Thus the identity in God between existence and essence is seen not as something closed in on itself, but rather as involving a form of becoming which is a perfection

of being and of which the becoming of created temporal being, due to
the real distinction between essence and existence that constitutes it,
is a deficient but true copy.[15]

If give and take are characteristic of the ever-greater love of the
Trinity, then so too are all the other modalities of love such as wonder,
surprise and that distance within unity whose economic forms we
have already seen can issue in forms such as divine anger, jealousy,
pain and so on. The temporal life of Jesus indicates the space for these
different modalities to be present and alerts us to a third feature of the
liveliness of eternity: it is a way of being which allows various, even
apparently conflicting, modes of love to be simultaneously present
and reconciled. This is part of the very real earnestness with which we
must accept the notion of the ordered liveliness of a trinitarian event
of love, a love whose utter freedom of expression Balthasar invokes to
overcome the logical difficulty of speaking in the same breath about
absolute being and ever-greater event.

But before examining this logical difficulty more closely let us first
note how Balthasar speaks about eternity in the light of the three
preceding viewpoints. The most significant feature here is his description of eternity as a 'supra-time' rather than an absolute 'non-time'.[16]
He is well aware that such a description is open to misunderstanding,
and so he takes care to explain what he means by it. What he intends
is to avoid the position which asserts a complete antithesis between
time and eternity, such that eternity is understood in terms of a
Platonic *nunc stans*, thereby excluding its application to the trinitarian
God of Christianity whose mode of being involves the kind of liveliness
just described.[17] But he is equally careful to counter the suggestion
that eternity is simply a matter of infinite time, in the sense of a
consecutive form of duration without beginning or end.[18] He argues
for a basic incommensurability between time and eternity so that the
qualitatively different reality of eternity cannot be measured in
temporal terms. However this difference does not preclude a certain
analogy between time and eternity such that eternity is described as
possessing all the liveliness, the movement and lovableness of time
without being subject to the latter's consecutive form of extension.[19]
It is because eternity possesses these perfections of time that Balthasar
can refer to it as 'infinite', 'eternal time', or God's form of 'duration';[20]
it is because this possession is non-temporal, in the sense of different
from the consecutive, extended form of time, that he can also refer to
eternity as 'timeless'.[21] But – to return to our logical difficulty, in
another form – how may one begin to understand eternity in the

paradoxical terms of a non-temporal possession of the perfections of temporality?

Balthasar's main approach to this issue is to contrast in different ways the extendedness of temporality with the intensity of eternity.[22] The contrast is intended to point to the possibility of the existence of a variety of states and happenings within a divine intensity of life which is not subject to the extendedness of time. The intensity of eternity would then be the medium in which the aspects of newness, increase and creativity – the 'ever-greater' – of the trinitarian event are expressed. The validity of this approach is grounded in our human experience of the real difference between extension and intensity. In a very early work Balthasar had remarked on the way in which progression by intensification characterised the 'existential' thought of St Gregory of Nyssa, in contrast to a more 'notional' thinker.[23] Here and elsewhere he speaks of the extended, horizontal, latitudinal aspects of time being found preserved but transformed into the intensive, vertical, longitudinal nature of eternity.[24] The image is varied: eternity contains an elasticity which is such that happening occurs without transitoriness (in this sense there is a future but no totally past dimension to eternity), while one may also speak of the circle of eternity containing within itself the linearity of time.[25] But Balthasar himself is not misled by such images into believing that he is thus able to offer a full account of what is meant by eternity as 'supra-time'. In particular it is clear that the validity of the principal approach he adopts – the way of the contrast between intensity and extension – is limited precisely by the fact that for us all experiences, however intense, are always also characterised by at least some minimal extension in time. Thus we are locked into our temporality so that eternity is ultimately unimaginable to us and a full account of it remains beyond our capabilities.[26]

However a limited, abstract account is possible: negatively by saying what eternity is not, and positively by stating what it must be without however being able to understand *how* it can so be. This logical difficulty is eased somewhat by the various images which Balthasar proposes and which may give us (as has been said of Augustine in a related context) 'a tenuous but precious metaphorical base for the leap that carries the contemplative mind towards the eternal: but the mind falls back before the impossible abyss is vaulted'.[27] It is worth noting too that whatever the particular detail of his approach may be, Balthasar is in agreement with many of his contemporaries in his desire to describe eternity is a less atemporal

way than has been traditional in the post-biblical era.[28] He is
accordingly part of a general movement which seeks to interpret the
position of Boethius (*aeternitas igitur est interminabilis vitae tota simul et
perfecta possessio*) beyond the medieval notion of a timelessness that
includes all time within it (in the sense of being present to every
moment of our time),[29] towards a notion which attempts to specify
how a transformed temporality is intrinsic to eternity itself. If this
thrust towards specification is ultimately doomed to failure – in the
sense that the positive meaning of the divine attribute of eternity
remains largely unknown – then it may still be argued that it points in
a direction more faithful to the biblical notion of eternity.

This return to a biblical understanding of eternity is characterised
by a further differentiation in Balthasar's thought concerning the way
in which the temporality of Jesus speaks to us about God's eternity.[30]
There are two main aspects of this differentiation, and it will be helpful
to indicate them here in order to underline the point that the 'being'
and 'becoming' aspects of eternity are grounded in a scriptural basis.
First, the time of Jesus expresses well the perfection and completeness
of eternity, that simultaneous all-at-once fullness contained in the
traditional philosophical notion whose classical formulation is the
Boethian *tota simul et perfecta possessio*. This expression is achieved by
the way in which Jesus gathers together the intrinsically transitory,
fragmentary nature of time by living every moment of his life in a love
of his Father which is shown in his obedience to the latter's will. It is
this loving fidelity which unifies the moments of Christ's life and
makes of them an expression of the unity of eternity. Similarly the
scriptural emphasis on the urgency and decisiveness of the time of
Jesus carries with it a sense of the fullness of eternity which relativises
all merely temporal progression. The weight of the time of Jesus,
with its characteristic stress on the 'now' of God present to all our
different times, once again expresses the 'ever-now' (*je-jetzt*), simultaneity of eternity.

Secondly, the fullness of eternity is not that of an immobile full stop:
the 'ever-now' refers to that 'ever-more' (*je-mehr*) or 'ever-greater'
(*immer-Größere*)within the divine eternity which is also revealed in
the mode of the temporal existence of Jesus as we have earlier
outlined.[31] Thirdly, Balthasar indicates how that paradoxical unity of
fullness and 'ever-more' is also grounded in the temporality of Jesus. A
theology of the different stages or seasons of Christ's life is instructive
in this regard.[32] On the one hand, since Christ is truly himself at every
stage of his existence it must be true that each stage (not just

adulthood as such, which is peculiarly suited to reveal the fullness of God) and every moment of his life are a revelation of the fullness of eternity. This corresponds well to the urgency of the scriptural 'now' to which we have referred. However, on the other hand it is also true that the stages of Christ's life complement one another in a way which suggests that movement from fullness into fullness which we have already noted – in other words, the natural succession of moments and seasons in Christ's life is a positive revelation of the 'becoming' nature of eternity which mysteriously coincides with its fullness of being. Furthermore, specific stages of Christ's temporal life – childhood, youth – are peculiarly suited to express that ever-new aspect of eternity.[33] In this way Balthasar seeks to ground scripturally that paradoxical unity of being and becoming in the eternity of God.

It should be noted, finally, that while the time of Jesus is the principal source of our knowledge about the eternity of God, Balthasar does attribute a similar, if subsidiary, role to our human time. In doing so he is consistent with his overall understanding of creation as being a reality within the trinitarian relationship and thus an expression of God.[34] Within this context there are two main aspects of human temporality which confirm what we have already discovered about God's eternity. First, that becoming which is proper to time is like a copy (*Abbild*) of its original image or idea (*Urbild/Idee*) which is the lively, ever-new, eventful aspect of eternity.[35] In this way time is not something merely negative but is a positive revelation of that intensity of eternity which Balthasar expresses with his use of the open comparative of the 'ever-more'. Secondly, there is a 'relative absoluteness'[36] discernible in the movement and structure of human time which points to the absoluteness and fullness of eternity. The transitory nature of time, the impossibility of ever possessing the present as it merges backwards and forwards into the past and future, is an indication of a tendency towards futility, nothingness and, ultimately, death. Yet it is precisely this ephemeral nature which reveals the positive side: time is a gift whose 'now' is precious, poignant, irreplaceable, never to be repeated and thus evoking urgency and decisiveness. This lends an exigency and uniqueness to the moments and stages of time, so that, ironically, in revealing its own non-eternity time points to the intense absoluteness and imperishability of eternity itself. Similarly, as human beings we make judgements (this is true) and decisions of commitment (I love you) in a way which may be conscious of the limitations which time imposes and yet which reveals an inbuilt dynamic to transcend those limits. The poet's claim to have built *monumentum aere perennius* is only giving voice to the dynamic of all human reason which, even with its relativity, is operational only within the horizon of the absolutely true and good.

The relationship between time and eternity

We come now to the nub of this whole issue. We propose here to outline the general structure and dynamic of the relationship between time and eternity and to offer the basis for Balthasar's position in his theology of Christ and of creation. A discussion of the problems which his account entails will follow.

Introduction

By way of a preliminary contextual observation it will be useful to indicate the parallelism between the shape of our present discussion and the general positions adopted when discussing the relationship between God and Christ (chapter 1 above) and God and the world (chapter 2 above). Just as in both previous issues the relationships in question involved the elements of dialogue as well as expression, so too in the issue under present discussion – time not only expresses eternity; there is also a dialogue and interaction between the two. This parallelism indicates an analogy between the present relationship and the ones previously under discussion: in particular, the specific models of the Trinity and the Hypostatic Union (which were used then to suggest ways in which there could be a difference-in-unity that allowed for the elements of both expression and interaction) can now be applied to the structurally similar relationship between time and eternity.[37] This will mean in particular that, just as within the trinitarian and christological relationships the unity that is involved does not in any way require the abolition of the differences (between the persons in the Trinity and between the natures in the Hypostatic Union), so too in the relationship between God's eternity and our time, despite the primacy of the former, there is no identity between the two terms of the relationship.

We have already dealt at some length with the expressive side of this relationship, indicating in particular how time reveals the absolute and 'ever-more' nature of eternity. Our focus now will be primarily on the interaction between the two.

Outline of Balthasar's position

Time and eternity are not two modes of being which are juxtaposed with one another in a contradictory or even neutral kind of way.[38] Rather, there is a relationship between them which is in a certain order. The main characteristics of this order may be described as follows: time is from eternity and is directed towards it; eternity has the primacy in their relationship; eternity breaks into time while time becomes part of eternity. We need to examine this short and rather bare description more closely in order to unfold its meaning.

In saying that time is from eternity Balthasar intends to affirm that both modes of being are real, that they are different, and that the reality of temporality is derived from that of eternity. They are real– and this means the ruling out of any suggestion that in being the Platonic image and even shadow[39] of eternity time has but an illusory reality. But neither is the felt weight of time allowed to dominate – the primary reality is that all-at-once intensity of eternity, and the extended duration of time is the created copy and image of the primary reality. Furthermore, time is directed back to its primary referent: in heaven we participate in God's eternity so that time as we know it, with its transitory and ephemeral features, will be transform-ed. This transformation will represent the fulfilment, not the annihilation, of time. This means that, once again, just as the distinction between creator and creature remains even in heaven, so too even in our heavenly participation in God's eternity there can be no question of our time being so transformed that it becomes simply identical to the eternity of God. Time may be said to be 'absorbed'[40] by eternity only in the sense that there is an 'end of time' when temporality survives in its perfected form, participating in, but never identical to, the eternity of God.

This primacy of eternity with regard to ontological status is also a feature of the dynamics of its interaction with time. Time is not 'cut out' from eternity as if the existence of the reality of time required an interruption in that of eternity. Nor is it the case that in order to interact with the temporal order eternity must itself acquire a temporal mode of being. Somehow eternity is present in and simultaneous with every moment of time without this involving a consecutive form of duration which would contradict its character-istic unity. This unity has, of course, its own differentiated liveliness and it is only within this notion of eternity as supra-temporal intensity that Balthasar can sometimes somewhat confusingly refer to a co-extensivity between eternity and time and to an extendedness within the intensity of eternity. His intention is, however, clear; the *form* of duration which characterises eternity is not affected by its interaction with time.[41]

It is the temporal form of duration whose destiny it is to be modified through this interaction, and we see this happening already in another aspect of the relationship between the two: the way in which eternity breaks into time. To the extent that this happens, temporality is experienced as a fullness and wholeness in contradistinction to its characteristically fragmentary nature. But until heaven the effect of this 'break-in' of eternity into time is limited, so that eternity in this life is experienced predominantly under the mode of the future, as that which is to come, albeit on the basis of a present experience. This future full integration of time into eternity will not, as has already been indicated, mean that the temporal is simply destroyed. Rather, all the positivity which time involves, the tensions between past, present and future which make our lives lovable and precious, will be present in a transfigured way in our experience of eternity. This means once again that the fullness of eternity is not homogeneous, but its supra-temporal intensity accommodates a differentiated presence (not just *awareness* – see p. 63 above) of our temporal past, present and future. There is no absolute past, then, in eternity (p. 93 above): our temporal lives are present there, not merely as memories but as present realities transformed in such a way as to be experienced all at once, in their diversity but reconciled. This can only be so as a participation in the eternity of God – and it is through this participation that eternity becomes a way of being in the perfect presence of trinitarian love which integrates the past and contains within it that future aspect of 'ever-more'.

If, finally, time becomes part of eternity, then there is implied a different content (not form – see p. 97 above) to eternity itself than would be the case without this temporal contribution. The intense liveliness of eternity contains within it all the positivities of a transformed temporality to which we have already referred. This applies both to God's eternity and to our participation in it. It is this aspect which indicates the real mutuality of the relationship involved, in that eternity is affected by time, albeit non-temporally. Of course the contribution in question, real though it is, cannot be understood as coming from a mode of being which is external to eternity. Time is in the lap of eternity.[42] Temporal reality is derived from eternal so that its relative independence is contained within eternity, analogous to the way in which the world contributes to God within the trinitarian relationship as described. In this way the primacy of eternity is maintained while the positive role of temporality is nevertheless acknowledged and integrated, thus ensuring a real dialogue between the two.

This account is abstract in so far as it remains unrelated to Christ's and our own experiences of time. We turn to these experiences now, both to establish the ground of the position that has been outlined and to illustrate its meaning in more concrete form.

The christological and created basis of Balthasar's position

It is Christ's time which mediates between time and eternity.[43] In this temporal mode of being as a coming from and going back to the Father he indicates that the derivation of time is from eternity, that the goal of time is eternity, and that eternity has the primacy in the relationship between the two.

In particular, through the incarnation there occurs that break-in of eternity into time: in different ways, especially through his faithful obedience, which gathers together the fragments of his life into a unified whole, and through the urgency, definitiveness and total uniqueness of his time as expressed in the scriptural 'now', the time of Jesus not only expresses what eternity is like but actually reveals its veiled presence among us.[44] This is also true, to a limited extent, of our own created human time. This time has its own 'relative absoluteness', instances of which we have already cited (pp. 95–6 above), and which is further exemplified in the sense of timelessness which great works of art achieve, the human ability to live for 'today', and the absoluteness of moments of sickness or death.[45] For the Christian this becomes even more pointed when through faith he shares in so many different ways in the fidelity of Christ's love which overcomes that dispersal characteristic of time and which can even overcome our fear of death. In this way, through being converted more and more to Christ the Christian may in this life increasingly experience the blossoming of that bud which is the presence of eternity in his time.[46]

In revealing to us the relationship between time and eternity. Balthasar gives a special place to the scriptural account of the forty days between the resurrection and ascension of Christ.[47] Here more clearly than before in the life of Jesus it can be seen that eternity and time are not juxtaposed in a neutral or contradictory way. The story of Emmaus shows 'the eternal allowing itself to be drawn into time and going along with it in genuine companionship'.[48] The resurrected Jesus is in a time continuous with our time, not divorced or estranged from it. There is the usual alternation and succession of words and action on the road to Emmaus, but there is too a sense of Christ's sovereignty over time, analogous to his ubiquitous sovereignty over space, which allows this resurrected time to reveal the fullness of eternity in a way which surpasses the revelatory powers of the more limited pre-resurrection time. But these forty days also show the way in which time becomes part of eternity: the fact that the marks of Christ's wounds are visible to Thomas is a revelation of the way in which temporality is integrated into eternity by being transposed and transformed.[49] These wounds indicate the presence of Christ's past in eternity not just as a memory but as a present reality – albeit, since they exist now in the resurrected, victorious Christ, as the presence of a transformed past which is part of that intensity of divine life whose perfection admits of differences which are real and are yet reconciled. Similarly, in his theology of the different stages of Christ's life to which we have already alluded, Balthasar wishes to maintain that the entire time sequence of Christ, with each of the stages of life that it enables, is present in a transformed sense in eternity.[50] And just as the entire temporal life of Christ is 'eternalised', so too all the positive aspects of our lives are transformed and 'eternalised' through participation in God's eternity.[51]

Christ's sovereignty over space and time as revealed in these forty days points also to the way in which eternity may be present to all our times without itself being measured temporally. In faith, through the Church and especially through the Eucharist, the eternal Christ is present to us without any temporal interruption of his eternity.[52] This is indicated most clearly by the way in which in the Emmaus, Thomas and other resurrection stories Christ can be present to human time with a wholeness and sovereignty which reveal the supra-temporality of eternity. These resurrection stories throw our notions of time into confusion: they show that Christ's time in being thus eternalised can be present to all times – in other words both forwards (to us) and backwards (to the OT) from his own time so as to contain all times.[53] There is no 'before' and 'after' in eternity, no points of time, but rather its fullness is always present at every stage of our temporal journey. Our notions of past, present and future (and so of eternity before, during and after time)[54] must be transformed when we speak about a supra-temporal eternity which, without temporal duration, nonetheless has an unimaginable intensive form of duration which is able to integrate while respecting the derived reality of our temporality. The intensity of eternity, then, is such that it can accommodate – and give rise to – the realities of temporal extension without thereby itself becoming 'temporalised'.[55] We are thus reminded once again that eternity is not properly described as coming before or after time, nor as a prolongation of time, nor as running parallel to time but without touching it, nor, finally, as clashing with it in order to destroy it. Rather, eternity is lateral to time, it is the open side of a totality which we can only approach now from the veiled, temporal side – and it is only from this open side that we may finally understand what we may now only affirm, that the two form a unity and harmony without prejudice to their differentiation and to the primacy of the eternal.[56]

With reference to the time of Christ and that of human beings we have been illustrating and grounding the position of Balthasar on the relationship between time and eternity. However we note, finally, that the way in which time expresses eternity is also further illustrated by the theology of Christ's time in the forty days after his resurrection. The glorified wounds of Christ live on: this, taken with the sense of present fulfilment and imminent return to the Father which characterise these forty days, reveals a notion of eternity in which, analogously, one may speak of a fullness of the present which contains within it the positivity of a transformed and reconciled past and the 'ever-more' of the future.[57]

Particular problems

In this outline of the framework and the relevant content of Balthasar's position on the relationship between time and eternity, we have largely ignored explicit treatment of the difficulties which attend this position. We turn to these difficulties now by focusing in particular on the various problems concerning the relationship between time and eternity which have arisen in the course of our enquiry thus far. By so doing we may expect both to sharpen the outline already offered and to indicate some of its limitations.

The incarnation and cross

The incarnation is treated in chapter 1 both as the expression of the trinitarian event of self-giving and as affecting this same event. Likewise the cross is considered under these two aspects of expression on the one hand and mutual interaction on the other. The image of the Slain Lamb points to the temporal incarnation and cross as expressions of the eternal reality in a way that aims to allow temporality to be seen as real, as derived from, contained by and fulfilled (by being preserved through transformation – see pp. 97–8 above) in eternity. We have expressed this in terms of the intensity of eternity which allows for so many different modalities of God's free love to be present and reconciled, including those modalities proper to the extended mode of being of temporality (pp. 90–4 above.) To this the open but glorified wounds of the Slain Lamb testify.

But despite his own intentions, does Balthasar really succeed in obviating the danger of downgrading the reality of temporality in this treatment of the incarnation and cross? This danger is inherent in any position which tries to assert the primacy of the eternal in its relationship to the temporal, and, implicitly or explicitly, this was the source of much of our questioning in this whole area throughout chapter 1. How real are the temporal incarnation and cross if they are so rooted in eternity and so impervious to the normal constraints of time as to become 'eternalised' and transformed? Balthasar's repeated assertions of the reality of time, and, in particular, of the historical nature of the incarnation and cross which lead him to a rejection of any Gnostic interpretation of the Slain Lamb image, are of course important. Important too are his carefully formulated affirmations of the effect of the temporal incarnation and cross on the eternal God. Nonetheless, despite all these safeguards, it is of course conceivable that, due to the peculiar difficulty of the whole topic, Balthasar in expressing some of the details of his own position fails to avoid those very pitfalls which by way of general principle he so clearly recognises. In other words, despite his own best intentions, does the thrust of his complex formulation of the relationship between time and eternity in fact imply some undermining of the temporal?[58]

It might be said that Balthasar successfully resolves this issue by distinguishing between the viewpoint of eternity and that of time. With this distinction in mind one might say that the incarnation – and also the cross – are always eternally true *sub specie aeternitatis*, while, speaking temporally, *sub species temporis*, they exist only at particular times (pp. 22–3, 28–9 above). But although the distinction is valid and helpful it does not on its own provide an explanation which safeguards temporality adequately. Rather than being an explanation this distinction is more like a linguistic device which affirms both positions (the realities of eternity and of time) and leaves them to exist side by side, without attempting to explore their relationship. This is valid because it is grounded in the fact that we have no common categories with which the notions of time and eternity may be described and their reality measured. It is useful because in refusing to go any further in the attempt to discover how our categories of time might relate to eternity it draws attention to our own inescapably time-conditioned approach to the whole issue and thus to the innately mysterious nature of the exercise. To speak of mystery is not necessarily to imply logical absurdity, and the distinction in question is helpful in adverting to the quite different respects with which seemingly contradictory statements about the same issue may be affirmed. But it does not bring us further than this in understanding the relationship between time and eternity, and so it does not demonstrate that Balthasar's position can meet the objections we have put to it.

More promising is the approach which describes eternity as a supra-temporality. This admittedly difficult notion offers a way of considering the unity of eternity not as a fixed point but rather as capable of integrating, without destroying, the scattered, consecutive reality of time. This intensive supra-temporality is capable of containing within it different modalities of both time and eternity in a unified way which does not destroy the distinctions between them. As the eternity of God, with its 'ever-more' dimension, it includes both the eternity of heaven, which involves that transformed temporality in which all the positive features and contents of time are 'eternalised' (the glorified wounds of Christ), and the temporality of earth with its good (the incarnation) and evil (sin). This inclusion is such that by a differentiated awareness and presence of past, present and future the reality of our temporality is preserved while nonetheless remaining only one modality within the intensity of eternity; another is that transformed temporality in which the negative features of lost time are redeemed and the positivity of time is fulfilled. Finally this inclusion is also such that temporality in its extended form does itself contribute to the richness of the intensity of eternity: the reality of interaction is preserved.

Does this approach work? Can an intensive mode of being contain what is extended without giving the impression that the extendedness in question is truncated so that time is reduced to nothing but a twinkle in the eye of eternity and the real drama of the temporal incarnation and cross is relaxed? Before returning to this vital question we turn to the other particular problem areas which arose in the course of our enquiry.

Creation, its history and end

The major themes treated in chapter 2 (creation, its history and end, and the divine attributes) confirm the main lines of Balthasar's approach to the relationship between time and eternity. Time is real and is the expression of eternity, and the interaction between them is such that the primacy remains with the eternal whilst there is a real contribution from the side of the temporal.

A particular problem which emerged in the context of these themes concerned the difficulty of grasping how God in his eternity could be present to all our temporal lives without impugning either his eternity or our temporality. This problem surfaced in different ways when we discussed the immutability of God's providence with respect to our lives, the nature of petitionary prayer, the interaction between infinite and finite freedom in history and the presence of mystery and a supra-hope within God himself. The basic difficulty arising in all these areas may be formulated as follows: if God's omniscience is such as to ensure the universality and immutability of his providence, does it not also, by the same token, undermine both our freedom and God's own originality and supra-hope in dealing with us? The difficulty is eased by the hints which were scattered throughout chapter 2 and which have now been collated in a more systematic form in our thematic discussion of the relationship between time and eternity. First, then, the omniscience of God is not to be confused with a divine pre- or fore-knowledge: such temporal categories are not suited to describe the eternal mode of knowing.[59] Secondly, it is affirmed that the supra-temporal intensive richness of eternity is such that it can interact in total originality with the extendedness of our time. This intensity can combine complete knowledge, a differentiated awareness of past, present and future, and a love which goes beyond the dead certainty of knowledge and opens up the realms of hope and mystery in a way which does not threaten its unity-in-difference. This means that time is not a matter of going through the motions of something that is 'already' always known and decided in eternity, rather as a genius chess-player might quickly foresee the whole course of a game and move his pieces through a game which for him is already over, or like the filling in of a figure already drawn in dotted lines.[60] Instead the full reality and seriousness of time are maintained by invoking the co-presence or co-extensivity of the intensity of eternity with our extended, temporal lives and in a way which allows for creative interaction without taking from the primacy of the eternal. We have already referred to the image of a drama which is conceived, produced and acted all in one to describe this unique relationship (pp. 63–4 above). Finally, to say that the difficulty is eased does not imply that the problem is solved. We have eased the difficulty by removing one mistaken, if common, approach and substituting a different one. We have yet to offer a final assessment of the adequacy of this latter approach.

Assessment of Balthasar's position

We are now in a position to address ourselves to the required assessment of Balthasar's theology of the relationship between time and eternity.

We begin with a predominantly positive set of comments. We accept in general Balthasar's principal affirmations concerning the nature of time, of eternity, and of the relationship between the two. They are scripturally based, respectful of philosophical traditions and innerly coherent. They are conclusions of arguments which are probably true – and it is useful to observe that in dealing with this whole issue we are for the most part involved in matters of theological understanding rather than of undisputed faith, so that probability and not certainty will be the appropriate 'note' of our judgements.[61] We accept, then, the insistence on the reality of time, on the notion of eternity as a supra-temporality in which the perfections of temporality are preserved, albeit in a different form, and on the relationship between time and eternity in which eternity has primacy but within which the reality and contribution of both 'pure' and transformed temporality are acknowledged. The significance of these affirmations for the issue of divine immutability resides in the fact that Balthasar has sketched a notion of eternity as both event and state, and as capable of being both transcendent to and yet affected by a temporal mode of being. If eternity is not just present to all times but itself integrates temporality in its pure and transformed modes, and if temporal creation does make a real contribution to the divine eternal life as described in chapter 2, then it is clear that the reality of temporal history is far from being undermined or 'swallowed up' by God's supra-history.[62] Nor, since this integration is understood to involve duration of an intensive kind, is Balthasar's position open to the objection that it implies an eternity which is merely an extended infinite time and thus bereft of transcendence.

But it is precisely at the level of understanding that we encounter the limitations of the position and are required to introduce some nuances to our positive assessment. Within what one might refer to as the general area of theological understanding one may distinguish further between acts of judgement and of understanding properly so-called.[63] The former in this case are those affirmations which are made about the issue and with which we have expressed substantial agreement. The latter have to do with how these affirmations are understood, the insights which ground such an understanding. In this case (if one excepts the important references to the models of the Trinity and the Hypostatic Union) the principal insight resides in the distinction between intensity and extension. Now it is quite normal that within the general area of theological understanding true affirmations may be made without an accompanying full explanation.[64] This is normal because in theological matters we are most often dealing with mysteries which lie beyond the proportionate powers of human reason: in such cases, on the basis of our faith in God's revelation and on the connections between different revealed mysteries,[65] we are able to make true statements which are without full understanding. Thus we may say that in a general sense the Christian 'understanding' of the Trinity, based on faith in the scriptural message, came to be expressed in true affirmations which in themselves are not capable of full explanation or understanding in the more proper sense. In this present instance our understanding is even more partial: the distinction between intensity and extension in Balthasar is not by any means as thoroughly or as systematically grounded as the traditional ways of trying to understand the Trinity in terms of a distinction between what is absolute and what is relative, a distinction which is elucidated further by the so-called psychological analogy of Augustine, which is then rigorously developed by Aquinas and later by other modern interpreters.[66] This is shown in particular by the fact that Balthasar's distinction between intensity and extension is advanced without any substantial discussion of the different approaches in modern philosophy (often in dialogue with physics and mathematics) to the issues of time and eternity. Chapter 5 redresses the balance somewhat.[67]

We have already by implication acknowledged this limitation (pp. 93, 100–3 above). In particular we have noted that the positive sense of the divine attribute of eternity remains largely unknown: what is being offered by way of positive understanding lies even more clearly at the metaphorical end of that continuum between metaphor and analogy which we referred to in justifying the 'due imprecision' of our speech about the attributes of God. The image of intensity (which, for us, is in any case always accompanied by at least some minimal extension in time) does not easily accommodate the slow maturation or disintegration that are so characteristic of time as we experience it. It fails, then, to convey how God's eternity in its non-consecutive form may yet, unimaginably, integrate the extended form of our temporality. It fails to explain how the integrity of our temporal mode of existence is maintained in its interaction with eternity. These and other deficiencies in this image indicate how it is possible to accept Balthasar's principal affirmations and still be uneasy about the thrust inherent in the way such affirmations are explained. In particular, then, it is possible to accept his repeated assurances concerning the reality of time, and the way in which its perfections are present, transformed, within eternity, and yet to caution against a too-literal interpretation of the distinction between intensity and extension as a means of grounding these assurances. The distinction in question cannot in fact bear the full weight of an explanatory function in the sense that it cannot tell us how the various affirmations about time and eternity are to be understood in themselves. What it can do is provide an image which, in conjunction with the many other images which Balthasar uses to convey the total sense of his position (p. 93 above), suggests a direction in which to look for an understanding which is professedly partial and respectful of mystery. Such an understanding is more descriptive than explanatory.

But one could also overstress the deficiencies of Balthasar's approach. The image of intensity does convey well the sense in which a scattered, consecutive multiplicity may be present in a lively but differentiated unity. And by being aware of its predominantly metaphorical rather than analogical application, as well as by using it in conjunction with the other images referred to, one may safely avoid the misunderstandings which might otherwise arise. Moreover it is noticeable that Balthasar himself lays greater stress on adherence to the models of the Trinity and the Hypostatic Union as normative guides in outlining the relationship between time and eternity than he does on any direct treatment of the issue through the use of all the images to which we have referred. The relationship between time and eternity is structurally similar to that between Christ and God, and, in particular, to that between the world and God. This latter relationship may be grasped according to the models of the Trinity and the Hypostatic Union in which there is ordered difference within unity. This structural similarity is not a mere parallel but constitutes a true analogy: it does so because, as we indicated at the start of this chapter, time and eternity are not beings in themselves but rather modes of being (of the world and God respectively). This means that their intelligibility is to be sought within that of the relationship between God and the world, and accordingly displays the same basic pattern as this relationship. In this way Balthasar very clearly obviates the 'identity' or 'absorption' dangers inherent in the use of the term 'intensity'. But again this is not to say that a full explanation has been offered – the use of the trinitarian and christological models does not address in a direct way the peculiar difficulties for intelligibility which are proper to the issue of the relationship between time and eternity. However it does mean that a normative context has been provided within which any distortions intrinsic to the partial explanation that has been presented may be corrected. We have already noted how some critics have suggested that in his own theological thinking on other issues Balthasar himself falls prey to the defective thrust inherent in his position on time and eternity by, for example, giving too little room to a treatment of the material aspects of human history. But it is sufficient for our purposes at this stage to have established in a provisional way that in principle his position is satisfactory, and is so even with the qualifications we have mentioned.

Conclusion

As with our discussion on the attributes of God, so too at the end of our search into the relationship between time and eternity we find ourselves in the realm of mystery. This is entirely proper for an enquiry which is explicitly anti-Gnostic:[68] time and again, in different ways, Balthasar draws attention to what for us as creatures is the ultimately insoluble nature of the relationship between time and eternity, an unimaginable mystery which admits of no synthetic overview.

Of course it is at least conceivable that a less metaphorical approach might be possible, even allowing for that appropriate imprecision which we have identified as intrinsic to Balthasar's modification of traditional analogical discourse (p. 81–7 above). This is worth mentioning because there is not the same detailed thematic treatment in Balthasar of the explanatory aspects of the relationship between time and eternity as there is of the issue of divine suffering. And because of this it remains an open question as to whether a more precise explanation might not be possible (as in the example of the Trinity – p. 77, 106 above), without in any way dissolving the mystery that is involved. We may wait for a more definitive assessment of Balthasar's position until we have examined its application to the issue of divine immutability (chapter 4) and have compared it with other approaches (chapter 5).

However, once again it is important to recall the positive side of Balthasar's achievement. He has presented an account of the relationship between time and eternity which is consonant with (if not absolutely required by) the scriptural tradition. This account provides a coherent set of affirmations which enables us to give probable answers within the context of faith to the difficulties which present themselves. Furthermore it is an account which provides a limited but genuine basis of understanding with which to support the affirmations in question.

We note finally the significance for the issue of divine immutability of our provisional acceptance of Balthasar's position. The notion of eternity as a supra-temporality, within whose intensity the extended-ness of time can exist in both its 'pure' and transformed way, opens up the possibility of allowing for the 'ever-greater' of the trinitarian event and of doing so in a way which is respectful of the distinct if dependent contribution of created temporality. It is this event which ultimately grounds Balthasar's modification of the traditional axiom of divine immutability, and it is to this event that we now turn.

4

Is the trinitarian God immutable?

Introduction

The theme of this chapter is the immutability of God, the central issue of our enquiry, which in Balthasar's treatment is rooted in his account of the analogous event of inner-trinitarian love. The hypothesis that this event lay at the heart of Balthasar's theology of the divine immutability was amply verified in both the christological context and in the context of the relationship between creation and God. In the course of our treatment of the many topics which lay within these two main contexts we often referred to the need to examine this event in greater detail in order to come to a more precise grasp of its intelligibility and of the way in which it leads to a careful modification of the traditional notion of divine immutability in the theology of Balthasar. As always, we limit ourselves to those aspects of Balthasar's account which have a direct bearing on his position on the divine immutability. Accordingly, the scope of our treatment does not extend to a comprehensive account either of his theology of the Trinity or indeed of the Trinity as divine event. However it *is* within our scope to describe and explain this event in such a way that his position on the divine immutability becomes clear, and the required final assessment is made possible. We begin with a general description of Balthasar's account, which will be followed by a more explanatory treatment.

Description of Balthasar's trinitarian 'event'

Balthasar accepts the traditional credal and Conciliar teaching on the Trinity as normative for his own theologising.[1] This means that his theology of the trinitarian event is developed from within an explicitly traditional Christian view of the Trinity.

Often he likes to present this view of the Trinity in contrast to the polytheism of myth and the absolute but impersonal One of the ancient philosophical world, in order to bring out the original way in which the Christian God as triune is both transcendent and yet truly personal. But apologetics is not the source of this teaching; it is the scriptural revelation of Jesus, integrating while modifying the monotheism of the OT, which alone allows us to speak of God as triune. In particular the scriptural (and especially Johannine) texts of 'sender/sent', of the Son going out from and returning to the Father in his mission, harmonise well with the later traditional account of those processions within God who, mysteriously, is one in nature while being three in person or hypostasis, this distinction in persons being real and identifiable where there is a 'relationship of opposition'.[2]

Again, in the traditional sense, Balthasar means to assert that the divine nature is one in the sense of numerical identity, and not just with reference to generic sameness or likeness. There are not two or three gods. Equally, of course, he insists on the real distinction of Persons, brought out so clearly in the NT, and rejects any Modalist interpretations which threaten the reality of these distinctions. This assertion of unity and distinction constitutes the deepest mystery at the heart of Christianity, a mystery which is not dispelled by the many human attempts to approach it.[3] One way of pointing to this mystery is to speak of the fact that in God relation to self and relation to other is identical: in speaking thus, Balthasar is already drawing attention to the reality that to be a person in the Trinity is to be a pure relation, to be for another, and, accordingly, that love is at the heart of the trinitarian *circumincessio*.[4]

The purpose of this brief presentation has been not merely to give evidence of Balthasar's professed orthodoxy, but also to identify those elements in the tradition itself which help us to understand his transition from talk of the Trinity to that of the trinitarian event. The language of 'processions' and 'love' is full of movement and life, but Balthasar clearly believes that these inherently dynamic elements have not been exploited sufficiently by the tradition itself, with the result that the Trinity has appeared as a rather abstract, undramatic, fixed order of relations, with the notion of immutability both adding to this distorted appearance and being itself distorted by its context.[5] Of course it is over-simplistic to speak merely in terms of a move from the static to the dynamic:[6] Balthasar is also well aware of the dynamic elements proper to the tradition, and indeed of the need to retain what is properly static in any true notion of God, however contemporary. What he wants to do himself is to focus more sharply on the dynamic side of what the tradition correctly identified as the processions of love within the Trinity; in this way he is attempting to interpret the difference-in-unity at the heart of traditional trinitarian theology in a manner which brings out the interaction within trinitarian love.

The trinitarian event

Balthasar's clear intention in speaking about the trinitarian 'event' is to do greater justice to the liveliness of divine love, without denying or reducing the absolute transcendence of God. In the early philosophical work *Wahrheit* there is already a going beyond the essentialism of neo-Thomistic thought by the manner in which inner-worldly truth is treated under such headings as history, situation, and the uniqueness and mystery of interpersonal revelation, as also by the espousal of a more dynamic notion of the *actus purus* of being itself.[7] This overall direction harmonises well with many of the tendencies of contemporary theology, including, indeed, the use of the category of event.[8] However, what is distinctive among theologians like Balthasar is precisely the explicit attempt to combine the static with the dynamic, to preserve the category of state while being open to that of event, to avoid the rationalism of an essentialist ontology not by giving priority to the notion of 'process', but rather by retaining the ontological, without denying the abiding truth of the notion of 'becoming'. In Balthasar himself, then, the *Theodrama* can never be separated from the *Theologik*: goodness and truth, with the other transcendentals of unity and beauty, must together help us to form our notion of the trinitarian God of Jesus Christ, a notion in which the philosophical elements are quite explicitly inspired by (while being able to contribute to) the theological, in that symbiosis between theology and philosophy in which Balthasar insists on the priority of the former.[9]

Such, in a general sense, is the intention of his attempt. It is an attempt which is professedly at odds with the systems of Hegel and Process thinkers: not only is the relationship between being and becoming different in Balthasar, but also he is insistent on the abiding difference between creator and creature so that there can be no attribution of a created 'becoming' or 'event' to God who is eternal. This has important terminological and semantic implications. It means that when Balthasar speaks of the trinitarian drama or conversation in terms of an event or happening his speech is non-univocal and expresses a liveliness in the triune God which is actual not, as in us, because it is accompanied by a need which is a lack in perfection, but rather because it expresses a holy love that is unchanging and groundless.[10]

These introductory remarks are the context within which the relevant features of Balthasar's theology of the trinitarian event of love may now be outlined descriptively. The trinitarian processions already imply movement in God: these processions are explicated by Balthasar (with the support of scriptural motifs such as the mutuality of giving, handing over, glorifying, that are present in God)[11] as a movement which is an event of love. The mysterious divine nature is constituted by this giving and receiving of love.[12] The Father in God reveals himself by expressing himself completely in the Son. This means that fatherhood in God is the total giving of all that the Father is and has to the Son. In this eternally actual generation the Son both receives his being from the Father and returns it to him in a love which is equally without reserve. This filial love is full of thanksgiving (eucharist) for the gift of the Father and expresses itself most properly in a free 'obedience' to the Father which is without the subordination of creaturehood. And again because this event between Father and Son is eternal, and implies no 'before' and 'after', the Holy Spirit is the fruit and personification of their love without any implication of subordination (as there is in the created analogy to the procession of the Holy Spirit drawn from the child as fruit of the human parents' love).[13] Once again that which is most proper to the Holy Spirit, personhood, is constituted by being utterly the love of the other two in the Trinity and thus by being in this scene 'expropriated'.[14]

What it is most important to grasp about this description is the contention that love is this way always, eternally, in God. The processions in God do not just explain how the persons originate, as if, this having been explained, there is no longer any movement between them. Rather, just as it makes no sense to speak of a Father 'before' the Son, of a Father as God on his own, so it is maintained that the nature of God is always both possessed and given, it is constituted by this eternal giving and receiving between the persons. So, for example, the Father is always generating the Son, and the Son is always both proceeding from and returning to the Father – it is this mysterious interchange which constitutes their being and its liveliness. And furthermore, while there is obvious sense in which it is the Father who gives while the Son and Holy Spirit both receive, still, on further reflection, it is clear that all three persons give and receive – so that, for example, the Father receives in the sense that his love is accepted and returned by the Son, while both Father and Son are united in their difference by the gift of the Holy Spirit.

If there exists this liveliness of interaction within the Trinity, and if (as Scripture reveals to us through the incarnation and cross of Christ) the Persons are not just distinct, but also assume different modalities within the power and freedom of their united love, then we may, again descriptively for now, further specify the love that is in God in a way that goes beyond some traditional boundaries. This is a love, then, which has an inbuilt open or ontological comparative to its nature – it is 'ever-more', 'ever-greater' than the reality which is present to the Persons themselves in their perfect knowledge of one another. In other words there is present in God's love those elements of surprise, wonder and difference which are proper to the mysterious self-giving and inter-penetration (*circumincessio*) of free love and which transcend the level of knowledge, however complete.[15] In this sense we may say that the Holy Spirit is constantly showing the Father and Son that their perfect love is more than they themselves had expected. There is no boredom in heaven. This daring way of speaking about trinitarian love, when combined with the equally untraditional stress on the receptivity of this love and the different modalities it can assume, leads to the positing of some other rather surprising divine attributes. Within the framework of analogical discourse as described, one may speak of such immanent modalities of trinitarian love as renunciation, prayer, faith and hope, longing and fulfilment. Within this same framework one may also speak of those economic modalities of this love such as anger and jealousy, and even something corresponding to pain, all of which, in turn, are modalities of the immanent triune love within which their original images reside. One may dare to use this rather shocking way of speaking because of Balthasar's conviction (the explanatory basis of which we have already outlined) that the transcendence of God may be maintained while allowing for the different reality of the contribution of dependent creation to the 'ever-more' of trinitarian love. Finally, in the extreme revelation of this trinitarian love in which sin is confronted and overcome, the positive personal distinction and difference between Father and Son assumes the modality of opposition and abandonment, and may do so because of the way in which the Holy Spirit continues to be the guarantor of that unity-in-difference which constitutes the trinitarian love. Indeed the freedom of divine love to assume such diverse modalities and still remain itself is evident in the economic leading of the Son by the Spirit in apparent contradiction of their immanent order in God; this 'trinitarian inversion'[16] Balthasar ascribes to the aspect of the Holy Spirit as objective witness of that difference-in-unity of trinitarian love, as witness, in other words, of precisely that freedom of this love to assume such diverse modalities and still remain itself. This reference to the sameness of divine love reminds us of Balthasar's constant care to integrate the notion of 'state' within his theology of the trinitarian event. The dynamism of God's love, with its diverse modalities, occurs eternally, without need, and in this sense is compatible with both the perfection and the immutability of God.

Summary

We have described Balthasar's theology of the trinitarian event by presenting in a unified way data which, for the most part, may be found in more scattered form throughout our account so far.

In intimate human relationships it may be granted that the presence of mystery increases rather than decreases as lovers become closer to one another in knowledge and love. This is a faint analogy for the reality of mystery within the transparency of the divine Persons to one another in God's love.[17] This mystery will be acknowledged from our side by a conscious awareness and acceptance in speaking about the trinitarian event that whether we use clearly pictorial language or more exact and properly analogous terminology we still always move within a universe of discourse which is non-univocal. We have already adverted to the 'due imprecision' which this situation entails for the theologian; however we have also adverted to his proper task in making the mystery more precise, and, in particular, in indicating that while the realm of mystery transcends that of human logic it does not simply contradict it. On the basis of our summary description we may now begin to ask about the ultimate intelligibility of Balthasar's theology of the trinitarian event.

Four main questions will help us to focus on this issue of intelligibility, so crucial for our final assessment of Balthasar's position on the divine immutability. First, can the unity of God really be preserved when so much emphasis is laid on the differences between the trinitarian Persons? Next, can the personal distinctions within the Trinity really serve as an explanation for the way in which God deals with sin? Then, can the traditional notion of God as pure act be modified to include some notion of receptivity? And finally, can we be satisfied with a notion of God as 'ever-more' in which being and becoming are somehow one? The last two questions in particular have obvious relevance for the issue of divine immutability, the major concern of our enquiry; but all four of them will allow us to enter in a deeper, more explanatory way into Balthasar's theology of the trinitarian event and thus to meet this concern.

The intelligibility of Balthasar's trinitarian 'event'

The unity of God

The question concerning the unity of God arises due to the emphasis in Balthasar's theology on the proper identity and roles of the three Persons both within God and in relation to the economy of salvation. This emphasis is clearly based on his interpretation of the scriptural account of the relationships within the divine unity of being.[18] The trinitarian processions are understood already to involve in God an interaction of an inter-personal and dramatic nature, the different modalities of which are then expressed in the economy of salvation, and in particular in that most extreme moment of the cross where Father and Son are distinct to the point of apparent separation. Does this 'theodramatic' notion of the trinitarian processions imply a downgrading or indeed elimination of the divine unity?

As a first approach towards an answer we must repeat Balthasar's own clear statements adhering to the credal and Conciliar teaching in defence of the traditional position on the unity of God. Thus there is the explicit rejection of ditheism and/or tritheism: there is no multiplication of substances or beings in God; the mystery resides in the fact that each person is identical with the one divine essence or nature (which is not itself reified as some kind of 'fourth' in God) and yet different from each other due to the opposition of relations within that nature.[19] At the level of intention and affirmation, then, we may be satisfied that Balthasar does indeed preserve the unity of God. Of course the difficulty arises due precisely to the mystery to which we have adverted and the need to express it in ways which embody these affirmations: the absolute unity and indivisibility of the Christian God go beyond the definitions of unity accessible to unaided philosophical thought, and must somehow take account of that plurality of relative realities which has been revealed by Christ.[20] It may not do so by reducing this plurality to some kind of an appearance of that which in reality is only one – the Father is not the Son, and options which inherit the legacy of traditional Modalism are to be rejected just as firmly as those which are polytheistic in character.[21] Balthasar's stress on the proper (and not just 'appropriated') roles of the three Persons in God means that in expressing his understanding of the true affirmations concerning the unity and threefold nature of God he needs to be particularly sensitive to ensuring that the divine unity is not dissolved (whereas with Rahner it is the danger of Modalism that needs to be avoided).[22] How does he express this sensitivity?

A first indication of his awareness of the need for balance in this whole question is his refusal to use on their own, in whatever form, either of the two traditional analogies for understanding the Trinity (the psychological analogy of Augustine and Aquinas, and the social one of Richard of St Victor). An intra-subjective approach is best suited to convey the unity of God in a way which the grossly anthropomorphic aspect of the social analogy cannot do; nonetheless the intersubjective aspect of the latter is needed to convey the reality of the real person I/Thou within God to which Christ gives witness. Both seemingly opposed approaches are necessary and their reconciliation is effected within the mystery of God in a way which is invisible to us.[23]

However Balthasar focuses chiefly on the notion of love as a clue to the way in which unity and plurality in God may be reconciled.[24] The groundless self-giving of love in God is the basic attribute and constituent both of the one divine nature and of the three divine hypostases. It is the existence of otherness within the unity of the triune God which allows us to speak of God as love in a transitive and not just an intransitive sense. Otherness is positive within love. Of course our created experience of love involves the coming together of two distinct beings, and so is different from that unique unity-in-difference which constitutes God. Nonetheless the way in which even created love reconciles the realities of difference and unity may be understood as a pointer at least to the existence without contradiction of these realities in God. The analogue of human inter-personal love, with its social and psychological integration of difference and unity, is used, then, to point to an ontological unity-in-difference within God which, due to the omnipotence of divine love, can embrace the kind of extreme differences which appear to us as separation and division without in fact undergoing such a dissolution of unity.

This extension of the analogy of created inter-personal love from the moral to the ontological level, when applied to God, is evident once again in Balthasar's treatment of the common decisions and activity of the one God which yet allow for a differentiation of identity and role. Again, there can be no question of three wills or three separate centres of consciousness in God; however there is a real I/Thou relationship within God so that the one divine freedom is possessed differently by each hypostasis, and the unity of the divine will is always present and yet must also be considered to be the integration of the intention of the different hypostases within the divine conversation.[25] The danger here, of course, is that one thinks again of three separate beings with their own aims which are then afterwards integrated into a common policy and decision. But Balthasar insists that this process is eternal, without a 'before' or 'after', and argues therefore that the divine *circumincessio* involves a creative freedom of the Persons which is such that their unity, while always existing, may also be spoken of in the daring terms of a result or synthesis. Such daring is more easily acceptable when one considers the traditional way of speaking about the Holy Spirit as being both the love of Father and Son and as being the fruit of that love. In particular then it is the Holy Spirit who personifies this mysterious unity of divine love which embraces interpersonal mutuality and difference without multiplying beings.[26] This kind of differentiated unity is apparent in God's decision to create and save us and in the actual execution of the divine plan, so that, for example, all three Persons in God are involved together, if differently, in the cross of Christ, while there is no question of the eternal unity of God being interrupted in any way by the incarnation of the Son.[27]

We turn now to the issues which arise when this theology of God's unity-in-difference is used to address the reality of sin.

The trinitarian distinctions and sin

We have already outlined at some length the trinitarian presuppositions of our creation in the theology of Balthasar. The 'eccentricity' of creation, and even sin, was located within the 'concentricity' of the trinitarian life of love.[28] Much of this thinking was uncontroversial; we do need, however, to restate Balthasar's position on the trinitarian background to sin and to the related event of Christ's death, in order to establish that his position on divine unity may be maintained in the face of its most extreme threat. May one really speak about the personal distinctions in God in such terms as 'distance', 'diastasis', 'separation' and 'alienation', when one treats of the divine response to sin? May one conceive of the trinitarian I/Thou, based on the traditional formulation of opposed relations within God, in terms of opposition in the hostile sense?

The key to these questions is in Balthasar's interpretation of the Trinity in terms of a love of self-giving and receiving that is absolute in respect of freedom, power and richness. The power of this love is shown by the way in which the other in God is allowed to be infinitely other without detriment to unity. Its richness and freedom are shown by the variety of modalities which this love can assume.

Within this framework[29] we saw how experiences such as suffering and anger might have a positive original image in God, while in an inverse way the possibility of human sin and of God's overcoming of sin was also contained in a positive sense within the power of divine love. It was clear from this that no ontological negativity was being posited in God: the non-univocal renunciatory reality involved in the kenotic aspects of inner-trinitarian love was viewed as compatible with the divine perfection and beatitude, and the similarly non-univocal economic modalities which flowed from this reality in response to sin (for example, God's anger and 'supra-suffering') were negative in appearance only, being in reality a positive answer to sin. This is the context within which the plan of God to save sinners is realised by the death of his Son. We saw how realistically Balthasar described this death – to the point of Christ's experience of the 'second death' of the sinner in hell. It is Balthasar's argument that the trinitarian personal distinctions, based on the opposition of relations, are indeed sufficiently real and infinite to embrace, without loss of unity, the kind of opposition between Father and Son which is involved in their common plan to overcome sin. This is so because divine love has the power freely to unfold its richness in such different modalities that the Son's experience of opposition in a hostile sense remains always a function and an aspect of his loving relationship to the Father in the Holy Spirit.

This means that the unity of God is maintained. It also means that the supra-space which Balthasar posits in God, referred to on the cross in such terms as 'diastasis', 'distance', 'separation', 'alienation', an 'abyss', is a metaphor which does not imply any ontological separation.[30] Once we are careful to realise the non-univocal nature of this way of speaking we may discover its evocative power. There is a rhythm of nearness and distance in relationships of love:[31] the way in which intimacy may sometimes be better nourished by a letter from afar than by actual physical presence becomes a faint human analogy for the way in which nearness and distance are mutually reconcilable within the unity of God's love. In particular, then, when distance is used as a metaphor for what is experienced as negative, the way in which human abandonment and the wounds of suffering may also serve to increase the bond of love becomes analogous to that substantial unity in God which arises out of the kenotic self-giving of the persons to one another. The renunciatory character of this inner-divine self-giving, this 'kenotic inhibition',[32] means that one may speak of a 'pre-sacrifice' (*Voropfer*)[33] within God which is ontologically prior to incarnation and cross. But again this inner-divine supra-kenosis is not negative – it remains an integral part of God's infinite perfection and happiness, for which the co-existence of human joy and suffering provides a faint analogy. Nor does it lead to a pan-kenoticism in God: the kenotic, renunciatory quality of the divine processions is but one aspect of a love whose drama and liveliness are also constituted by the joy and wondering surprise which character-ise what is, above all, the perfect beatitude of the inner-divine self-giving and receiving.[34]

Human love values difference, and may use suffering and even the combating of evil to increase inter-personal unity. But human love may also be broken under the burden of differences, may not be strong enough to survive separation and opposition. Furthermore self-love is not the highest example of human love – rather, one loves another being in a unity that is moral but not substantial.[35] In God, however, the unity is substantial, so that self-love and love of the other mysteriously coincide, while the richness and power of divine love are sufficient freely to take care of differences, however extreme. It is within this pattern of similarity and dissimilarity that Balthasar uses the analogy of human love to maintain the unity of God even while interpreting the distinction of persons according to the opposition of relationships in a way which harmonises with this theology of the cross of Christ. It may be noted finally – in answer to an earlier query – that Balthasar's soteriological position is supported by this framework which ensures that the particular negativity inserted into the Trinity due to the free representation by Christ of sinners remains within the scope of the ontologically positive divine love.

We have been focusing, in these two questions concerning unity and difference in God, on some structural aspects of the theology of the trinitarian event. We turn now to the more dynamic aspects of this event.

Receptivity in God

In the discussions concerning the obedience and temporality of Christ as expressive of the divine nature, the contribution of the world to God within the trinitarian relationships and the possibility of ascribing something like a supra-suffering to the Trinity,[36] we have remarked how time and again Balthasar argues for some kind of receptivity within God. We have also drawn attention in these discussions to the problems this position causes a traditional way of speaking about God in terms of pure act and omnipotence. Traditionally it was always possible to ascribe something analogous to an active potency in God (thus allowing for the freedom of creation), but not anything analogous to that passive potency which in us is grounded in our nature as creatures. Receptivity then, as a passive potency proper to the imperfection of a creature, could not be attributed to God, who is perfect: after all, how could God who is and has all be thought to be receptive? Our aim, then, is to present in a more thematic way Balthasar's case for considering receptivity as a divine perfection. The stakes are high: if his position is accepted then the way is at least open to an acceptance of all those other modalities of love – such as surprise, joy, renunciation – which he has placed within an event described in terms of a conversation, a reciprocal dialogue or exchange.

The great revelation of receptivity as a divine perfection is of course the incarnate Christ, whose mission, accomplished in obedience, is a manifestation that passivity of this kind is an integral element of the love which is at the centre of the inner-trinitarian event.[37] Supported by this scriptural basis Balthasar distinguishes two aspects of that love which indicate how receptivity may be passive and yet positive.[38] First, there is the aspect of love considered in relation to the trinitarian processions and origins of the hypostases in God. It is because of the self-giving of love that the Father generates the Son, that Father and Son are source of the Holy Spirit. This means that the Son and Holy Spirit in particular receive their being: and yet because they are both God it also means, very significantly, that within this reality of love to receive is just as divine as to give. Furthermore, since the giving of the Father is incomplete unless received by the Son, receptivity is part of the active giving of the Father: fatherhood in God is given with the divine nature only because this nature is intrinsically inter personal through being distinguished by opposed relations, so that there is a real sense in which the Father receives from the Son, despite the predominantly active being of the Father as origin within God. This means, to return to the objections of the traditional approach, that there is something at least analogous to passive potency within the *Actus Purus* of the omnipotent God. This is not of course identical with that passive potency in us which is grounded primarily in our being as creatures, *ex nihilo* – receptivity in God has nothing to do with lack of being. Nonetheless there are positive elements even in created passive potency which do indicate its likeness (*Abbild*) to what is originally imaged (*Urbild*) in God. In this context Balthasar refers to the analogy of human sexual intercourse and conception as a pointer to what occurs in God (without of course implying that love in God is sexual as it is in us). The human inter-penetration of activity and passivity, giving and receiving in sexual love points to the way in which receptivity is positive in God's love.

The love which is at the origin of the trinitarian hypostases continues to be their mode of relating: it could not be otherwise in God who is eternal. The hypostases do not stand against one another in some dead vis-à-vis; rather they continue to exist in a *circumincessio* of giving and receiving, and this second aspect of the mutual interaction and exchange involved in trinitarian love is used by Balthasar to indicate again how receptivity may be viewed as a perfection.[39] In this exchange, made possible by that unity-in-difference to which we have often referred, there is that free revelation and giving of the Persons to one another which involves as well that receiving of the other proper to inter-personal communication. Part of the divine joy consists precisely in *receiving* the love of another, as well as the different modalities of that love, and this always remains a mysterious occurrence within the intensity of divine eternal life because it involves, beyond knowledge, the creatively free revelation and self-giving of a person. Receptivity, then, is intrinsic to the perfection of the dialogical I/Thou relationship within God: and we are given a hint here as well, in the reference to the intrinsically mysterious nature of inter-personal relationships, about the 'ever-more' aspect of the trinitarian event.

This notion of the positive nature of receptivity within inter-personal love is deepened by Balthasar's use, once again, of the pertinent created analogy. In the early study concerning truth[40] he details the way in which the subject/object relationship is characterised by a receptivity on the part of both subject and object, as shown, for example, in the non-prejudicial welcoming of the other into one's own realm of being. The openness of this receptivity means that there is an inherently active, creative, spontaneous element in its passivity, and by distinguishing an ascending scale of subject/object relationships in the created realm, going from the realms of inanimate to animate and then human spiritual being, Balthasar establishes the fact that the higher one reaches on this scale the more apparent it is that this kind of passivity is indeed a potency, *viz.* a power, with these active elements in it. At the top of this scale is that relationship between subject and object when it takes the form of that between subject and subject. In inter-personal dialogue it becomes evident that truth is ultimately derived from and directed towards love – the ground of the world is ultimately free self-disclosure of a personal nature, at the heart of which are both mystery and a welcoming, active receptivity.

It might be argued that just as God is not a sexual being, so neither does he attain truth as we do, so that analogies of this kind are, at best, simply redundant. But Balthasar is very clear about the abiding difference between creator and creature: in particular, with regard to this analogy, he knows that God is creative of truth from his own being and so cannot really be said to 'attain' truth in our sense. Nonetheless, within this dissimilarity he believes that one can point to a helpful similarity. All created being is *ex nihilo*, and the passivity of the subject/object relationship is due partly at least to this ontological difference between the world and God. In this sense it is rooted in deficiency. However the curious and helpful aspect to which Balthasar draws our attention is that the higher up the scale of created reality one goes the more this passivity increases, along the lines of the open receptivity proper to human inter-personal encounter. What he is suggesting here is that this kind of passivity is not just a deficiency, that it also has its positive side. And if it is positive as well then it is not simply contradictory to what is in God, but may be the created copy of an original in God. By holding on to the ontological difference between creator and creature, with the implications for dissimilarity which this involves, the transcendence of the trinitarian *Urbild* over the human *Abbild* is maintained. But Balthasar has also identified the positive similarities between created receptivity, traditionally regarded as a deficiency only, and the analogous positive reality within God's love. It should be noted finally that the use of human analogies is entirely subsidiary to the fact that this kind of receptivity in God has been established by its revelation in the life of Christ, the primary source of our truth about God.

Balthasar has shown that while there is no pure potentiality or passivity in God, there is an active receptivity which is the original image of passive potency in the created realm. This can be understood as perfection when it is allowed that the omnipotence of God is primarily the absolute power of love, and thus involves the giving and receiving of trinitarian exchange and mutuality in which we too participate, so that God's relationship to the world may be characterised as containing elements not only of the masculine *Deus faber* but also of feminine receptivity.[41] This is an eternal 'giving and receiving', not a frozen, past 'given and received'. What Balthasar has argued for is a notion of God as *Actus Purus* in which, because of the revelation of absolute power as love, God remains primarily active but the form of divine activity is such that it may integrate passivity positively. The discussion, then, is moved beyond the traditional categories of potency and act, within which passive potency could be seen exclusively as non-divine (positive only in differentiating the world from God) and without any analogous existence in the trinitarian life.[42]

But if one may allow that Balthasar has indeed indicated how receptivity may be a perfection, there remains the niggling worry that his position is ultimately incoherent. That God, who is and has all, can receive and indeed receive more – is this not an absurd proposition, despite all the supporting evidence and argumentation?

The 'ever-more' of the trinitarian event

We are already familiar with Balthasar's paradoxical attribution of an 'ever-more', 'ever-greater' element to God who is perfect. Based on the scriptural revelation (in particular concerning the time of Jesus) we noted his contention that temporal, created becoming pointed to an uncreated, eternal, but real and positive becoming and liveliness in God. Such an analogical divine becoming was evidenced in the dramatic notion of God arising from the christological context of incarnation and soteriology, as well as the theology of creation, its history and end. This dramatic notion involved a trinitarian love with different interacting modalities, including a receptivity in God within himself and to us, which required us to attribute to him something like wonder and surprise, as well as increase. The notion of eternity as a form of intensity rather than a Platonic *nunc stans* facilitated speech about God in terms of an ontological comparative rather than the traditional superlative.

We need now, however, to bring together in a more thematic way

Balthasar's argument for these crucial contentions. For we are now at the nub of the matter: can event and state, absolute being and happening, really be reconciled?[43] The question of the validity of such speech is clearly of decisive importance in determining the issue of divine immutability. How does Balthasar argue against the apparent logical absurdity attending talk of self-transcendence within divine perfection?[44]

Part of his argument is based on a Patristic image which is both helpful in itself and possesses a certain authority due to its use by the Fathers. The image in question arises from the general context of a discussion concerning the way in which creation, especially human-kind, participates in the eternal life of God.[45] With Platonic and neo-Platonic precedent, and faithful to the main thrust of Irenaeus, Gregory of Nyssa proposes that there is a paradoxical identity of rest and movement in God's eternal life, an identity which involves none of the tragic opposition associated with the position of Origen. Gregory's proposal means that, in full recognition of the connection between movement and creaturely deficiency, there is nonetheless a positive aspect of movement and desire which he attributes to the ever-richer life of God. By doing so he is affirming that the opposition between being and becoming is overcome in God. In order to throw light on this paradoxical affirmation, and to illustrate how God may be *semper major* not just to us (gnoseologically) but also in himself (ontologically), Gregory uses the image of a spring or fountain. The divine life in Scripture is more than just living water: it is a fountain of living water which, in its constant springing forth, has an appearance of fullness and sameness and yet is always renewing itself from within. The fountain is an image of the paradoxical unity of repose and movement in God; and the onlooker is amazed at its infinite streaming forth from within so that the whole is never seen and there are always new outpourings in and from the same depths. The image of course is pointing to the ultimately indescribable reality of God's triune love, which reconciles repose and movement so that even such an Aristotelian thinker as Maximus the Confessor (who saw movement principally in teleological terms and thus as foreign to God) was able to acknowledge this reconciliation in his use of the image of the 'holy dance'.[46]

The image used by Gregory is related by Balthasar to the themes of fruit and fruitfulness in the NT, especially in their Pauline use.[47] The divine fruitfulness and abundance are likened to the way in which one might believe (if one did not know that it was nourished by underground sources) that in pouring water out of itself in every instant a fountain creates its own waters anew. Once again the image is transferred from the realm of nature to that of free inter-personal love in which renewal is experienced in giving and in which fullness is maintained precisely through the passing on of the overflow. A fountain is identical with itself in this process of flowing over; and in being so it is an image of the fullness of trinitarian love which is ever-more than itself. This divine excess[48] and extravagance is revealed in so many ways by the ever-more self-giving being and activity of Jesus.

The Patristic image of a fountain evokes some sense of the possibility of the unity of rest and movement in God. But it needs to be inserted into an ontological framework in order to avoid misunder-standings and to fulfil its potential as a pointer to how God may be both perfect and ever-more. The second part of Balthasar's argument addresses itself to this required insertion. It depends for its efficacy on two principal considerations. First, there is an irreducible difference between God and the world within a unity, however intimate.[49] In particular there is a fullness of being in God, who simply is, which may be expressed in terms of an identity between essence and existence in contrast to the real distinction between essence and existence in creatures who exist dependently, participating in the existence of God. This dependent, creaturely existence, *ex nihilo*, is distinguished at every stage by a becoming which is characteristic of that which comes into being and which is in process towards its final state of participation in the fullness of God's being. This becoming, then, characteristic of creaturehood, is rooted in radical need, deficiency and dependency, and cannot apply to God. This basic ontological foundation means that Balthasar is in fundamental disagreement with the approach of Process thinkers or any others who posit some kind of univocal becoming (or change, or suffering) in God. It means that, whatever the resulting cost in imprecision, there can at most be only an analogous becoming within what remains as the basic reality of God's fullness of being.

Secondly, in order to make room for and conceive even this analogous becoming in God, Balthasar focuses on the reality and specific nature of love, which is, as before, at the absolute centre of his approach. The whole story about God is not that he is the fullness of being, but rather that he is love.[50] This scriptural stance, along with the equally scriptural axiom that humankind is made in the image and likeness of God, allows Balthasar to sketch a trinitarian ontology in which the primary metaphysical question about why anything at all exists is answered with reference to the 'why-lessness' of the trinitarian self-giving.[51] This groundless self-giving is beyond freedom and necessity in our terms in being characterised as natural but without being caused by anything outside God. Such a convertibility between being and love is saying that reality in its ultimate source and finality is due not simply to the existence of being or God as substance, but to this substance understood in terms of gift. Love is what is first in being. If God and his fullness of being is the primary reality, then what is primary in God is trinitarian love. The I/Thou relationship between the hypostases of the Trinity is what is ultimate in God and that which is the basis of God's entirely free decision to create us; reality is a 'given' not in the sense of a bare fact but rather because it is due to the self-giving in love of Father, Son and Holy Spirit. This means that truth too, being the truth is what *is*, is rooted in and in service of love, so that true knowledge goes beyond the notion of a formal corre-spondence between the mental concept of the subject and the reality of the object to embrace the notion of inter-personal self-giving.[52] It is in specifying further the nature of this inter-personal love, with its primacy within being and truth, that Balthasar opens up a way to point to an analogous becoming in God.

He does so by noting how intrinsic to the notion of inter-personal self-giving is a respect for the enduring otherness of the lovers and for their freedom to offer themselves to each other ever-anew, in a way which eliminates the primacy of knowledge or possession. The lover 'possesses' the beloved only in the latter's free gift of self, and this gift is not a commodity which corresponds to a knowledge that is 'already in the picture',[53] but is a free personal self-communication which involves a constant giving and allows the beloved to reveal and give new aspects of the self while retaining his own otherness. Within the intimacy of inter-personal love, then, there are a reserve and discretion which allow and want the other to be other in a way which preserves the freedom of self-giving and the creativity, wonder, surprise and mystery which accompany this freedom.[54] It is part of the joy of love's perfection, then, to fulfil expectations in a way which surpasses the highest expectations and yet does nothing to induce satiation; and this is due precisely to its nature as free personal giving and receiving to which increase and 'ever-more' are intrinsic. In other words, it is part of the perfection of love that the delight of the lovers is constantly renewed by the different modalities contained within the fullness of self-giving. It is only where love grows cold that the lover tires of looking at the beloved because knowledge and habit persuade him that there is nothing new to be seen. Where love is alive there are an excess and overflow which rule out boredom. And if love is not just what is first but also what is last in being, then this means that faith[55] and mystery are intrinsic to reality and truth in that they are appropriate elements in the inexhaustible richness of inter-personal love which grounds everything that is. Such a notion of truth goes beyond an essentialist form of knowledge, in which both subject and object are treated as things to be labelled, and opens out to the realm of truth as rooted in personal love. In this realm otherness is respected and, along with it, the freedom of the other to express and give his self in a way that includes the delight of surprise in being 'ever-more' than any knowledge of each other, however complete, that the lovers genuinely possess.[56]

It may be objected that this description of the nature of love applies to humankind only, and not to God. A consideration of the reply to this serious objection will help to fill in the detail of Balthasar's position as outlined above. First, it is clear that, as always, our speech about God is analogous, allowing for dissimilarity, so that Balthasar is saying once again that within God's love there exists the original image (*Urbild*), and not the created form, of such elements as creativity, increase, reserve and discretion. Then, as before, he will claim that one may specify this analogous love in God to some extent (for example, its dynamic nature is not due to any deficiency in being; it exists within that intensity of eternity which is different from, although not directly opposed to, the extendedness of time, and it exists too between three divine Persons who are distinct but who are nonetheless, mysteriously, only one divine being), while being obliged to remain satisfied with a use of language in which an appropriate imprecision points to the presence of ultimate mystery. However, even within such a framework might one not object that the 'ever-more' aspect of human love is due precisely to the inability of humans ever to give themselves to one another totally, and so, willy-nilly, is rooted in deficiency and ought not to be attributed even analogously to God? In particular, is not the 'excess' of love over knowledge due to the unavoidable partial nature of human knowledge and so, once again, unattributable to God, who is omniscient? The answer to these objections follows the same approach as that taken to the objections against considering receptivity as a perfection of divine love – first, that an analogous 'ever-more' is more true to the scriptural and, in particular, the Johannine account of the liveliness of trinitarian love,[57] and secondly, that far from decreasing as human love grows in knowledge and fullness it can be seen that the more perfect human love is, and the more transparent the lovers are to one another, so too there increases the aspect of 'ever-more'. In this way Balthasar appeals both to the scriptural evidence and to the created analogue in support of what we may consider to be his hypothesis that there is a dynamic, 'ever-more' element intrinsic to the fullness of divine love.[58]

There is then in God, who is infinitely free, that eternal increase of love, personified in a special way by the Holy Spirit, who is the fruit of Father and Son and may be understood in terms of the comparative which guarantees the superlative at the heart of God's free love.[59] The Holy Spirit is, metaphorically, the future aspect[60] within the ever-present intensity of God's eternity. Within this eternity the infinite richness of divine love may assume ever-new aspects and modalities as, in accordance with the absolute freedom of the divine being, Father and Son allow themselves to be surprised by the love they have for each other.[61] This love, it is true, is given totally and once for all, but is so *in statu nascendi*,[62] in a mode which respects the interaction and increase at the heart of the perfection of intimacy. This analogous surprise and increase apply of course not just to God's life in itself, apart from us, but also to our effect on his life within the framework we have outlined. This means that, for example, in the exercise of God's providence there remains, despite the divine omniscience, a truly reciprocal dialogue between God and us in which creative originality is maintained by means of God's 'latency', his free decision not to let 'his left hand know what his right hand is doing',[63] thus allowing us to participate in the 'ever-more' modalities of trinitarian love in accordance with its absolute freedom. It should be noted here that this absolute freedom in God, so central to Balthasar's attempt to reconcile the apparently irreconcilable elements of fullness and increase within divine love, is not to be conceived of in a Nominalist spirit as something arbitrary.[64] It is a freedom rooted in truth, with a logic that is rigorous and may be costly, as our soteriological account indicated. For Balthasar, then, there is no recourse to contradiction or strict philosophical dialectic as means of resolving the difficulties which arise in grasping the relationships between truth and freedom, between fullness and increase, in God's revelation.

We have been considering Balthasar's attempt to formulate the unity of fullness and 'ever-more' within God. The evocative Patristic sub-personal image of a fountain was inserted, with a view to a less exclusively metaphorical expression, into a scripturally inspired ontology of inter-personal love, within which an analogous becoming was conceived within the perfection of trinitarian life. The ontology in question distinguished carefully between the 'ever-more' proper to creation as such, in its mode of absolute dependency on God, and that 'ever-more' which was seen as a perfection of inter-personal love. This latter perfection, attributed hypothetically to God, was grounded in the enduring otherness and freedom of the persons of the Trinity (within however intimate a union), which allowed the richness of their love to be expressed in many different modalities and which constituted the source of an eternally renewed delight in each other without prejudice to the absolute and total nature of their knowledge and original self-giving. Balthasar's attempt would seem to be successful in illuminating the paradox of a unity between fullness and 'ever-more' in God without claiming to have a full solution of the logical difficulty. He is very happy to admit and indeed to insist that there can be no fully adequate philosophical account of what is a mystery in God and therefore ultimately indescribable.[65] In particular it may quickly be granted that we have no direct, full experience of how eternity may be supra-temporally intense in the way that is required for his account, nor, even more centrally, do we have a direct, full experience of that 'ever-more' of perfect love untouched by the needy becoming which is intrinsic to created being and love. Instead, with theological and philosophical support, we have been given a pointer at least as to how the mystery may be maintained without lapsing into either logical absurdity or mystification.

Summary

The intelligibility of Balthasar's theology of the trinitarian event has been discussed with reference to the central areas of unity, sin, receptivity and 'ever-more'. In different ways it emerged that love was the key to the intelligibility of all four areas. Having argued that the ontological ground of all truth and Being is the inner-trinitarian love of the Father, Son and Holy Spirit, Balthasar went on to establish how one could address the issues arising from all four areas by reference to the nature of this love. In particular it was argued that the aspects of receptivity and 'ever-more' are intrinsic to the perfection of love and, accordingly, that they exist analogously in God.

The immutability of God

The issue of divine immutability (and impassibility)[66] is central to Balthasar's concerns, but is treated by him only rarely in those precise terms. More usually, as we have seen, the matter is addressed through his theology of the trinitarian event. Our task now is to outline in a concluding, synthetic account Balthasar's theology of the divine immutability, drawn from his few thematic references[67] but also, and more importantly, from his more indirect treatment. This theology is, for the most part, already present in scattered form throughout our work.

Outline

We saw how the question about the immutability of God arose in many different contexts: the incarnation of Christ, his cross and its soteriological meaning, the creation of our world, its relationship with God through history and the eschatological aspect of this relationship. The answer was couched in terms of the ever-greater liveliness of the trinitarian event of free love.[68] Given a certain understanding of time and eternity it was argued that this liveliness involved a supra-mutability within God; furthermore, again given an understanding of creation within a trinitarian framework, God freely enjoyed a reciprocal relationship with his creatures so that this supra-mutability included a contribution from the world. This dramatic image of a God whose omnipotence was seen to be that of absolute love required a modification of the traditional notion of divine immutability.

It was clear what this modification did not involve. First, God does not change, or become, or suffer in a created, temporal sense. Balthasar time and again rejected any univocal attribution of change to God, associating such an attribution with a position which claims that God needs our world in order, through his relationship with us, to become his full self. This position, attributed in different ways to Hegel, Process thinkers and Moltmann, was rejected on the grounds that it presents a mythical God, without transcendence, who is a product of the titanic impulse in humankind, albeit often with the laudable intention of making God less remote. Balthasar insisted that even in God's most intimate dealings with creation, in the incarnation, there remains an abiding distinction between the created and uncreated orders of being. Change in us is a characteristic of creaturehood and so is rooted in deficiency and imperfection: he will refuse to say that God is mutable. Secondly, although immutability certainly conveys the fidelity of God's love in relation to his covenant with us, it may not be reduced to an economic divine attribute of ethical significance only. God loves us in this way because of who he is in himself: there is an inner link between the economic and the immanent, the ethical and the ontological. Thirdly, while Balthasar's continued references to God as immutable included some kind of responsiveness and growth ('ever-more') within the divine love in a way which clashed with the traditional, classical philosophical meaning of the term immutability,[69] this did not by any means involve an outright rejection of philosophy. The philosophical tradition, going back to Plato,[70] was right in rejecting any attribution of creaturely change to God and in holding open the distinction between God and humankind. Nonetheless Balthasar does reject the austere classical notion of immutability which sees God's love for us in purely altruistic terms,[71] affecting us but not himself.

Balthasar explained how one might give positive expression to a modified notion of divine immutability by showing how it needed to be understood within the context of the absolute freedom and liveliness of the event of 'ever-more' trinitarian love which is central to the being of God. Within a trinitarian ontology of being this love was understood to possess a receptivity and increase analogous to what are present in human inter-personal love. The similar and dissimilar elements of the analogy were capable of specification to an extent; in God the dynamic nature of love was not due to any ontological lack, but was a little like those aspects of responsiveness and 'ever-more' which are intrinsic to the perfection of human love. Within this pattern of similarity/dissimilarity we were reminded by the greater difficulty in ascribing negative attributes (such as suprasuffering) to God that there is a certain imprecision intrinsic to this whole area, an area in which one may range from metaphor to a more properly analogical attribution. However, even allowing for this imprecision one could, with this understanding of love, at least point to a mutability in God which is a perfection of immutability, and to an intense richness of life in which all the different modalities of the ever-greater trinitarian love are contained. The intensity in question is made possible by the supra-temporal nature of God's eternal being, which can interact reciprocally with the extended reality of created temporality. This is a *modified* notion of immutability, because Balthasar clearly stated that it must be dynamic enough to describe the divine being which contains within it the original image of all created, temporal becoming and liveliness. But this original image, eternal and without deficiency, transcends its created copy: in this sense it still remains true to speak of the *immutability* of God, not merely to indicate his reliability, but more importantly to point to that perfect divine fullness of being which can yet be reconciled with the element of 'ever-more', a reconcilability which is remotely hinted at in this understanding of trinitarian love.

A more considered account of the limited nature of this attempt to reconcile what are usually believed to be mutually contradictory opposites will be offered in our section on theological discourse. Here we simply note that the evocative power of Balthasar's approach does not derive from the realms of imagination and metaphor alone but is supplied and controlled as well by a strong ontological framework.

Some details

Our outline requires some further detail in order to serve as an adequate account of Balthasar's theology of the divine immutability. In particular we need to look at the relationship to Rahner on this issue, as well as the kind of conceptual framework and linguistic usage which is employed.

Balthasar's reference to Rahner on the issue of divine immutability is both instructive and curious. On several occasions, and as recently as 1985 and 1987,[72] when this issue arises, in whatever context, Balthasar makes it clear that he is not himself offering a comprehensive thematic account; but he refers approvingly to Rahner's account and, in particular, to the latter's formulation that while God remains immutable 'in himself' he can himself change 'in the other'.[73] The curious aspect of this reference is that while Rahner's formulation may indeed be interpreted along the lines of Balthasar's own treatment of divine immutability, this is clearly not the interpretation which Rahner himself proposes. Rahner adopts what he himself refers to as a 'pure Chalcedonian'[74] interpretation, in which it is made quite clear that God in himself (the divine nature is unmixed, unconfused with the human) is absolutely immutable despite the fact that we also must assert, dialectically (but in a non-Hegelian sense),[75] the mystery that God changes in the other. Balthasar, as we have seen, goes further than this:[76] within his notion of the christological analogy of being he understands the human to be different from but also an expression of the divine, and so can posit something like a supramutability and suffering within God himself so that the distinction between inner and outer, God in himself and God in the other, is maintained, but in a less exclusive, separatist mode. In his one extended thematic treatment of the notion of divine impassibility Balthasar more directly acknowledges this difference from Rahner:[77]

and elsewhere, especially in his criticism of Rahner's failure both to acknowledge the full sense in which soteriologically Christ acts as our representative in affecting God and to allow a real inter-personal relationship to exist within the Trinity, it is clear that Balthasar's interpretation of the Rahnerian formulation posits implicitly an analogous mutability and passibility in God quite at odds with Rahner's own account.

Of course, Rahner too has moved from the strictly traditional interpretation of divine immutability with his acknowledgement that God himself changes 'in the other'. And perhaps it is this movement, and the fact that the formulation in question is at least open to the interpretative development accorded it by Balthasar, which explain this curious repeated reference despite the implicit and more direct rejection of Rahner's own meaning. However there is also the instructive possibility that by not treating the issue of divine immutability in a thematically comprehensive way Balthasar has simply failed to notice the full significance implicit in his own ontology of the trinitarian event, and in particular how his own position on divine immutability is quite different from the Rahnerian formulation as interpreted by Rahner himself. This possibility is made more likely by the fact that in his one extended treatment of the related issue of impassibility Balthasar does more directly repudiate Rahner's position. In any case this whole matter serves as a very useful reminder to us that however central the issue of divine immutability may be to Balthasar's theological enterprise, it is only rarely discussed by him in explicit terms. This certainly means that it is futile to look for precise definitions or formulae on this matter from Balthasar himself; and it may also mean that his treatment of the issue results in a notion of divine immutability of which Balthasar himself did not realise all the implications.

It is also instructive to examine the conceptual framework within which Balthasar treats the issue of divine immutability. The Christian use of the term immutability as applied to God had its roots deep within the Greek and classical philosophical tradition. Within this tradition a philosophy of being developed in which, in different ways, the immutability of the One was contrasted with the mutability of the many. In particular, by using the terms 'potency' and 'act' to explain change, and the terms 'substance' and 'accidents' to explain respectively the immutable and mutable principles of the being which changes, a notion of the immutable God developed in terms of pure act, of absolute (subsistent) being without accidents.[78] But – to adopt the language of K. Hemmerle[79] – what is immutable, what remains, in the NT is described in terms of love, not in terms of an immutable substance. This means that Christianity must modify the traditional philosophy of being, which was constructed within a primarily cosmological world view and without any developed personalist categories. Balthasar agreed that the Patristic and Conciliar categories of nature and person did not do justice to the full scriptural revelation, and that in general, despite real progress, there emerged an essentialism in Christian thought which obscured the dynamic inherent in the description of God as pure act and which presented an overly-rigid notion of the divine immutability.

It is Balthasar's view that it is part of the vocation of the Christian to offer a specifically Christian contribution to human thought and that in our age we are peculiarly well placed to do this.[80] Consistent with this view in his own attempt, which is explicitly indebted to a scriptural and indeed trinitarian foundation, to sketch a philosophy of being in terms of inter-personal love and in this way, by modifying the traditional conceptual framework, to produce a more adequate notion of immutability. The main lines of this sketch are already familiar to us: they focus on an ontological account of the difference between God and creatures which is grounded in a metaphysics of love. This metaphysics uses more developed personal and relational categories so that the perfection of the trinitarian God includes elements of analogous becoming and receptivity. This new image of God retains its ontological foundation, but the category of event is reconciled with that of state thanks to the trinitarian – dialogical basis of this ontology, which respects the relative validity of the substance-based natural metaphysics of the classical philosophy of being.[81] In addition, of course, we have noted Balthasar's view that in order to do greater justice to the biblical account of God as trinitarian love theological discourse must integrate very many aspects which are often considered disparate and beyond the proper range of theology. In this respect we noted his attempt to include an affective as well as a scientific dimension within theology so that spirituality, prayer and poetry all become integral elements of theological discourse. This means, of course, that the notion of conceptual framework is itself broadened beyond its more traditional abstract connotation to include what is concrete and metaphorical.[82]

Finally it remains to comment on Balthasar's linguistic usage within this conceptual framework. Why does he continue to speak of the immutability of God when the reality signified is so much more complex? For there can be no doubt that he himself expressly avoids saying that God is mutable, and cautions others against such a use of language.[83] He does of course refer to the supra-mutability of God, and, with great care, to something like a divine supra-suffering.[84] However, it would seem that in the absence of any ideal third term which would describe the complex reality more adequately, Balthasar has decided that by a qualified use of the term 'immutability' he may best convey that perfection of trinitarian love within which there is this intrinsic supra-mutability. The grounds for this choice are perhaps reinforced by the inherent probability that to call God mutable would be to invite even greater misunderstanding, besides which, as already indicated, Balthasar dislikes 'fashionable' theology and prefers to renew and modify traditional and conventional terminology rather than abandon it or even turn to a directly opposite linguistic usage.

Conclusion

The difficulty remains, of course, that on the face of it the term 'immutability' conveys a simple negation of its opposite, 'mutability', while in fact Balthasar wishes to attribute to God a much more complex combination of these two seemingly mutually contradictory terms. This is why, as we noted earlier, he could answer both 'yes' and 'no' to the direct question, does God change? The danger with such a nuanced razor's-edge approach is that in seeking to avoid extremes one may end up using a traditional term in such a modified sense that the term (because of its association with its original meaning) is unable to carry the new sense. This danger is made more acute when the modification in question contains an intrinsic imprecision so that a suspicion of semantic obfuscation may be aroused.

Does Balthasar's approach in fact overcome this danger? Does it supply a satisfactory basis for his linguistic usage? Ultimately this question concerns our final assessment of Balthasar's overall position on divine immutability: but in order to make this assessment possible we must first tackle the issue of theological discourse, which is implicit in the question. After all, given our account so far, to say that God is absolutely immutable would seem to be both true and absurd:[85] is this an instance of paradox, or dialectic, or mystification – and what notion of theological discourse can justify it?

Theological discourse

Our intention is not to offer a full account of Balthasar's position on theological discourse,[86] but rather, by focusing on the specific difficulty we have adverted to in the use of the modified language of immutability, to arrive at a notion of theological discourse sufficiently adequate to contribute to our final assessment of his theology of the divine immutability.

The difficulty in question is due to the attempt to modify the language of immutability so that terms are used in a non-technical, poetic way which combines apparently irreconcilable meanings and seems to contradict their original meaning. Within this context the question arose as to the justification and status of such language. We know already the main lines of Balthasar's reply: a differentiated acceptance of anthropomorphic speech about God is acceptable and indeed necessary in a theology which is respectful of mystery.[87] He did allow, of course, that such speech could range from the broadly metaphorical to the more properly analogical, and that more precise indicators of semantic adjustment could be employed depending on what specifically was attributed to God. However there was also an inbuilt imprecision to be reckoned with, again entirely proper in discourse which treated of God, who is transcendent. This imprecision increased the nearer one approached the metaphorical end of that continuum of human speech about God. Our further question to this general reply of Balthasar is whether the degree of imprecision present in his own language of immutability is not so great as to make such language simply mystifying. In fact, if this language is suggesting the reconcilability of what, in our experience, is irreconcilable, ought we not perhaps to remain with the more prosaic, traditional terms in their original, unmodified sense, even while admitting their inadequacy to convey the fullness of the mystery which they describe?

Balthasar's reply is to argue that his own linguistic approach is through paradox, not dialectic, and that this involves a controlled use of imagery and metaphor which point in a direction more faithful to the scriptural revelation. We turn now to this argument for a wider notion of theological discourse.

Mystery as paradox

We have already referred to the notion that Jesus reveals God as concealed.[88] This paradoxical affirmation is not due to any inability on the part of Christ, in his humanity, to disclose clearly what God is – the revelation of God in Christ is fully adequate and exact.[89] Rather, the paradox is rooted in the intrinsically mysterious nature of the divine being itself. This is a being of trinitarian love with the freedom, creativity and, hence, inherent mystery which inter-personal love involves. Furthermore, it is this trinitarian being which is the ground of all reality and Being, and of truth itself. In this way Balthasar has argued that mystery is immanent to truth, and that the more truth is revealed the more there is of mystery too.

The implications for human logic and discourse of this notion of truth are what chiefly concern us here. Balthasar's general position is that the expression of the divine mystery in human terms involves a transcending of formal human logic in such a way that the principle of non-contradiction is respected, there are seemingly opposed affirmations made about God, and we may go some way to showing that such affirmations are not in reality mutually contradictory.[90] This means that there is no question of a philosophical dialectic in which, in the manner of Nominalism, God's freedom is such that the truth may consist in mutually contradictory statements or, in the manner of Hegel, in which God's freedom is denied.[91] The term 'dialectic' may be used mainly in the qualified sense which admits the truth of the Hegelian logic in pointing out that partial truths can and must be complemented through contrary ones, while denying that a real contradiction exists within the mystery of full truth.[92] The Scriptures[93] do speak dialectically in this qualified sense, and it is again the task of the theologian to show that no contradiction exists and to point in the direction of how the seeming contradiction may be resolved. This means that it is his task to indicate that the mystery is paradoxical rather than purely dialectical, and to set about softening the hardness of this paradox.[94]

This whole approach of Balthasar may best be illustrated at precisely the point where it undergoes its most severe test: the paradox is hardest of all in the death of Christ and his separation from the Father on the cross, and in the descent into hell.[95] In this context Balthasar is able to give full weight to the concerns behing the *sub contrario* formula of Luther[96] and Kierkegaard's 'absolute paradox'.[97] Nonetheless these concerns ought not to issue in a formal rejection of human logic, or in the development of a logic which claims to set to one side the principle of non-contradiction. Rather, Balthasar argues, the identity of the crucified with the resurrected one (made possible in turn by the identity and unity of the Logos in the abiding difference of his divinity and humanity) overcomes the seeming contradiction by adverting to the trinitarian presuppositions of the cross. These allow us at least to point in the direction of an understanding of the crucified Christ, in his obedience, as the supreme revelation of God's love. The scandalous paradox of the cross, then, in which the Son who is God may be rightly said to die and to be separated from God, is illuminated by this reference to the freedom and power of trinitarian love in which difference and otherness are positive. In this way the truth of the cross is shown to be beyond, but not opposed to, human logic, while its mystery is not left as a 'pure' or static paradox, but an attempt is made to throw light on the obscurity of what, in unaided rational terms, is incomprehensible. It is through being confronted in this way by the insoluble problem of the limits of human discourse that we encounter the much richer reality of the mystery that is grounded in the truth of inner-trinitarian love.

This way of speaking about God may not be developed into a system susceptible of precise measurement and evaluation.[98] Instead of dialectic Balthasar speaks of dialogic, of the divine, trinitarian (theo)logic of love which expresses itself so exactly in our language but cannot, because it is instrinsically mysterious, be explained exactly by human logic.[99] Nonetheless, in the qualified senses given to these terms, we may say that Balthasar is proposing an analogous approach to God which takes into account the *major dissimilitudo* between creator and creature and so includes a dialectical component.[100] He argues[101] that such is the scriptural way of speaking about God, in which the basically positive revelation is balanced by a *via negationis* and *via eminentiae*. It is within this differentiated rhythm of speech about God that any Christian negative philosophy or theology of God is to be evaluated and distinguished from non-Christian negative approaches. In particular Balthasar warns against a tendency, even within Christianity, towards an anti-incarnational stress on the negative way which undermines the radically positive, if mysterious, revelation of God in Christ. A specifically Christian negative approach will take central account of the positive revelation at the heart of the negative event of the cross; its silence will be one of worship and prayer before the ever-greater mystery of God's love. In this sense, just as the non-word (*Unwort*) of the cross is always contained within the supra-word (*Überwort*) of trinitarian love, so too the dialectical and apophatic components of theological discourse exist within a positive framework of analogy. This means that while Balthasar accepts the traditional dictum that we cannot know what God is, nonetheless he maintains that the thrust of Scripture is to point in the direction of saying what God is, and that this ought to be the aim of the theologian also.

This overall position on mystery as paradox has an important implication for the language of divine immutability. It is clear that etymologically this language focuses on what God is not (not mutable like us), and because of this might be considered to be on safer ground than attempts to say what God is (supra-mutable). It would seem that Balthasar might indeed concede that there is a greater certainty in this negative approach, and, moreover, that it is an indispensable part of correct speech about God. But it is also clear that he would wish to go further, to attempt to say something positive about God, and in doing so to argue that we are advancing with less certainty but within the realm of mystery to which we are called. Sometimes there is a hidden assumption in the approach of an exclusively negative theology that one is in fact speaking not just with greater certainty but also more adequately about what God is; Balthasar's argument is that on its own the negative approach does not yet say anything positive about God, that it must be used in the function of an attempt to speak positively, and that as soon as it is so used it is open to the same necessary and indeed proper uncertainty that is inherent in the differentiated structure of a fundamentally affirmative analogical approach – it is difficult to express positively what is meant by the immutability of God.[102] On these grounds, then, there is no *a priori* etymological reason for an absolute preference for the term 'immutability' over the term 'supra-mutability' in our discourse about God. The term 'immutable' is linguistically standard and has the advantage of being the one used traditionally, with a certainty and precision due to its negative sense; its disadvantage is that it can be open to much misunderstanding when one tries to translate it positively. The term 'supra-mutable' has the disadvantage of being linguistically artificial and of imprecise meaning; it does however convey the mystery at issue in a positive way. Both terms are needed to complement one another in order to express Balthasar's meaning, and his own choice of one or the other seems to be related to the appropriateness of particular contexts rather than to any more absolute criteria. If there is a more pronounced preference for the term immutability, this would seem to be for reasons of traditional usage and linguistic acceptability.

Mystery and theological discourse

The exact revelation of God in Jesus Christ does not imply that theology, or any system of human logic or discourse, may verbalise this revelation exactly.[103] There is a gap between objective expression and subjective appropriation. This relative inadequacy of theology is due to several reasons. First, it is Jesus Christ alone who as the Word is the full expression of God – we participate in this expression but are not identical to it, and so our theological enterprise is characterised by the incompleteness which is involved in this non-identity. Then, it is clear that Jesus Christ reveals God not just in words alone but through his whole life, death and resurrection, through the entire range of human expression including deeds and silence as well as words; theology has only words at its disposal. Furthermore, God is revealed as mystery in a way which includes not merely a doctrine about God, but also the deeds of God's love – and, once again, we are aware of the limitations of language in expressing mystery and the kind of truth which involves the personal freedom of self-giving. All this means that theology cannot be our only response to God's revelation: our deepest response to God's word must be one of discipleship, involving our whole lives. Nonetheless, theology must be part of this response, and there are more or less adequate ways of doing theology. A key factor in determining such adequacy is the kind of theological discourse one chooses to employ. We must now try to specify a little further what Balthasar's approach is in this area of theological discourse.

At the heart of his approach is the concern to be true to the scriptural revelation of mystery by combining abstract, conceptual language with more metaphorical and image-laden terms.[104] He considers this combination necessary in order to do justice to the particular, individual, historical and concrete aspects of the scriptural mystery as well as to the more general, essential aspects. If theology is to convey the living form of scriptural revelation then the flesh of a more metaphorical approach must be used together with the bones of a more abstract one. A conceptual approach on its own fails to convey the unique and personal dimensions of mystery; it tends to systematise too easily and so to resolve paradox by abstracting from differences. Its limitation in expressing the prose and poetry of Scripture may be compared to the attempt to express the meaning of a Mozart symphony in concepts alone.[105] But neither is an exclusively metaphorical, pictorial approach sufficient: the ultimate reality of God is unimaginable, besides which images may be inexact in a way which leads to misunderstandings and error. There remains, then, a combination of the two approaches, which involves an enriching and corrective complementarity which Balthasar expresses in the words of G. Söhngen: 'Metaphysics without metaphor is empty; metaphor without metaphysics is blind.'[106] This combination recognises the value of the concept which is formed by abstraction, through insight into data that is available to the senses. But it recognises too the need for a continuing *conversio ad phantasmata*, in order that our inseparable spiritual and physical way of knowing may be reflected in the discourse which expresses our knowledge. A metaphorical, poetic way of speaking, then, may be used in the 'quasi-science'[107] of theology, but not in a manner unguarded by the more exact abstract approach. Similarly, the notion of analogy to be used in theology must have ontological foundations, but cannot be reduced to the ontological alone without loss of its power to convey what is personal and unique.

Balthasar is not much more specific about the dynamics of this complementary combination. As before, and as is the case in Scripture itself, he is content to say that the boundaries between different forms of discourse are fluid, so that there is a continuum of human speech about God, ranging from the broadly metaphorical to the more properly analogical and abstract.[108] It may be more or less easy in any particular instance to determine these boundaries, but it is proper to the treatment of mystery as paradox that there be this continuum of speech with its inbuilt imprecision which escapes anything like an exact mathematical measurement. Just as, then, the speech of Jesus belongs to no system, but may be likened to that of an organ with many different registers, so too it is not to be expected or desired that theological discourse should conform to the precise criteria of a philosophical linguistic analysis, or, indeed, even to those of biblical exegesis.[109] This inbuilt imprecision remains even when one takes into account all the various factors which contribute to the proper expression of theological truth, including the roles of the Holy Spirit, of believing and holy Christians and of the Church as a whole.[110]

It is, however, desirable also that to whatever extent possible the discourse of theology should be exact and accurate.[111] This should be so both when proposing a theory of theological discourse in general and in the application of this discourse to particular issues. It has been suggested that at both general and applied levels Balthasar himself fails to be sufficiently precise.[112] We have already noted instances where there is a degree of imprecision in his discourse which may be open to correction. Nonetheless, I believe that the main thrust of his position on theological discourse is acceptable; he has argued persuasively that a combined conceptual and metaphorical approach is needed to evoke a response in us to the scriptural presentation of mystery. This position is consistent with the knowledge we have from our own lives of the necessity of this dynamic between more abstract and more concrete ways of thinking and speaking when we tackle those issues which concern us most deeply. It is in this way, Balthasar argues, that theology makes progress, a progress he speaks of in terms such as 'pointing in a direction', 'softening' or 'illuminating' the paradox.[113] Given the acceptance of the main thrust of Balthasar's approach at the level of theological discourse in general, it now remains to ask to what extent this approach may apply to his own discourse on the immutability of God.

The theological discourse of divine immutability

We have outlined Balthasar's position on theological discourse in general: the mystery of God revealed in Scripture may best be expressed in paradoxical terms by theology, in a mutually corrective combination of conceptual and metaphorical language, in which by means of this 'limit discourse'[114] the appearance of literal contradiction is removed and a partial knowledge is gained which leads us to the possibility of a deeper encounter with the mystery. If, then, the notion of God as revealed in Scripture is richer and more mysterious than the particular, traditional terminology of immutability has conveyed, then this terminology must be modified. Balthasar has argued that the scriptural data does justify such a modification: he introduces the term 'supra-mutability' into the discourse in order to try to express the mystery positively. He argues that this term has a sufficiently precise meaning to obviate the charges of obfuscation and absurdity, and thus that one is justified in moving beyond the use of traditional terms in an unmodified sense. This precision is due to the way in which the use of metaphor is controlled by being combined with an ontology of love. One might distinguish further by noting that the term 'immutability' belongs to the more abstract, traditionally ontological level of speech about God, while the term 'supra-mutability' comes from the metaphorical level. It is Balthasar's contribution not so much to have reconciled these two levels in a systematic way (he repeatedly warns against encapsulating the word of God in any system), but rather to be aware of the distinction

between the levels, to use both levels in a complementary combination, and to have argued for their systematic irreconcilability by
highlighting their positive function in pointing to mystery.[115] The
unavoidable imprecision which remains, then, would be due to the
fact that in the realm of mystery our knowledge is necessarily
incomplete; it would be analogous to our human experience of being
able to say that something is provable without ourselves having the
proof.[116] It would also be consistent with the generally accepted
theological approach to mystery within which true affirmations are
made on the grounds of a limited but genuine understanding, so that
the reconcilability of what, in our experience, is irreconcilable may
indeed, for good reasons, be affirmed without being systematically
understood. Within this context Balthasar's ascription of the status of
'pointer', and not possession, to knowledge of this kind would seem
both to have an acceptable meaning and to be accurate.

What has been established is a formal compatibility between
Balthasar's position on theological discourse in general and his
discourse concerning the divine immutability in particular. This is
important: it provides further grounds to support the continued use of
the term 'immutability', while investing it with a modified meaning.
In this way the attempt is made to soothe an understandable
impatience with the language of paradox arising from the suspicion
that such language may in fact be in the service of mystification and
not mystery.[117] But this formal compatibility must be supported, in
turn, by a positive assessment of the whole of Balthasar's argument in
order that his position on divine immutability can be actually justified.
On the grounds of the case made from the argument of theological
discourse, then, Balthasar's position on divine immutability is indeed
sustainable. But this position also involves all the other material steps
of the argument that have been taken from the beginning of our
enquiry. Our task remains to assess the coherence and validity of this
whole argument.

5

Balthasar and other approaches

Introduction

A critical assessment of Balthasar's position will be facilitated by situating it more precisely vis-à-vis other contemporary approaches. These approaches will be considered in so far as they relate to Balthasar's own position and without claim to comprehensive coverage. A further aim of this chapter is to go beyond Balthasar in initiating a dialogue between his position and that of an English-speaking world to which he rarely adverts. This aim functions as another criterion with regard to the selection of authors considered, authors who represent an important contemporary approach but with whom Balthasar himself has had no explicit dialogue.

There will be no further consideration of the position of Process philosophers and theologians within this dialogue. The general lines of Balthasar's rather sweeping rejection of the explanatory details of the Process understanding of God have been spelled out with great particularity and with more nuances by many other thinkers,[1] several of whom present the Process case very sympathetically. There is, accordingly, no need to go back over this ground here. It will be sufficient to note that emerging from this discussion there is a general unease with two basic positions in the Process understanding of God. First, the notion of an ontological dipolarity in God's nature (between primordial–abstract nature and consequent–concrete nature) seems to involve an unsatisfactory duality in God, with the primacy given to the concrete in a way which necessitates creation and so threatens the divine transcendence. Secondly, the concept of becoming (creativity, increase) is given such prominence that it seems itself to be a primary metaphysical principle to which even God is subject, and so once again divine transcendence is called into question. I believe that these two criticisms are fair, that they are basic to Balthasar's rejection of the Process approach, and that the main concerns, as well as many of the valuable insights, of this approach are grounded better within Balthasar's own theology of the trinitarian event. We turn now to some other contemporary approaches within the English-speaking world of philosophy and theology which have not received the same critical consideration in dialogue with Balthasar's position.

Brian Davies

We may take the recent book by Brian Davies, *Thinking About God*,[2] as a competent modern exposition of the traditional Thomist position on divine immutability. Davies argues carefully that one of the ways in which God is different from the material beings of this world is that he is not a composition or mixture of form and matter, or of *suppositum* and nature or essence. This is the doctrine of the divine simplicity. It means that one may not 'distinguish between God and his nature, so we might just as well say that he is his nature and that he is, therefore, his attributes or properties'.[3] Within this context it makes sense to speak of God's eternity and immutability in the strict sense of an unchanging state, without temporal succession, because the necessary connection between life on the one hand and time and change on the other applies to material beings only – the divine simplicity involves a changeless and full life 'all at once', as Boethius puts it.

Davies advances further, related reasons why God must be immutable. As explanation of a world characterised by change, God must himself be unchanging and unchangeable. Since he is infinite, and thus unlimited, God cannot change – temporal realities change precisely because they are limited and deficient. All this means, of course, that creation cannot in any sense act on God, so that God's providential involvement in our world must be understood in terms which deny any effect on God. He acknowledges that many find the notion of an immutable God unlikeable, in particular its association with impassibility. But, Davies argues, following Chalcedon it is correct to limit the suffering of Jesus Christ to his human nature, and anyway it is mistaken to admire God for being defective (which is what divine suffering would imply), or to contend that love needs what is in effect the limitation of suffering to be true. With reference to the biblical way of speaking about God as mutable Davies is clear that it is the function of philosophy to reflect on scriptural imagery so as to distinguish metaphor from a more properly ('literal') analogical approach. And within this context the Thomistic attribution of immutability to God is not unscriptural.

Finally, in a section which goes beyond philosophy to consider the distinctively Christian notion of God, Davies notes how the doctrines of the incarnation and Trinity allow us to speak about God as love and to understand how God is always love (even without creation, so that creation is seen clearly as a free divine act). Furthermore they allow us to speak, in terms surprising to philosophy, of God's love for us, despite the inequality between the partners to this love. This means that while we may think of God philosophically as detached, remote and unable to relate to us, nonetheless 'we are entitled to balance such thoughts by other ones if the doctrine of the Incarnation is true'.[4]

This Thomistic position of Davies is further strengthened when one develops the divine simplicity in terms of the notion of pure act, without any mixture of potency (as in Kondoleon, McCabe, Weinandy and Dodds),[5] so that the dynamic nature of the immutable divine *esse* is conveyed. It is an innerly coherent position which has the great advantage of obviating any reduction of God to the mythological level of a changing Zeus or Apollo, ultimately as helplessly embroiled in the ambiguities of world history as the devotees to whom they respond.

Balthasar accepts the basic position, with important differences however. These differences are due largely to his understanding of the way in which theology influences philosophy – and, in particular, to the way in which a theology of trinitarian divine love may affect a philosophy of God as Pure Act. Within this latter context he retains the foundational philosophical conclusion that there can be no created change or suffering in God. He does so because he accepts the reasoning which comes to such conclusions, and judges that the metaphysical system supporting these reasons is adequate to account for an understanding of the finite world and to point in the direction of its infinite creator. That God is simple would accordingly be acceptable to Balthasar at a basic level. He suggests, however, that the inner-trinitarian relations involve a receptivity and 'ever-more' within the Pure Act and simplicity of God which is somewhat analogous to created potency, becoming, change and suffering. In doing so he goes beyond the use of the Trinity as support for the fact that God can be love without creation to a use which transforms the philosophical notion of being. This trinitarian ontology retains 'the correct philosophical conclusion that there can be no created change in God, but develops the philosophical account of God as Pure Act in a surprising but, it has been argued, intelligible way. It is a way which can integrate talk of the divine simplicity, infinity and perfection with a responsiveness and liveliness in God that go beyond the notion of an unchanging, altruistic love. It is a way then which broadens the classical philosophical system of Thomism (in particular by giving new prominence to the notion of relationality) so that the latter's concepts and conclusions are accepted but also developed and transcended. If as Christians we already believe that the divine simplicity and Pure Act may be understood (beyond what is suggested by philosophy) to include a unity that is relational in a threefold way, then we perhaps have *a priori* grounds at least to be open to the paradox of considering an analogous receptivity and increase as perfections, not deficiencies, in God. And these *a priori* grounds are further supported by the analysis of love given by Balthasar, with its ontology based on the trinitarian revelation.

Davies himself admits that theology 'balances' philosophical talk about God in a surprising way. He fails, however, to follow up systematically on how the doctrines of the Trinity and the incarnation might do this. Dodds does suggest a way forward, drawing on Aquinas to do so.[6] He notes that for St Thomas 'act is an unbounded or unlimited priniciple', and this is expressed in the immanent motion of the 'never-ceasing yet ever-changing activity of knowledge and love' within the Trinity, as well as in the transient motion of the activity of the Trinity in relation to creatures. Dodds speaks of 'the motion of the motionless God' and affirms that predicating 'motion of God in this way does not contradict but rather complements the predication of immutability'. Without yet identifying with the developed lines of Balthasar's trinitarian ontology Dodds nonetheless speaks in terms which are at least open to this kind of development.

The Thomist position of Davies is a reminder once again that while the hypothesis of a receptivity and 'ever-more' in God may seem to be demanded by the theological evidence, it points to a very mysterious reality within God for which we have no exact created corre-spondence. But here again Balthasar may be correct in persuading us that metaphor – and not only analogy properly so-called – is needed for speech about God, provided that it is used in a way which 'perfects' rather than 'destroys' the metaphysical nature of such speech.

I have focused on the central point in Davies concerning the immutability of God in himself. We need also to focus more on God's relation to creation and on how Balthasar's position here may be assessed in relation to other thinkers on the same topic.

Kenny, Stump and Kretzmann

We turn first to Anthony Kenny,[7] whose extensive discussion on the relationship between creatures and God results in conclusions very different from those of the traditional Thomism of Davies. Kenny's discussion focuses on divine omniscience and omnipotence, and he concludes that one cannot provide a coherent philosophical explanation of how these attributes may be predicated of God. In the course of his discussion he claims in particular that omniscience and immutability are contradictory, and that the notion of an atemporal eternal personal being is radically incoherent. It is interesting to note that Kenny, whose Thomism is very much in dialogue with modern British analytic philosophy, is not very impressed by the teaching of Aquinas on being. This teaching is of course (as Davies and Mann[8] in their accounts of the divine simplicity note) foundational for the teaching on the divine attributes. However for present purposes we may concentrate directly on the notions of omniscience, immutability and eternity as discussed by Kenny.

Kenny notes the traditional dilemma that if God knows future contingent events then these events must necessarily happen, so that human freedom is denied. He outlines the traditional answer to this dilemma: since God is eternal, outside time, then all times are present to God, so that God may know with certainty what we do freely in the future. The famous illustration in Aquinas to support this solution is that 'of a man who is walking along a road (and) cannot see those who are coming after him; but a man who looks down from a hill upon the whole length of the road can see at the same time all those who are travelling along'.[9] Kenny contends that this is a misconceived solution, and in support of this view he gives two reasons that are important for our purposes.

First, if God knows everything as present (even the past and future) then God is not omniscient, since without any temporal qualifications of his knowledge he cannot know in time as we do. Of course Kenny concedes that God may know timelessly events that are future (or past/present) to us, and know that they are future (or past/present) to us. However, the point of his objection is that while one may make a valid distinction between an item of knowledge and the way in which the knowledge is expressed (and so argue that God knows timelessly the same things that we know in time), nonetheless the way in which knowlege is known in time does add something different to the item that is known. So, using Arthur Prior's example,[10] to know now that exams are now over brings with it a pleasure that is due to the temporal nature of the item of knowledge, and may not be regarded as identical with a timeless knowing of the same truth. Kenny, then, is arguing for the irreducibility of tensed propositions, and their inaccessibility to an immutable, eternal God.[11] Kenny's second reason for rejecting the solution of Aquinas points to the apparent radical incoherence of the concept of a timeless eternity, the whole of which is simultaneous with every point of time. Simultaneity, he argues, is ordinarily understood as a transitive relation, so that if A happens at the same time as B, and B happens at the same time as C, then A happens at the same times as C. 'But, on St Thomas' view, my typing of this paper is simultaneous with the whole of eternity. Again, on his view, the great fire of Rome is simultaneous with the whole of eternity. Therefore, while I type these very words, Nero fiddles heartlessly on.'[12] Clearly such a conclusion is absurd and so the premises upon which it is based must be rejected. Finally Kenny notes that it might be objected that 'no argument could, or should be given of how God knows the future; we must simply assert *that* he knows and not expect to be able to shed any light on the mysterious and unique nature of his knowledge'.[13] In other words, might it not be sufficient to establish that there is no flat contradiction in the notion of God's certain knowledge of things which occur freely in the future? Kenny's objection to this minimalist position is due precisely to what he understands as the inescapably contradictory nature of the notion itself. And it is clear right through Kenny's presentation that this contradiction can be avoided only if one accepts some version of the teaching of Aquinas on the eternity of God, which Kenny has also argued to be contradictory.

A consideration of some responses to Kenny's position will be helpful in our attempt to relate this discussion to the position of Balthasar. Barden[14] correctly notes that divine omniscience is incompatible with human freedom only if one speaks of God's *fore*knowledge and not his eternal knowledge of future events. However it is precisely this notion of eternal knowledge of temporal events that Kenny calls into question. Davies[15] responds to Kenny's second reason for calling this notion into question. He argues that Kenny is mistaken in speaking of a temporal event as simultaneous with eternity in the same way as one may speak of simultaneity between temporal events. According to Davies the significant point about eternity is that it does not 'occupy' time and so may not be spoken of in any univocal sense as simultaneous with temporal events. This means that Kenny's argument against timeless eternity simply does not engage with the position it is supposed to be attacking. This becomes clearer in the very enlightening discussion on eternity by Stump and Kretzmann[16] to which we now turn.

These co-authors are aware of the crucial importance of the

concept of eternity for issues which as the divine omniscience and immutability, and our prayers of petition. They argue that this concept is not incoherent. Two misunderstandings of the concept are to be avoided: it does not mean limitless duration in time, nor does it mean simple atemporality in the sense analogous to an isolated static instant. Rather, following on from the definition of Boethius (trans- lated as 'the complete possession all at once of illimitable life'), it involves a fullness of life whose infinite duration is atemporal and which is present to all mobile, created time. This means that there is duration without succession in eternity, a form of extension that is not temporal, and a form of extension that is present, but not identical to, a temporal present. The coherence of this difficult notion is argued for in a discussion of simultaneity which addresses Kenny's second difficulty. Stump and Kretzmann distinguish between temporal and eternal simultaneity. Temporal (T-) simultaneity involves existence or occurrence at one and the same time; eternal (E-) simultaneity involves existence or occurrence at one and the same eternal present. The relationship between the two (ET-simultaneity) must take cognisance of the fact that one is speaking about two different, irreducible modes of existence, without any common third mode. If there is co-existence then it must be conceived of as outside the same mode of existence. As an analogy for this possibility Stump and Kretzmann point to the fact that within an Einsteinian relativistic notion of time 'events occurring at different places which are simultaneous with one frame of reference will not be simultaneous in another frame of reference which is moving with respect to the first. This is known as the relativity of simultaneity.'[17] The example given is of a fast train struck by lightning at each end, observed as simultaneous by an onlooker from the ground but as one after the other by someone on the train. This means that simultaneity must be related to the reference frame of a given observer. This kind of difficulty in specifying exactly what even the temporal simultaneity with which we are familiar involves is analogous to the difficulties in spelling out an acceptable definition of ET-simultaneity. Furthermore, it points to the kind of definition that is required. It must be one that is constructed in terms of two reference frames and two observers, acknowledging that E-simultaneity refers to one and same present rather than to the one and the same time of T-simultaneity. The details of the definition given by the authors need not detain us[18] – enough has been said to indicate the logical coherence of their position and the fact that, given the two different frames of reference, the *relata* in the simultaneous relationship are not transitive in the way that Kenny's *reductio ad absurdum* suggested in his positing of simultaneity between Nero's musical performance and his own typing of his manuscript.

Stump and Kretzmann go on to outline the very fruitful implications of a coherent concept of eternity. Temporal events are present to God's knowledge in a non-sequential way which knows that they are sequential for us. This does not involve a metaphysical relativism apparent, for example, in the claim that the death of Richard Nixon is really future for us and really present for an eternal entity. Rather, reality, although objective, 'contains two modes of real existence in which two different sorts of duration are measured by two irreducibly different sorts of measure: time and eternity'.[19] This means that while Nixon's death is future, and not simultaneous, to us, it is ET-simultaneous with the life of an eternal entity, without this involving logical incoherence. Furthermore there is no incoherence in positing a duration that is atemporal as intrinsic to eternity: an analysis of time reveals how evanescent temporal duration is (the past has gone, the future is not yet, the present is passing). It is not incoherent, then, to suppose that 'eternity, not time, is the mode of existence that admits of fully realised duration'.[20] Similarly, while life normally involves process in us, and so the concept of eternal life might seem contradictory, nonetheless there are aspects of the mind (knowing, willing) which do not involve temporal process and can help us see how life (and indeed a plurality of activities) may be reconciled with atemporal eternity.

A further implication of a coherent concept of eternity is the possibility of coherent speech about the activity of an eternal being in time. Stump and Kretzmann argue that an eternal being may act in time without existing in time if one notes that it is the effect of this activity which is temporal, and not the cause. This provides a reasonable argument for speech about creation, providence and petitionary prayer. Stump and Kretzmann are aware that the issue of the incarnation represents a distinct case – here one is dealing not simply with the temporal effect of eternal activity but with the claim that the eternal itself in some way is a component of the temporal. However they appeal to the orthodox Chalcedonian teaching on the two natures of Christ to alleviate at least the *a priori* incompatability and incoherence of this reality. According to this approach Christ's temporal activity would be *qua* human, not divine: the second person of the Trinity then has two natures eternally, and at some temporal instants, all of which are ET-simultaneous with both these natures in their entirety, the human nature of the second person has been temporally actual. Finally, with this notion of Et-simultaneity Stump and Kretzmann argue that God may know what time it is now without this threatening the divine immutability. This position goes against an earlier denial of this possibility by Kretzmann himself, a denial which Kenny uses to support his first reason for rejecting the concept of an atemporal eternity and which Davies too was inclined to accept as valid.[21] The argument in question, based on the notion of ET-simultaneity already advanced, maintains that there is nothing incoherent in suggesting that an omniscient being always knows in the eternal present what time it is in the temporal present, and so this knowledge does not involve mutability.

We will conclude by relating this discussion to Balthasar's position. We have confirmed the crucial significance of the notion of eternity for an understanding of divine immutability. Furthermore, the arguments proposed against Kenny's position that the concept of an atemporal eternity is incoherent are substantially persuasive. The understanding of this eternity in terms of an extensive duration without sequence is remarkably similar in reality (if not always in formulation) to Balthasar's notion of eternity as a supra-time with an intensive form of duration. The logical basis for this notion in Balthasar has been given added support by the analysis in Stump and Kretzmann, in particular by their development of the notion of ET-simultaneity based on the distinction between absolute and relative notions of time and the use of this distinction as an analogy for the relationship between eternity and time. However there remains some validity to Kenny's first reason for rejecting the concept of eternity, a validity which Davies indirectly acknowledges,[22] and which Stump and Kretzmann do not satisfactorily address. It would seem clear that Stump and Kretzmann, with their notion of ET-simultaneity, do allow us to speak coherently about the eternal God's knowledge of time, but that in doing so they have not yet addressed Kenny's objection that the item of knowledge is known differently by us from by God, and that this difference is significant. I would suggest that this difficulty runs right through the assertions of Stump and Kretzmann that the two modes (eternity and time) are irreducibly different, so that in the interaction between the two (especially in the key instance of the incarnation) it is unclear how Kenny's advertence to the emotional richness of temporality may be accommodated in the mode of eternity. In this respect I would suggest that Balthasar's notion of eternity as supra-time is preferable. This notion goes beyond Stump and Kretzmann (and the traditional Boethian position) in seeing time as analogous and not simply antithetical to eternity, so that, as in the neo-Chalcedonian interpretation of the two natures of Christ, the irreducibility in question does not prevent an analogy according to which the richness of temporality is present in the distinctive otherness of eternity. Also in response to Kenny's difficulty, Balthasar does of course note the primacy of love over knowledge, and his insistence on attributing surprise and wonder to God, his way of accommodating the effects we have on God within the divine supra-time, do allow for the richness which Kenny associates with created temporality.[23]

It would seem, then, that Balthasar's account of the distinct forms of time and eternity is strengthened by the presentation of Stump and Kretzmann; that his own understanding of the analogous relationship between these forms helps to meet the very valid concerns of Kenny about the proper richness of temporality; and that while one is still left without much positive understanding of how the richness of time may be present in the different form of eternity, this lack does not in itself entail a flat contradiction.

Peter Geach

Peter Geach[24] agrees with Anthony Kenny that the traditional notion of eternity is not an adequate solution to the problem concerning the omniscience of God in relation to the future. According to Geach we may not speak of the future as being somehow already there, in existence, but invisible to us. He rejects the idea of a determinative future in this sense. Rather, we may speak in terms of changing the future, of acting now in such a way that what is going to happen will not happen. It is misleading, then, to imagine time as a fixed straight line, with past and present visible to us, and future invisible. The best we can do within this picture is to imagine the future as a line which breaks out in different directions, only one of which will in fact be what happens. Changing the image, the future is as yet unconceived: it is not like a series of foetal existences, hidden for now within the womb of time. The future, then, *is* not (unlike the past and present), and therefore 'seeing the future is a self-contradictory notion'.[25]

If a proposition is self-contradictory an appeal to God's knowledge cannot remove the contradiction or make sense out of nonsense. If the future does not exist, then, it is incoherent to say that God sees the future. Aquinas is therefore incorrect to speak of God seeing from the high tower of his eternity the course of future events. To say that God sees future events as present involves either a misperception or a flat self-contradiction: a misperception if God sees as present events that are really future, a flat self-contradiction if God sees events as both future and simultaneously present.

Geach goes on to propose how we may understand the immutable and eternal (although not timeless) God to be also omniscient with respect to the future. God knows the future (which is really future both to us and to God) by controlling it. Geach means by this that God's knowledge of the future is like a man's knowledge of his own internal actions, not like that of an ideal spectator. Because God's knowledge is perfect he may control the course of the universe (be the cause of what happens) rather as a Grand Master might control a game of chess, without any interference in the freedom of the other players. In other words, 'no line of play that finite players may think of can force God to improvise; his knowledge of the game embraces all the possible variant lines of play, theirs does not', so that God 'cannot be surprised or thwarted or cheated or disappointed'.[26] Geach admits that difficulties arise within this understanding with regard to the reality of sin; must one say that God's foreknowledge brings it about that we sin? His approach is to note the difficulty we have in understanding the surd that is sin, and to point to the parallel difficulty that a philosopher has in trying to describe a position that is philosophically confused (if the description is clear the confusion is not conveyed, if the description is confused then no insight is communicated). This, Geach maintains, is a difficulty concerning God's foreknowledge of sin, but not a plain contradiction; and so we are entitled to hold on to an account of divine foreknowledge which appears capable of answering other questions but can give no satisfactory answer to this one.[27]

The main value of Geach's analysis is to bring out the difficulty in speaking about God's knowledge of that which 'is not' (the future). This joins a metaphysical with an epistemological difficulty concerning knowledge of the future. But Geach's own approach to this difficulty is vulnerable to the critique levelled at it by Kenny, who argues that Geach's Grand Master can know only all the possible moves of his opponent and not the actual ones. While such knowledge would be sufficient to ensure victory in the game, it would limit God's knowledge of the future to possibilities (at best, present 'actual unfulfilled tendencies'), and deny God the range of knowledge of the actual future traditionally ascribed to him.[28] Furthermore, it is difficult to see how God may have new contents of knowledge (in the case of the realised future) without thereby changing. Geach argues that God only apparently changes in so knowing; there is not real change in Socrates) in Plato's *Theaetetus*) when Theatetus grows taller than him, so that similarly we may have to say different things at different times about God's knowledge concerning temporal events without thereby saying that God's mind changes.[29] But the argument fails because the parallel is not exact: rather, on Geach's own account it is difficult to avoid positing a real change in God if one takes seriously the fact that the future does not yet exist and thus can only be known now as a range of more or less likely possibilities, so that a different content exists in God's mind when one of these possibilities is actually realised.

It would seem that we may best formulate God's knowledge of the future if, like Geach, this knowledge comes through self-knowledge (not through observation), but also (unlike Geach and Kenny, but like Davies) if that self is eternal and thus present to all times. This formulation addresses the epistemological and ontological issues concerning knowledge of the future. The actual future, then, 'is not' in terms of our time, but 'is' for God, who knows it through knowledge of his eternal self and its effects. Our understanding of how these effects may be present to God (so that the condition for certain knowledge of contingent events may be fulfilled) remains unclear, however. This places the difficulty back at the point of our own limitations in coming to any positive understanding of the mode of existence of an eternal being and its relationship to temporal beings. A lack of positive understanding need not in itself imply a lack of true knowledge of God, as both Kenny and Geach recognise. In this case the argument for the acceptance of the hypothesis of divine eternity is based on an understanding of other divine attributes (especially the simplicity of God), and this hypothesis does itself provide satisfactory ways of answering other positions about the divine knowledge and will.

One is brought back, then, to the issue concerning the coherence of the concept of eternity itself. Stump and Kretzmann, as indicated, deal with this issue in a satisfactory way. This does not yield a positive understanding of how eternity is present (not temporally present) to all our times, but does allow us to speak coherently of this presence while holding on to the reality of time. The lack of positive understanding may then be likened to the analogous difficulty in spelling out even a very crude acceptable definition for temporal simultaneity in the light of relativity theory, or, in the realm of theology, to the difficulty experienced in giving positive expression to the mysteries of the Trinity and the Hypostatic Union.[30] Geach's own presentation of God's knowledge of temporal events as deriving from self-knowledge rather than observation does, however, point in a direction towards some positive understanding of the presence of temporality to the eternal God.[31]

Balthasar's suggestion that the richness of temporality is present to eternity helps to maintain Geach's emphasis on the reality of time. It does so in a way consistent with Stump and Kretzmann's account, transcending it in arguing for an analogous relationship between eternity and time, and not simply for a radical distinction between the two. Furthermore, some hint of what this analogous relationship might involve may be seen in his insistence on the primacy of love over knowledge in God. Here Balthasar opens up a more personal and mutual understanding of the relationship between God and us in a way which overcomes the difficulties of Geach's chess image, which suggests either too much control on God's part or (as Kenny has pointed out) too little awareness of the actual moves which the other participants make. In this Balthasar modifies the traditional view by noting how God freely allows himself to be surprised by the actual moves of the other participants. His position suggests to us a way of understanding how the richness of the future (the surprise element in love) may co-exist with the omniscience of an eternal present.

Jonathan Kvanvig

Jonathan Kvanvig is concerned primarily with a defence of the doctrine of divine omniscience.[32] A secondary concern is to offer 'a limited defence of the compatability of timelessness, omniscience, and immutability'.[33] While this secondary concern is of more direct significance for our own discussion, a brief account of Kvanvig's overall position is required in order to situate his particular contribution to the debate on divine immutability.

One of the principal difficulties arising in connection with the doctrine of divine omniscience is the problem posed by knowledge of the future. Kvanvig argues in favour of the strong intuitions human beings have that the future may be an object of knowledge. The argument focuses on the premise that the objects of knowledge are propositions, that we may make true propositions about the future, and thus (against Geach)[34] that we may know the future as real without this implying the present existence of the future. Kvanvig realises, of course, that it is insufficient, if useful, merely to establish that human beings may sometimes know the future – God's essential omniscience is at once more extensive in range than our knowledge of the future and, crucially, it involves an absolute certainty which seems to call into question the possibility of human freedom. Kvanvig attempts to solve this difficulty by arguing that infallible knowledge about the future involves a logical and not a causal relationship; certainty of knowledge is not to be confused with causality of the known, so that things need not come about with necessity, even though known with certainty.

But if there is not necessary imcompatibility between divine omniscience and the future actions of free individuals, how may we conceive in a positive way of the possibility of this kind of omniscience? Kvanvig dismisses as inadequate the traditional approach laid down by Augustine and Aquinas, which would propose that God's knowledge is the cause of truth and reality rather than (as in the case of human knowledge) the derived effect of already existing reality. According to this model of practical knowledge – similar to Geach's account of God's knowledge of the future through control and not through observation – God would know the future by knowing his own essence and those possibilities within that essence which he has willed to exist. This model, whatever its other attractive features, is flawed in a central way by its incompatibility with the reality of human freedom. Since, according to Kvanvig, 'no action is free unless brought about only by the agent himself',[35] then in order to safeguard human freedom it ought not to be proposed that God knows future acts through causing them.

Kvanvig proposes instead a Molinistic account of divine omniscience.[36] According to this view God, in addition to knowledge of possibilities and actualities, has a third kind of knowledge (*scientia media*, or middle knowledge). This is the knowledge of what an individual would do if placed in certain circumstances where many possible decisions might be taken (this freedom of the individual, involving our partial responsibility with God for the actualisation of our world, is referred to as a 'maximal subjunctive of freedom').[37] The intuitve idea behind this theory is that there are true statements about what a person would freely do, were s/he in certain circumstances: 'If one leaves a child in the kitchen in clear view of a full and reachable biscuit tin, what that child will do is obvious: he is going to eat a biscuit (or two).'[38] Such knowledge is possible ultimately because individuals, including human beings, have basic natures or essences which allow of knowledge of their future actuality, a knowledge which God has before creation.

Kvanvig is clear that his position so far does not depend in any way on an acceptance of the timelessness or immutability of God. It is appropriate, then, at this stage to comment on the issues raised by this position, given the intrinsic link between omniscience, eternity and immutability proposed by Balthasar. A persistent and central difficulty about Kvanvig's position stems from his propositional account of knowledge. This account does not seem adequate to an understanding of knowledge which focuses on the commensurability, equality and conformity between the understanding of the knower and the object known, as found in thinkers like Lonergan and Kasper.[39] According to this latter account knowledge is present in the judgement of what *is*, a reflexive judgement which is possible only through verification of one's understanding in the light of the data to be understood. Even God's knowledge, which is the cause rather than the effect of the known, requires that this known exist for the knowledge in question to be verifiably certain. It is difficult without recourse to the notion of divine eternity to see how the contingent future of free, indeterminate human activity can exist in a way which allows a verification leading to certain (and not just probable) knowledge. The Molinistic appeal to the middle knowledge of essences is valid only if these essences are determinative of free action, which seems to deny true freedom; while a non-determinative future can surely only be verifiably known when it has happened, so that before it has happened Kvanvig's God seems rather like Geach's Grand Master, able to see all possible moves and sure of winning the game, but, as Kenny notes, unable to know future *actual* moves. Kvanvig himself knows that the justified true belief of a proposition is determined by whether or not it reflects the way the world is, and he argues too that his Molinistic notion of omniscience allows him to affirm a more than *probable* divine knowledge of the future.[40] But despite these affirmations it is difficult to see how, within his admittedly reductionist propositional account of knowledge, he is able to maintain an ontological grounding for the verification required for infallible knowledge of future free actions. This ontological grounding *is* present in the traditional account as presented by Lonergan,[41] who stresses that God's certain, verified knowledge of the future is possible because God knows the future in an eternal 'now' to which

everything is present. Admittedly our understanding of how everything can be present in this way is obscure, but it does occur in such a
way that, *pace* Kvanvig, God's knowledge and will are indeed the
cause of our free acts, so that the primary source of divine knowledge
is self-knowledge.[42] This latter assertion is supported by a nuanced
notion of transcendent universal instrumentality which allows of
secondary causality and, in particular, of human free activity as being
the effect of both divine and human causality acting in relationship
(thus overcoming the simple disjunction implied by Kvanvig's
contention, already quoted, that 'no action is free unless brought bout
only by the agent himself' – my emphasis: Augustine would not have
been too happy with this formulation!). However it should be noted
once again that, without spelling out all the philosophical implications, Balthasar has modified this traditional account to allow for the
element of surprise to exist within God's certain knowledge. So truth is
more than a formal correspondence between the knower and the
known: ultimately truth is mystery, the mystery of love with its
creative freedom and originality which enjoys a primacy over
knowledge. Because of this Geach's chess image implies an overly
rigid and controlling notion of omniscience; Balthasar's image is that
of an original drama, conceived, produced and acted all in one. In this
way he wishes to suggest that akin to the reserve and discretion which
preserve the creativity and freedom of love within the trinitarian
relationship of the omniscient Father and Son, there is a divine
'latency' with respect to creation which allows us also to share in the
Son's surprising of the omniscient Father. The extent of the divine
knowledge and the strength of the divine love guarantee the success
of the drama, but Balthasar offers no more precise philosophical
account of this interplay between knowledge and love in God.

Kvanvig goes on to show that, while his account of divine
omniscience does not require the doctrines of divine timelessness and
immutability, it is nonetheless compatible with these doctrines. We
may use our account of his admittedly provisional position to indicate
some features of his thought which illuminate Balthasar's text. First,
Kvanvig deals with the objection by Prior that a timeless God cannot
know what time it is now – this is the issue concerning the
relationship between time and tense to which we adverted in our
discussion of Kenny, who also refers to Prior.[43] Kvanvig replies to this
objection by citing the omnipresence of the eternal 'now' to all
temporal moments, explaining this by the treatment of simultaneity
in relativity theory, and referring explicity to the analysis of Stump

and Kretzmann. Kvanvig would strengthen this argument if he were able to see his way towards accepting the traditional answer to God's knowledge of empirical matters, *viz.* that God's knowledge is the cause, not the effect, of created things.[44] One would then be close to Balthasar's notion that the richness of temporality is present to eternity – the positivity of the effect (time) is present in the cause (eternity), this cause which is exemplary in being the original idea (and not the simple antithesis) of its effect.

Secondly, Kvanvig addresses the question of how a timeless, immutable and omniscient God can participate in the history of human affairs.[45] To explain how this can be so Kvanvig develops the notion of an *eternal action*. The intuition behind this notion is that there is a valid distinction between that aspect of an act which is internal to an agent and that which consists of some effect produced by the agent, and that this distinction may involve a temporal difference. So, for example, 'Jim might try to kill Joe by shooting him on Tuesday, though Joe does not actually die until Friday.'[46] Analogously it may be argued that while the worldly effects of God's actions are in time, the divine action itself is timeless. Consequently, 'instead of saying that in 7 BC God had not yet sent His Son, but that by 7 AD He had, we should say that God performed the following actions (or omissions) eternally: not sending His Son in 7 BC, and sending His Son at some time earlier than 7 AD'.[47] This gives us an interesting illustration of the way in which opposites may be reconciled in God without contradiction. It suggests that Kvanvig's notion of eternal action is a fruitful explication of the traditional notion of God as Pure Act, an explication which, without the same trinitarian development, has much in common with Balthasar's 'trinitarian event'. Interestingly Kvanvig does not go on to consider the special case of divine participation in human history, with its trinitarian implications, which is entailed by the incarnation; our treatment of Stump and Kretzmann indicates how such a consideration leads towards Balthasar's notion of an analogous relationship between eternity and time. Even without such a consideration, however, Kvanvig notes that his notion of eternal action may be used as a further grounding for God's timeless direct grasping of what is temporal.

Three main conclusions in relation to Balthasar's position emerge from this discussion of Kvanvig. First, the difficulty which attends the Molinistic account of divine omniscience without the ontological grounding given by the notion of divine eternity suggests that Balthasar's adherence to a modified form of the basic elements of the traditional notions of omniscience, eternity and immutability is justified. The ultimate ontological ground of all these attributes may indeed, as Davies and Lonergan[48] also contend, be the divine simplicity. Secondly, the view that eternity is a coherent notion is reinforced, and Balthasar's proposal that the perfection of time is present in eternity may be understood as a constructive way of tackling some modern objections concerning the apparent uniqueness attaching to the temporal way of knowing. Thirdly, Kvanvig's notion of eternal action is a helpful explanation of at least some of what Balthasar intends by his 'trinitarian event'. In particular it allows us to posit without contradiction a multiplicity of apparently conflicting actions in God.

D. H. Mellor and A. H. Williams

We have already adverted to the lack in Balthasar of any substantial discussion of the different approaches in modern philosophy (often in dialogue with physics and mathematics) to the issues of time and eternity.[49] One such approach is that of D. H. Mellor.[50] Mellor's position does not address the various questions concerning the relationship between the temporal universe and the eternal God which has such bearing on the issue of divine immutability. Nonetheless his position does have implications for these questions, as a brief outline of the relevant parts of his discussion will indicate.

Mellor's basic position is outlined succinctly in the Introduction of his book;[51] its grounding and development occupy the rest of the text. He holds that while time is real, J. E. McTaggart is correct in asserting that tense and the flow of time are not real. The distinctions between past, present and future, then, are not objective differences to which a real past, present and future correspond. Rather, past, present and future refer to the relations all events and things have to earlier, simultaneous and later times, *viz.* the tenseless relations of being later, simultaneous and earlier than them – 'so far as time goes, in short, the truth of a tensed statement depends only on how much earlier or later it is made than whatever it is about'.[52] Therefore the B-series of temporal positions (e.g. 1948), which uses dates to locate earlier or later events, is more foundational than the A-series, which locates things and events by their past or future distance from the present (e.g. twenty-one years ago). This 'token-reflexive' account of what makes tensed statements true or false does not deny that tensed statements are indispensable and untranslatable; they are inescapable objective truths about what is past, present and future, and to us who act in time tense 'is an inescapable mode of perceiving, thinking and speaking about reality'.[53] However tense itself is not an aspect of reality and 'nothing is really past, present or future in itself'.[54]

But things *are* earlier or later. Mellor grounds this real distinction in the notion of causation – causal order fixes temporal order. It does so in the tenseless sense that my seeing x precede y means first seeing x, and this seeing of x is somehow recollected in my seeing of y, so that the causal order of perception fixes the temporal order. This relationship between causality and temporality is then exploited to explain how we can affect some future events and perceive (be affected by) the past; but how does one explain our inability to perceive the future or affect the past? Mellor argues that ultimately this inability is due to the fact that we 'cannot affect what we have already perceived, i.e. one event cannot both affect and be affected by another'.[55] In other words the past event is perceivable because it has affected me, which entails (given the non-reciprocity of cause and effect) that I cannot affect it, while the future event is something I can affect, as cause, which entails that I cannot perceive it (because to do so would be to be affected by it, to be its effect). Only if causes and effects formed 'a closed loop in and via which each event indirectly affects itself'[56] could one both perceive and affect the past, affect and perceive the future. The argument is given to support the contention that there is no such closed loop.

The implications of Mellor's position may be indicated briefly. If it is incorrect not only to reify time and eternity[57] but also to ascribe objective reality to what is intended by the notions of past, present and future, then it would seem that in principle at least it may be easier to understand God's simultaneous eternal presence in all our times. After all, if the asymmetry between our knowledge of past and future events is due not to the non-existence of the future but rather to our inability to perceive events before they occur, perhaps an eternal God may have access to these existent dimensions of reality which, because of our temporal natures, are inaccessible to us. Mellor himself, incidentally, indicates briefly his own scepticism with regard to the notion of the Deity being 'outside time',[58] but this is not a developed position and so we are not required to engage in critical discussion with it. But if tense is in our heads rather than in reality, then it is easier to assert that the whole of reality may be present to God (provided in addition that one can also show that God is eternal cause in a way which obviates the difficulties presented by Mellor's 'closed loop'). It is also, of course, clear that the difficulties which Prior, Kenny, Davies, and Kvanvig had with regard to God's know-ledge of tensed propositions become less acute. In these respects Mellor (although he himself would probably not share this view) would seem to offer some ontological grounding for Balthasar's view that temporal reality may be present to God non-successively.

Mellor's position, with its espousal of a B-notion of time, is of course far from being accepted universally.[59] If ontologically the past and the future are just as real as the present, then what account is one to give of birth and death that acknowledges the existence and not just the occurrence of things? To what extent, then, is Mellor's notion of causality an adequate explanation of the being of existents which come into being, and not simply of the occurrence of already (and always) existent beings? Whatever allowance is made for the existence of things in the eternal ideas of God, or God's own eternal presence to things which temporally really do come into being, it is difficult to accept that on its own, without this more transcendent framework, Mellor's position can do justice to the intrinsic tempor-ality of being. Finally, in the light of our criticism of Balthasar's lack of dialogue with physics-based philosophies of time, it is interesting that Mellor, although clearly well informed himself, believes that the authority of physics in this matter is over-valued and that 'philo-sophers of late years have been altogether too deferential to the metaphysical speculations of physicists, especially about time'.[60]

It remains to indicate briefly another approach to time which is more directly related to the theological issues of our concern. Arthur Williams,[61] in discussing the Trinity and time, distinguishes between two basic views of time, the Parmenidean and the Heraclitian, and suggests that the principle of complementarity be invoked to recog-nise that both are valid and that it is not a question of choosing between contradictory alternatives. Briefly, the Parmenidean view relates time to spatial motion and change; this is S-(Space-) time, and its discrete units can be measured. The Heraclitian view uses the dynamic unity of process as its model for time: each phase is continually transformed into its 'opposite', that is into a qualitatively different phase, in a way which resists a strict application of the law of non-contradiction. In its modern form it is connected with the idea of the continuity of introspective experience, the stream of conscious-ness, and may be known as D-(Duration-) time. It is not measurable in any exact way but is related to consciousness in such a way that the passage of time is notoriously variable, as in the saying, 'How time flies when you are having fun.'[62] Williams argues that both S- and D-time are valid, suggesting that this may be so within an Einsteinian cosmology which acknowledges the legitimacy of different frames of references. An analogy from the physics of light is adduced to support this argument – in physics light is a continuous wave-motion or a stream of discrete bundles (photons); the principle of complementarity states that both sets of evidence are to be accepted and affirmed.[63]

Williams goes on to show how the two views of time are needed within theological discourse. In particular, D-time allows us to understand the past in terms of diminished immediacy co-inhering in our consciousness, rather than as points on a line that recede from us and create a 'gap' that needs to be 'bridged'. With D-time, then, we are able to draw an analogy with memory and to renew the vividness of the past in celebration, song, ritual and so on – time is not just a series of points on a line, but is a whole life that grows organically. With specific reference to our own concern Williams comments on the notion of Theophilus of Antioch that the first three days of creation are a 'type' of the Trinity. He suggests that with a D-view of time one may understand this in an orthodox way – the first day of our lives is never lost to us, but persists all our lives as a part of who we are; every succeeding day is truly different, but all days come together to form a unity. This may be called the Perichoresis, the co-inherence of time.

There are two aspects of this account of Williams which are significant for our own dicussion. First, the notion of D-time, with its roots in the Heraclitian view of a process which reconciles opposites and its application to the trinitarian circumincession, is a good image for the eternity of divine life which Balthasar refers to under the leit-motif of intensity. Secondly, the appeal to Einsteinian cosmology and to the principle of complementarity recalls the approach of Stump and Kretzmann, as well as Kvanvig, in their attempt to show the coherence of the view that the eternal God interacts with temporal creation.[64]

Conclusion

It remains to comment in a summary way on the main points arising from this dialogue which we have initiated between Balthasar and some representatives of the English-speaking philosophical world.

The discussion with B. Davies and the Thomistic position focused directly on the issue of divine immutability. The strength of the traditional philosophical position was underlined, while an opening towards a theological modification of this position, which would involve a metaphysically-rooted use of metaphor, was indicated. The debate with Kenny, Stump and Kretzmann, Geach and Kvanvig focused in a general way on the relationship between the world and God, and in particular on the difficult question of God's knowledge of the future. From this debate it emerged that a helpful approach towards an understanding of the divine omniscience with respect to the future depended on a nuanced grasp of the eternity of God. While this was consistent with Balthasar's notion of the divine immutability, it was clear also that the discussion had questioned the precision of Balthasar's more general account. In addition, illuminating suggestions were made by Kvanvig and Stump and Kretzmann in particular about the notion of divine eternity. Finally, the focus of the discussion with Mellor and Williams was quite specifically on the notion of time. Mellor's position on the non-objectivity of past, present and future did provide support for Balthasar's views on the presence of time within eternity, but the position itself is so controverted that it is best omitted from any attempt at a formal assessment of these views. More promisingly, the account given by Williams of D-time offered an approach consistent with Balthasar's position on time and eternity.

This dialogue between Balthasar and the other contributors is mutually enriching despite the very real differences in presuppositions, language and tone which make it difficult to mediate the sense of the discussion between the two sides. A particular point which is unique to Balthasar may help to illustrate one of the key differences between his own theological metaphysics which is at home with metaphor and the more formally philosophical approach of the discussion partners with their greater emphasis on linguistic precision.[65] The point in question is his insistence on the primacy of love over knowledge and the way in which this allows for the freedom of surprise to be compatible with the divine omniscience. This emerged at several stages in the dialogue as an important contribution to grasping how the liveliness and freedom associated with time, and the temporal future in particular, might be reconcilable with divine eternity. Now this point is itself based on an analogy with human inter-personal relationships of love where, it is suggested, as people get to know one another better there is, if anything, an increase in those aspects of surprise, mystery and freedom which are characteristic of love. The intuition that this is the way things are in human relationships is, I would argue, a sound one, and hence its application to the divine life (with suitable modifications) is helpful. Nonetheless it is not so clear that this intuition may be understood conceptually in a way which can reconcile omniscience with surprise. In this there is a challenge to Balthasar from the more formally philosophical approach (of Kenny, Geach and Kvanvig in particular) to develop a more precise understanding, while from Balthasar's side there is the reminder of the necessary imprecision in such matters, and hence of the proper contribution of metaphor.

We may turn now to a more explicit final assessment of Balthasar's position.

6

Final assessment

Brief synopsis of Balthasar's overall position on divine immutability

In our first chapter we examined the reasons why Balthasar considered it necessary to propose a modification of the traditional Christian teaching on the divine immutability and impassibility. The main lines of this modification were sketched in a general way; from the revelation of God in Christ, with its trinitarian presuppositions, and within the context of a christological analogy of being, one argued to an event of love in God. Further reasons were given in our second chapter for positing such an event in God, this time deriving from an examination of the relationship between creation (its history and end) and God. Here it was argued that the trinitarian presuppositions of creation, with the positive significance they gave to otherness and difference without detriment to unity, allowed one to speak in terms of the effect of creation on God, without elimination of the divine transcendence. Within an analogical context (which, in attempting to convey the uniquely personal nature of the God/human relationship, could use language extending on a continuum from the metaphorical to the purely abstract) it was possible to attribute some very untraditional characteristics to God, including forms of surprise, receptivity, self-transcendence ('ever-more') and something that was remotely and mysteriously like suffering. It was possible also, to a limited extent, to specify the adjustments required when transferring language from the human to the divine spheres; nonetheless an intrinsic imprecision was also noted, appropriate to the partial nature of human knowledge in respect of the abiding mystery and transcendence of God. These first two chapters indicated that while it will not do to attribute created mutability to God, the divine immutability must nonetheless be understood in the context of the liveliness of inner-trinitarian love.

But these two chapters also raised the crucial issue of the relationship between time and eternity, to which our third chapter was devoted. How could the lively immutability of the eternal inner-trinitarian event be understood to interact mutually with temporal beings? A way forward was found by proposing that eternity and temporality were not simply antithetical, but that there was a positive and mutual relationship between the two in which the primacy rested with the eternal. Within such a context there emerged the notion of eternity as a supra-temporality, with an intensive form of duration which could interact with the extended form of temporal duration without detriment to the integrity of either form.

We moved on in our fourth chapter to a thematic consideration of the eternal trinitarian event in itself. Here the reconciliation of unity and difference, as well as that of state and event, and the inclusion of the aspects of receptivity and 'ever-more' within the Trinity, were all accomplished in different ways through a scripturally-inspired trin-itarian ontology of love. In such an ontology one used the analogy of human love and applied it hypothetically to God, making adjustments to cater for the ontological difference between God and us, so that it was possible at least to hint at the way in which various modalities of human love could exist analogously in God as perfections, and not as deficiencies. Within this context divine immutability was interpreted as that perfection and fullness of free inter-personal love, intrinsic to which are the receptivity of mutual exchange and that mysterious ontological comparative, the ever-more of self-giving, which may be described as a supra-mutability. A notion of theological discourse was proposed in support of the appropriateness, and indeed requirement, of paradoxical speech in theology, with a differentiated use of metaphor and more abstract terminology, in order to indicate even remotely the scriptural revelation of mystery. Finally, in our fifth chapter Balthasar's position was brought into discussion with other contemporary English-speaking approaches.

Such has been our presentation (in the absence of any sustained thematic treatment in Balthasar himself) of the way the whole looks when the scattered fragments of his theology of the immutability of God are gathered together. What has emerged is clearly different from the traditional understanding of Scripture on this issue; is this difference an instance of genuine theological development, or is it mistaken?

The strengths and weaknesses of the position – final assessment

The main issue

The great advantage of Balthasar's position on the divine immutability, presented in the form of a theology of the trinitarian event, is that it allows us to speak coherently about God as transcendent and yet as intimately involved with us. It does so in conformity with scriptural revelation and Christian experience but in contrast to some of the traditional terms of Christian theism, by showing how creation is distinct but not separate from God and, crucially, is an analogous expression of God. Balthasar has identified and developed the similarity, within dissimilarity, of the created and divine spheres in their analogous relationship (revealed primarily in Christ) in such a way that he may speak about a supra-mutability and suffering in God which are clearly not identical with and yet relate positively to created change and suffering. In this way he avoids the appearance (common in other approaches) of a 'split' in God, whether between God in himself and God in the other, or between the economic and immanent realms, or between the human and divine natures of Christ, while being able to maintain the distinction proper to the divine transcendence. Within this trinitarian ontology of love, then, he offers a nuanced[1] and developed[2] theology of the divine immutability.

This nuanced approach of Balthasar, however, is part of a general theological vision which has been criticised as involving in different ways a denial or neglect of the reality and importance of creation in its temporal, historical and social dimensions.[3] If what is primary and normative is the eternal, non-created event of trinitarian love, is there room any more for the distinct contribution of the incarnate Christ, and, more problematically, of other men and women? This sense of an excessive spiritualisation is apparent in Balthasar's tendency, in his unashamedly theocentric theological approach, to spend rather more time in dialogue with the tradition than with contemporaries, so that, unfashionably, modern concerns are relativised in a way which increases the 'other-worldly' impression of the discussion. Some of this criticism is deserved; there is a regrettable lack of more serious engagement with contemporary concerns, and we have already drawn attention to the dangers of downgrading temporality which are inherent in some of the ways in which he formulates an understanding of the relationship between time and eternity. However it does seem to us that with regard to the specific issue of divine immutability Balthasar's theology is not in principle vulnerable to such criticism. This is so because he has found a way to establish that creation is real and that God is involved in it, without reducing God to creation and without making God's involvement any less real by preserving his transcendence. He has gone beyond a more traditional interpretation of the Chalcedonian two-natures teaching by positing the original image of change and suffering among the modalities of the liveliness of inner-trinitarian love itself. This is done in such a way that this original image, however different and however imprecise, is sufficiently similar and determined for us to be able to affirm that it is an even more serious and primary reality than the very real change and suffering which we experience at the created level. The fact that supra-mutability and supra-suffering are perfections, are free modalities of love, and are mysterious and are non-created does not imply that they are any less real than, or incapable of interaction with, their created copies. In this way the primary reality of the original image, the secondary reality of the copy and the abiding distinction between the two are maintained without any downgrading of the different realities involved. This is the God who is affected by and involved, but not entangled, in created reality; the divine transcendence does not rule out a very real immanence.

Balthasar's position is, however, more vulnerable to criticism because of its imprecision, although here again careful distinctions need to be made. We have already noted his predominantly metaphorical approach to understanding that enormously mysterious relationship between time and eternity, and the difficulties which Geach's questioning of the ontological basis for God's knowledge of the future poses to this approach. Nonetheless, we also recall that the coherence of Balthasar's position in this area, which we argued for in our third chapter, is well supported by the thrust of the discussion in our fifth chapter, and, in particular, by the analysis of Stump and Kretzmann. There is also some imprecision about Balthasar's attempt to ground the 'ever-more' in God in an ontology of love in which there is a primacy of love over knowledge: this imprecision emerges most clearly when, as in our fifth chapter, one examines in greater detail the philosophical implications of this position for God's providential omniscience. Nonetheless, here too we have argued that Balthasar's basic hunch, that true knowledge of the heart allows for the surprise of love, is valid. Finally, Balthasar's way of interpreting Scripture in close association with the Christian tradition of spirituality makes it more difficult to offer a precise assessment of his theology of the divine immutability. This is so because when the Christian experience of sanctity and prayer are accepted as theological loci they introduce subjective factors into the theological equation concerning the interpretation of Scripture, factors which are themselves difficult to assess and which accordingly make more complex the assessment proper to the usual canons of biblical exegetes. This is important: after all we have claimed that Balthasar's theology of the divine immutability is scripturally inspired, not that it is always the only or necessarily the correct interpretation of Scripture. However, giving an intrinsic theological role to Christian experience in this exercise is arguably valid (despite its complicating effect) and in accord with the much respected traditional dictum *lex orandi, lex credendi*. The intrinsic intelligibility of Balthasar's own position, his critical dialogue with exegetes, and his concern to be in conformity with Church teaching are further counter-balances to the subjective dangers inherent in his approach. Nonetheless a more precise assessment of his overall position would require a more detailed scrutiny of his use of Scripture.

This nuanced criticism of Balthasar's imprecision must of course be further modified by the acceptance that there is an imprecision inherent in the analogous treatment of mystery, which, far from being vague, is the more proper and exact way to conduct a theological enquiry of this nature. Given that the central thrust of Balthasar's description of an analogous event in God is capable of sufficient specification to obviate charges of mystification, and given the inner consistency between the different parts of his account, the intelligible unity of his overall position, its ability to answer the questions which arise in this whole area, and its status as a valid possible interpretation of Scripture, then it is reasonable to suggest that where his account can and should be corrected it will be done in a way which will not contradict but rather further develop its main lines.

This structure of positive assessment combined with still inconclusive aspects suggests that Balthasar's position is best understood in terms of an hypothesis.[4] This is not meant to suggest that it is unreal: the hypothetical nature refers to a natural stage in the process of theological enquiry into a mystery. It is a stage where an unproven position is proposed in answer to difficulties concerning an issue which awaits resolution. The analogy with the development of the doctrine of the Trinity in the early centuries of Christianity is, once again, apposite: in an important sense the mystery always remains, and yet definitive steps forward may be possible and are signalled by the reception of the Church. Church reception in the issue of divine immutability as it arises today has not reached definitive status: one may begin to speak of a broad theological consensus concerning the need to modify the traditional teaching, and within the Roman Catholic Church there is some rather general but far from definitive support[5] for the main lines of the particular modification proposed by Balthasar, but it is much too early yet to speak of a consensus or any authoritative Church teaching with regard to particular positions on this issue. What this means is that Balthasar's hypothesis needs to be further tested in areas which we have already mentioned, so that a more definitive assessment of its status becomes possible.

This testing would involve in particular a correction of Balthasar's tendency to ignore opposing views or to dismiss them without detailed discussion.[6] This occasionally somewhat patrician tendency is impoverishing. In this context, while we considered that his basic critique of Process thinkers was justified, a more sustained treatment of the lively debate between such thinkers and those of a more traditional school would bring his own position into sharper focus.[7] It would also illustrate that despite radical differences Balthasar would seem to have many, for the most part unacknowledged, affinities with the Process approach. We also noted an apparent confusion, due mainly to this failure to enter into detailed discussion, in Balthasar's references to Rahner's formula concerning divine immutability. It should also be said that in proceeding in this way Balthasar's target is not individual thinkers as such but rather systems of thought, and in particular the starting-points of such systems with their inexorable ensuing logic.[8] This does allow him, by contrast with counter-positions, to make his own position more precise. However, even greater precision would be achieved by a more thorough discussion of other views. In this respect our own attempt to initiate a discussion between Balthasar's position and other, very different, contemporary approaches may be understood as a small contribution to this required verification procedure. Through it we discovered that Balthasar's overall vision stood up well and seemed to offer the possibility of informing the kind of philosophical detail which it still lacked.

In the absence of further testing and of a more complete ecclesial reception (with its combination of theological consensus and authoritative teaching) it is nonetheless possible to offer an appraisal of the present status of Balthasar's position. Given our predominantly positive assessment, in conjunction with our description of it as a hypothesis, it is our judgement that we may assess his position as being probably, but not certainly, correct. The uncertainty is due to the incomplete stage of the verification procedure. The probability is due to the intelligibility of the position proposed by Balthasar and the persuasive arguments which support it. In a very difficult area, with the need to keep a delicate balance in the inter-relationships between the witness of Scripture, tradition, Christian experience, the inherent logic and dynamic of philosophical systems and his own presuppositions and biases, Balthasar has provided us with a way of speaking about God which resonates with the intuition of the Christian faithful concerning God's consoling intimacy and yet his reassuring otherness. This razor's-edge approach of Balthasar, mid-way between the proponents of process theology and those of a strict traditional school, reveals a unity of complexity and inner consistency characteristic of the *lectio difficilior*[9] and thus more likely to be true to the scriptural revelation.

Subsidiary issues

Balthasar's position on our main issue of the divine immutability and his position on the subsidiary issues treated in our enquiry are, to an extent, mutually dependent. We need now, in the light of our qualified positive assessment of this theology of the divine immutability, to comment on the explanatory dynamic between these two sets of positions, and in particular on the assessment of one subsidiary issue of a controversial nature.

The first point to establish is that the unity and intelligibility of the complex whole which is Balthasar's theology of the divine immutability is in itself a strong argument for a positive assessment of the parts which constitute this whole. Since his unified position is innerly consistent, and answers the main questions which arise in a satisfactory way, then to that extent its intelligibility is established independently of a definitive positive assessment of each of his positions on subsidiary issues, provided at least that these positions are not in themselves contradictory. This means in turn that in a general sense our assessment of his position on subsidiary issues is more definitively favourable at the end of our enquiry.

But, next, to what extent does the qualified nature of our acceptance of Balthasar's position on the main issue affect our assessment of the subsidiary issue of soteriology which we have most particularly called into question? Our first point above applies: Balthasar's position on this issue is undoubtedly supported by our positive assessment of his position on the main issue. However, precisely because of the qualified nature of this positive assessment it is also true that this support alone is not sufficient to warrant a definitive acceptance of his position on the subsidiary issue. We have noted that if Balthasar's soteriology were rejected – in particular his notion of the representative abandonment of Christ as expressed most controversially in his theology of Holy Saturday – there would still be a strong case to support his attribution of a supra-mutability to God. This supra-mutability would be different from the one at present proposed – it would lack that aspect of conflict which Balthasar sees as possible due to the extreme nature of trinitarian love in its free response to our sin – but it would still contain a form of supra-suffering and 'ever-more' as before. This means that while we may retain our qualified acceptance of his main position, and while the status of his position on the subsidiary issue of soteriology is enhanced, this latter does not admit of conclusive assessment within the parameters of our discussion.

We note finally that Balthasar's theology of the divine immutability fits well into the notion of doctrinal development. It is a theology which does not contradict the traditional position but, in response to new concerns and in accordance with the scriptural revelation, moves beyond a fundamentalist reiteration of this tradition to a position that is consistent with it but is also a real advance. This consistency, due to Balthasar's nuanced, razor's-edge approach, is a reassuring indication of true development; but so too is the advance, that surprising 'ever-more' which is characteristic of divine love in its revelation and gift of self.

Conclusion

We have attempted to present in a systematic way Balthasar's thought on the immutability of God. Such a systematic presentation fails to convey Balthasar's own theological style. This is a style which, in its circular repetition and apparent glorious disorder, has a unified form which is complex, and is so in a deliberate attempt to be proportionate to the matter it presents.[10] This complexity of form, with its constant focus on the whole and its refusal to be drawn into extended treatment of individual theological tracts, has a beauty and originality which critics recognise.[11] However it can also be an obstacle to a wider reception of Balthasar's thought, in that it can create an impression of a slightly dilettantish, less than rigorous combination of spirituality and theological speculation. Our attempt to indicate the systematic 'bones' of Balthasar's 'living form'[12] may help to minimise this impression.

In Balthasar himself, of course, style and content combine intrinsically to create this living form. There results an inspirational momentum which refuses to linger in tying up every loose end, but which tosses up approaches and phrases which would be immediately suspect in a more conventional theology. We have tried to indicate that this living form moves on solid ground. Once again, however, this time in the specific area of scriptural grounding, it is important to note that our systematic account fails to convey the force of Balthasar's own approach, in which a meditative use of Scripture is central and combines with other strands to produce a theology which is scripturally inspired in a way which far transcends the use of particular 'proof-texts'. Still, one may learn a great deal from a skeleton about the living form. With all its limitations and omissions our systematic account of Balthasar's theology of the divine immutability does trace the outlines of his position in a way which indicates its strengths and weaknesses. This is helpful in coming to terms with the richness of the less flat, more complex and lively reality of Balthasar's own presentation.

On Balthasar's position itself, we have seen that he has moved away from the limited, rigid notion of immutability so congenial to the ancient world in its quest for stability.[13] Nonetheless he has done so without recourse to the opposite extreme of a titanism which would make God in our image. In doing so he has maintained the divine transcendence while allowing God to be involved in our world. This results in a far from insipid and ultimately enormously reassuring image of God, which requires acknowledgement of the full reality of human existence, including evil and the cross. It is an image of God which may also – although Balthasar himself has been less interested in developing this aspect – be helpful in inspiring Christians to engage in a committed, realistic search for justice in this world.[14]

With regard to the more general significance of Balthasar's theology, of which his theology of the divine immutability is a particular and characteristic instance, the impression persists, despite disagreement with individual points, that this is an approach to be reckoned with, which offers a strong challenge. The challenge is directed in part at an excessive rationalism in modern theology, whether it be in the reductively scientific presuppositions of some exegetes and liberal theologians, or in the over-emphasis on an anthropocentric approach which is common in more moderate circles. But it is also directed at all forms of theological fundamentalism, including an excessively fideistic adherence to a fossilised tradition. It is a theology to be reckoned with because with that slightly old-fashioned ring to its demanding, explicitly Christian and authoritative tone it jars with the secularist, relativist ethos of our age and opens up new perspectives. This was part of the original function of Christianity as 'good news', and a theology which has similar effects today may last longer than those approaches which are more obviously in tune with the spirit of the age. However this may be – and time alone will be the judge – it is clear that Balthasar's distinctive theology, besides being itself an exciting catalyst in the process of theological development, is also very well placed to offer a normative contribution to the dialogue between, on the one hand, contemporary theology, and, on the other, the long tradition of Christianity and the modern world to which the Gospel speaks. The particular position on divine immutability, then, opens up an overall vision of God and his relationship to our world which is of great significance for the major areas of theology, and indeed for the nature of theology itself.

The glory of God, as revealed in his deeds, is the truth of inner-trinitarian love. The liveliness of this immutable love allows for the truth of the reality of our mutable, created lives, and grounds the hope of our 'ever-greater' participation in divine glory.

Notes

Introduction

1 For a history of the notion of divine immutability, with its scriptural, philosophical and dogmatic aspects, as well as reference to the contemporary problematic, see W. Maas, *Unveränderlichkeit Gottes* (Munich, 1974). For what follows, see *ibid.*, 11–19, 176–189.

2 Some examples may be cited of those who, with different nuances, have attempted this major rethinking: in mainland Europe, Magnus Löhrer, Karl Rahner, Karl Barth, Bernhard Welte, Edward Schillebeeckx, Heribert Mühlen, Wolfgang Pannenberg, Piet Schoonenberg, Hans Küng, Dietrich Wiederkehr, Karl Lehmann, Alexander Dumas, Jürgen Moltmann, Eberhard Jüngel, Jean Galot, Joseph Ratzinger, Hans Urs von Balthasar; in Britain, John Macquarrie, E. L. Mascall, Sebastian Moore, Rosemary Haughton; in North America, the Process theologians, following on from Alfred Whitehead and Charles Hartshorne, and in dialogue with such partners as David Burrell, William Norris-Clarke, Joseph Bracken, William Hill, Joseph Donceel, Thomas G. Weinandy; in the East, Kazah Kitamori with his very influential book on the suffering of God; and in Latin America Juan Segundo, as part of the programme of Liberation Theology to bring about change in our world towards a more just society by invoking the image of a God who cares about and is involved in what happens to his creation. This list is clearly not intended to be exhaustive. More exact references to the authors cited may be found in Maas, *Unveränderlichkeit*; Balthasar, *TD*, I–IV; the Bibliography at the end of this book. The discussion in North American circles is particularly interesting since it is characterised by a constructive dialogue between the adherents of the Process school and those who derive from a more traditional Thomistic school. For an introduction to the Process approach to theology, see John Cobb and David R. Griffin, *Process Theology: an Introductory Exposition* (Belfast, 1976).

3 Maas, *Unveränderlichkeit*, 19–22 is clear that, despite much conciliar teaching on this issue, the immutability of God has not been defined dogmatically by the Roman Catholic Church.

4 'International Theological Commission: Theology, Christology, Anthropology', *ITQ*, 49(1982), 285–300 (especially 285).

5 'We have learned that in attempting to reflect on these matters human and theological reasoning encounter some of the greatest of all difficulties (such as "anthropomorphism"). But in a remarkable fashion they also encounter the ineffable mystery of the living God and realise the limits of thought itself' (*ibid.*, 299).

6 See Bibliography below, under the heading *Works about Hans Urs von Balthasar*, for a selection of the secondary literature on Balthasar. For a more complete list see M. Lochbrunner, *Analogia Caritatis* (Freiburg, 1981); M. Jöhri, *Descensus Dei* (Rome, 1981). For interesting comments on some of this literature see Jöhri, *Descensus*, 5–10; G. de Schrijver, *Le Merveilleux Accord de l'homme et de Dieu* (Louvain, 1983), 48–51. For Balthasar's own several accounts of his life and works, see:

  (a) 'Es stellt sich vor', in *Das neue Buch* (Lucerne), 7 (1945), 43–6.

  (b) Kleiner Lageplan zu meiner Büchern', *Schweizer Rundschau*, 55 (1955), 212–25.

  (c) *Rechenchaft 1965. Mit einer Bibliographie der Veröffentlichungen Hans Urs von Balthasar zusammengestellt von Berthe Widmer* (Einsiedeln, 1965). An adaptation of this, by K. Batinovich, NSM, appeared in English under the title *In Retrospect* in *Communio, International Catholic Review*, 2 (1975), 197–200.

  (d) 'Geist and Feuer. Ein Gespräch mit Hans Urs von Balthasar', *Herder Korrespondenz*, 30 (1976), 72–82. (The interviewer is Michael Albus.)

  (e) *Il filo di Arianna attraverso la mia opera* (Milan, 1980). This includes the account given in *Rechenschaft 1965*, with the addition of a description of his works from 1966–75 and an updating of the bibliography. For official bibliographies see *Rechenschaft 1965*, and *Il filo*, as well as *Hans Urs von Balthasar, Bibliographie, 1925–1980*, ed. Cornelia Capol (Einsiedeln, 1981) which is a more up-to-date version of Capol's own 1975 work.

7 T. and T. Clarke of Edinburgh have however embarked upon the publication of *Herrlichkeit*, the first part of Balthasar's theological trilogy, under the joint editorship of John Riches and Joseph Fessio; see Bibliography for this and other English translations of Balthasar's works.

8 H. de Lubac, *The Church, Paradox and Mystery* (Shannon, 1969), 105 (from the article in this book entitled *A Witness of Christ in the Church: Hans Urs von Balthasar*, 103–21). This article was also published in English in *Communio, International Catholic Review*, 2 (1975), 228–49.

9 See Béguin, preface to Balthasar's *Théologie de l'Histoire* (Paris, 1955). This preface (1–14) gives an interesting account of Balthasar's chaplaincy life in Basle in the 1940s.

10 See *In Retrospect*, 198, 205–7, 219.

11 See W. Löser, *Im Geiste des Origenes* (Frankfurt, 1976).

12 See *In Retrospect*, 199–204. For the change (*Wende*) that occurred around 1955 in Balthasar's attitude concerning the proper openness of

the Church to the world, see H. Heinz, *Der Gott des Je-Mehr* (Bern/Frankfurt, 1975), 82–4.

13 For this whole discussion see M. Kehl in the Introduction to *In Der Fülle des Glaubens, Hans Urs von Balthasar-Leserbuch*, ed. M. Kehl and W. Löser (Freiburg, 1980), 13–60 (especially 13–16). Balthasar's theology of Christ's descent into hell, of infant baptism and of the issue under discussion, the immutability of God, his rejection of neo-Thomism, his defence of the censured de Lubac and his decision to leave the Jesuits in order to set up a secular institute are but some of the many indications that he is much too complex to be labelled simply as conservative.

14 Published as *Theologie der drei Tage* (Einsiedeln, 1969); as *Mysterium Pascale* in *Mysterium Salutis*, ed. J. Feiner and M. Löhrer (Einsiedeln/Cologne, 1970), III/2, 133–326; and as *Paques le Mystère* (Paris, 1981).

15 *Theodramatik*, I (Einsiedeln, 1973); *Theodramatik*, II/1 (Einsiedeln, 1976); *Theodramatik*, II/2 (Einsiedeln, 1978); *Theodramatik*, III (Einsiedeln, 1980); *Theodramatik*, IV (Einsiedeln, 1983). For full titles see Bibliography.

16 The trilogy comprises the several volumes of *Herrlichkeit: Eine theologische Ästhetik* (published in the 1960s), *Theodramatik* (published in the 1970s and 1980s), and *Theologik* (the first volume of which is the re-issue of a work originally published in 1947 under the title *Wahrheit der Welt*). For full titles, see Bibliography.

17 This helps to explain the fact that while there is only one account from the secondary literature on Balthasar which deals directly with this theology of the divine immutability (see P. Sequeri, 'Cristologie nel quadro della problematica della mutabilità e passibilità di Dio: Balthasar, Küng, Mühlen, Moltmann, Galot', *La Scuola Cattolica*, 105 (1977), 114–51); this is limited to Balthasar's discussion in *MP* – see Seuqueri, 114–19), several of the other secondary works deal with the issue indirectly, e.g. H. Heinz, *Der Gott*; M. Jöhri, *Descensus*; G. Marchesi, *La Cristologia di Hans Urs von Balthasar* (Rome, 1977).

18 See *TD*, I, 118: Und da wir unweigerlich diesen letzen Fragen, die das Zentrum der Theodramatik bilden, begegnen: welcher Weg führt hindurch zwischen den beiden Abgründen einer Systematik, in der Gott als das absolute Sein nur das Regungslose ist, vor dem die Weltbewegung abspielt, und eines Mythologie, die Gott als eine der streitenden Parteien in den Weltprozeß hineinzieht?' See also *TD*, I III, 58–63; Heinz, *Der Gott*, 101; Jöhri, *Descensus*, 339–40. For Balthasar's own references to the centrality of *TD* in his trilogy and thus in his theological writings in general, see *In Retrospect*, 212–13, 216–17; *Il filo*, 50–3; *TD*, II/I, 9–10, 17–22; *TD*, III, 11–12; *H*, I, 9–11 (Foreword).

19 See *Kosmische*, 51.

20 This has in any case already been done with regard to the central themes of Balthasar's theology, and so the main lines are already established – see Marchesi, *La Cristologia*; Heinz, *Der Gott*; Jöhri, *Descensus*; Loch-

brunner, *Analogia*; Löser, *Origenes*; de Schrijver, *Le Merveilleux Accord*; A. Peelman, *Hans urs von Balthasar et la théologie de l'histoire* (Bern/Frankfurt, 1978).

21 See *Pneuma und Institution. Skizzen zur Theologie*, IV (Einsiedeln, 1974) (*Pneuma*); *Homo Creatus Est. Skizzen zur Theologie*, V (*HC*); *Spiritus Creator. Skizzen zur Theologie*, III (Einsiedeln, 1967) (*SC*); *Theologie der Geschichte* (Einsiedeln, 1950) (*TG*); *Das Ganze im Fragment* (Einsiedeln, 1963) (*GF*).

22 For the image of the thread that guides the way through the labyrinth, see *Die Wahrheit*, 27; and the title itself of *Il filo*.

23 See Marchesi, *La Cristologia*, 345; Heinz, *Der Gott*, 13, 289.

24 Balthasar himself is always concerned to show the presence of the whole in the fragments, as the title of his work *Das Ganze im Fragment* indicates.

1 Christ and God's immutability

1 *MP*, 17–28
2 *Ibid.*, 9.
3 See especially *TD*, III and *TD*, *IV passim*.
4 Historically too this was a stumbling-block, and led in fact to the denial of the divinity of Christ; see Mass, *Unveränderlichkeit*, 132–6 for the example of Celsus.
5 For what follows see *TD*, II/1, 64–5; *TD*, II/2, 50; *MP*, 202–4; *H*, I, 182, 323–7, 426–41, 463–526; *VC¹*, 87–119; *Die Wahrheit*, 27–9; Heinz, *Der Gott*, 168–299; Marchesi, *La Cristologia*, 12–13, 33–55, 388–90; Löser, *Darstellung*, 18.
6 We have used 'figure' to translate the German *Gestalt* because, although linguistically clumsy at times, it conveys Balthasar's sense of the full concrete reality of Christ as God's expression, while the term 'form' could suggest an abstraction from certain aspects of this full reality (e.g. his historical activity from birth to death). The English translation of *H*, I (*Schau der Gestalt*) has preferred to use the term *form* ('Seeing the Form') to translate *Gestalt* (19), and this is certainly justified so long as one realises that Balthasar time and again uses *Gestalt* to convey the full reality (and not just a distinct, formal aspect) of the object specified. For this whole discussion, see *La Gloire et las Croix* (French trans. of *H*, I, 1965), 12, note 1; G. O'Hanlon, *The Theological Metaphysics of Hans Urs von Balthasar* Dublin, 1980, (unpublished STL dissertation) 19, 27–30 (especially note 130); de Schrijver, *Le merveilleux Accord*, 322–4.
7 For what follows see *MP*, 202, 249; *TG*, 25–8; *Pneuma*, 139; *Warum*, 42f; *GF*, 282f; *H*, II/1, 353–61; *TD*, III, 463–5; *Au Coeur*, *passim*; Marchesi, *La Cristologia*, 28–33, 348–51, 389–90; Heinz, *Der Gott*, 168, 244–46; Jöhri, *Descensus*, *passim* and especially 9, 93–6, 320–1, 369–89; Löser, *Darstellung*, 21–2; J. Hyde, 'Another Method in Theology', *Horizons*, 13 (1979), 14–16 and 'A Dhia Mhóir – Seanliodán. Machnamh Diagaire', *Milltown Studies*, 3 (1979), 109–12.

8 See B. J. Lee, 'The Two Process Theologies', *TS* 46 (1984), 307–19; J. Keller, 'Basic Differences between Classical and Process Metaphysics and Their Implications for the Concept of God', *International Philosophical Quarterly*, 22 (1982), 3–20; S. Sia, 'The Doctrine of God's Immutability: Introducing the Modern Debate', *New Blackfriars*, 68 (1987), 220–32 and 'God, Time and Change', *The Clergy Review*, 63 (1978), 378–86; L. Scheffczyk, 'Prozeßtheismus und christlicher Gottesglaube', *Münchner Theol. Zeit.*, 35 (1984), 81–104.

9 *HAB*, 11; *GF*, 232; *H*, I, 167–8; *VC²*, 67–72; see also Balthasar's essay 'Regagner une philosophie à partir de la théologie' in *Pour une philosophie chrétienne*, ed. P-Ph. Druet (Paris, 1983), 175–87, and note 9, p. 202 below.

10 *MP*, 30, 33, 37, 202–3; *TD*, II/1, 112; *HNB*, 80; Marchesi, *La Cristologia*, 348–51.

11 For the importance of *MP* within the corpus of Balthasar's writings, together with an outline of its contents, see Jöhri, *Descensus*, 17–21, 80–96.

12 *TD*, III, 296; Jöhri, *Descensus*, 93, note 31. And so in what follows, unless otherwise stated, reference to the cross of Christ will always mean a reference to the Paschal Mystery in all its dimensions, unless the context makes it clear that we are limiting the discussion to the particular event of the cross.

13 See also *MP*, 47, 98–9; *HNB*, 196–7; *TD*, III, 227–8; Jöhri, *Descensus*, 19, 25–36; Marchesi, *La Cristologia*, 347–50.

14 See also *HNB*, 196–200 on Phil. 2, 5–11, especially p. 196 which states Balthasar's case for affirming that the subject of Phil. 2, 5–11 is the divine person, the pre-existent Son, and not the incarnate Logos; see also *CS*, 59–65.

15 See also M. Hengel, *Crucifixion*, 2nd ed. (Philadelphia, 1978), 62–3 for a similar position, 88–90 for the central significance of this divine kenosis.

16 *MP*, 31.

17 See *MP*, 78–9 for Barth's clarification of how this means that Chalcedon is objectively true but nevertheless what happens in Christ *does* tell us about who God is. See also Balthasar, *TD*, II/2, 202–10; *TD*, IV, 353–5; *HNB*, 196–200; Marchesi, *La Cristologia*, 348–9.

18 *MP*, 34–5 (see especially notes 58 and 59 on Augustine and Aquinas respectively).

19 *MP*, 35–6. Balthasar does however note that the position of Thomasius is close enough to the intuitions of Hilary – and in general one might suppose that the rejection is of Hegel and a school of thought which leads from him, rather than of individual theologians as such. See also *TD*, IV, 201–4 for a discussion of the position of the nineteenth-century German Kenoticists and that of Hegel himself.

20 See D. M. Baillie, *God Was in Christ* (London, 1948), 94–8 for a critical account of British Kenotic Theology, also J. K. Mozley, *The Impassibility of*

God: A Survey of Christian Thought (Cambridge, 1966); MP, 36–7; TD, IV, 201–2.

21 MP, 37.

22 See also TD, III, 291–2, 300–1.

23 P. T. Forsyth, The Person and Place of Christ (London, 1909); MP, 40, note 74.

24 Christus Veritas (1924); MP, 40, note 75.

25 MP, 40; Maas, Unveränderlichkeit, 136–8.

26 MP, 77–80. The references are to Karl Barth, Church Dogmatics, IV, 1 (Edinburgh, 1956), 132–5, 180–3, 188f, 185–8, 193, 203. See also MP, 203, note 79 (Barth, op. cit, 186f), in which Barth states that we know who and what God is from what Jesus tells us and this must mean that divinity includes such elements as finitude, suffering and passivity. God's freedom enables him to do more and be other than our human concepts of the divinity would allow – HNB, 197–9; Maas, Unveränderlichkeit, 186, note 60.

27 HNB, 198; TL, III, 187–8.

28 MP, 9–11.

29 Ibid., 10.

30 See especially HNB, 197.

31 For confirmation again of Balthasar's views on the difference between the Christian God and the gods of mythology, with special reference to the cross and pagan myths of redeeming gods, see Hengel, Crucifixion, 5–7, 12, 14–21.

32 HRM, 15–19, 43–281 (especially 143); MP, 64, 193 with reference to Phil. 2, 5–11; SC, 13–50, 244–9; TD, I, 121–2; TD, II/1, 75, 175; TD, II/2, 353; TD, IV, 43–5; GF, 53, 60–4.

33 TD, II/1, 9, 41–2, 55; TD, II/2, 209, 464–7, 471, 483–5; TD, III, 49–50; TD, IV, 151–5.

34 TD, III, 206.

35 TD, II/2, 479, also ibid., 209.

36 TD, II/1, 9

37 KT, 21–2. See also Heinz, Der Gott, 94–108, 167–71, 247–58.

38 KT, 22, 213; TD, II/2, 235.

39 KT, 22.

40 TD, 25–33; Heinz, Der Gott, 106.

41 TG, 33.

42 TD, II/2, 207–9.

43 KT 22; See also Heinz, Der Gott, 106–9.

44 MP, 38. The Slain Lamb motif is the eternal aspect of the historic cross – accordingly it points to 'un état du Fils, qui est coextensif à toute la création, et par là affecte, de quelque manière, son être divin'.

45 TD, IV, 289, 466–73; TD, II/1, 377.

46 TD, IV, 469–72 (which explains as well how the incarnation can be seen both as a limitation and as an enrichment of God). See also Heinz, Der Gott, 96–101.

47 See *TD*, iv, 458, 470 (note 25) in particular for very clear statements of this claim.

48 See Marchesi, *La Cristologia*, 335–6 for a discussion of how the cross as revelation and as saving event is central to Balthasar's christology. See also Heinz, *Der Gott*, 101 for a comment on these two aspects of the cross. R. Brown, *The Community of the Beloved Disciple* (London, 1979), 119, 122–3 notes the primary emphasis in John on the cross as revelation of God.

49 See also *HNB*, 187–217; Jöhri, *Descensus*, 39–96; Marchesi, *La Cristologia*, 329–84.

50 See also W. Mass, *Gott und die Hölle, Studien zum Descensus Christi* (Einsiedeln, 1979). Also *Pneuma*, 387–400 (from the article 'Abstieg zur Hölle'); *TD*, iv, 273–88; *GF*, 278–85; and, in particular, *TL*, ii, 289–329.

51 *MP*, 47–80, especially 47–8, 53–4, 63, 68–71; also *ibid.*, 139–44 for a treatment of the method to be used in approaching Holy Saturday.

52 *MP*, 139–44; *HNB*, 213. An even more radical account of the death of Christ is given in *TL*, ii, 314–29, where the phrase 'solidarity with the dead', used in *MP*, is described as a 'compromise' (*TL*, ii, 315, note 1) and the indebtedness to von Speyr is explicitly acknowledged.

53 *MP*, 62, 133–5, 159–65; *HNB*, 192.

54 *MP*, 161–5 (especially 164–5 for a discussion of the distinction between NT hell and OT Hades/Sheol), 170; *HNB*, 212–16; *TD*, iii, 53–4. For the experience of definitive timelessness that is involved in the 'second death', see *MP*, 48, 74–5; *HNB*, 209, 214–15; *TD*, iv, 251–2, 280–3. For the notion of sin detached from sinners, see *MP*, 165–7; *HNB*, 216–17; Jöhri, *Descensus*, 88–9 (note 19); *TL*, ii, 317.

55 *MP*, 49, 63–4, 168–70; *HNB*, 213–14; see also *Pneuma*, 206–9.

56 *HNB*, 187–200, 217; *MP*, 62, 77–80, 197–8, 202–4, 249; *TD*, iv, 223–43, 298; Heinz, *Der Gott*, 194–9, 225–6, 249; Jöhri, *Descensus*, 42–5. For similar approaches see J. J. O'Donnell, *The Mystery of the Triune God* (London, 1988), chapter 2 and W. Kasper, *The God of Jesus Christ* (London, 1982), 187–97.

57 *MP*, 62, 77–8, 133, 137, 195–212 (especially 208–9); *HNB*, 196–7.

58 Jöhri, *Descensus*, 88.

59 *MP*, 48–54, 73, 77–8; *HNB*, 196–200; *CS*, 59–65.

60 *MP*, 51–2, 59–60. For Balthasar's criticism of Luther's theology on this score, see *TD*, ii/1, 268–9.

61 Heinz, *Der Gott*, 193. For some reservations concerning Balthasar's theology of Holy Saturday, see Marchesi, *La Cristologia*, 351–2.

62 *MP*, 52–3, 65–8, 116–19; Jöhri, *Descensus*, 144–5.

63 *MP*, 64–5, 171; Heinz, *Der Gott*, 235.

64 *MP*, 54–63, 88–9, 106.

65 *TD*, iv, 367. See also Heinz, *Der Gott*, 102, 194–9, 255.

66 *MP*, 57–63, 88–9.

67 *HNB*, 197–200.

68 *MP*, 98, 135; Jöhri, *Descensus*, 52; Heinz, *Der Gott*, 194–9.

69 *TD*, III, 253–62.

70 Paris, 1980; originally given at a conference in 1978.

71 *MP*, 104; *Au Coeur*, 10–14, 28; *Pneuma*, 403–4; *TD*, III, 211, 218, 220, 223–4, 236, 310.

72 *Au Coeur*, 12–13. These four concepts are taken from Aquinas; see *TD*, III, 241–5. For a slightly different list of five Biblical motifs – sacrifice, substitution, redemption, divinisation, God's love – see *TD*, III, 221–5, 295f.

73 *Ibid.*, 10–11. For Balthasar's discriminating acceptance of the original theological contribution by Luther to this issue, see *TD*, III, 263–9, 276. For a short, succinct presentation of Balthasar's position on the meaning of the *pro nobis* formula, see 'Crucifixus etiam pro nobis', *IKaZ*, 9 (1980), 26–35 ('Crucifixus'); also 'Der sich für mich dahingegeben hat/Gal. 2, 20', *Geist und Leben*, 53 (1980), 416–19 ('Der sich'); *TD*, II/2, 224–5; *Epilog*, 94ff; *HNB*, 191–3; *MP*, 102–6; *Pneuma*, 401–9; *Kennt uns Jesus*, 35–9; *TD*, III, 219, 327.

74 *Au Cœur*, 21–6. See also *HNB*, 187–221; *TD*, III, 315–27; *TD*, II/1, 135–52; *TD*, IV, 240–3; *MP*, 100–2; 'Crucifixus', 26–35.

75 See also *TD*, III, 229. For Balthasar's attempt, based on the theology of A. von Speyr, to overcome what he regards as Luther's purely formal interpretation of the *admirabile commercium*, see *TL*, II, 305–29.

76 Balthasar's concern is to bring the notions of solidarity and substitution together – see *TD*, III, 245–6. For one-sided treatments of solidarity, see *TD*, III, 247–62, and of substitution, *ibid.*, 263–91.

77 Paul and John are most explicit on this notion of substitution, but Balthasar maintains that it is a common NT teaching. See *TD*, II/2, 219–220 (especially 220 note 12), 224–5.

78 *Au Cœur*, 27–33; *MP*, 133–4.

79 See also *MP*, 114–16, 134–5; *HNB*, 195–6; *Pneuma*, 402.

80 For a discussion elsewhere in Balthasar of his disagreement with Rahner's soteriology, see *Cordula*, 63–5; *MP*, 133–7 (especially 134, note 105); *HNB*, 202 (note 14); *Kennt uns Jesus*, 35–9; and in particular *TD*, III, 252 (note 35), 253–62 for a sustained treatment of Rahner's soteriology. For Rahner's relationship to Anselm, see *TD*, III, 240–1, 248, 253–7.

81 *Au Cœur*, 33–40; *Kennt uns Jesus*, 35–9; *MP*, 69, 73, 95–106, 113–19, 133–7; *HNB*, 147–64, 187–217; *TD*, II/1, 135–42; *TD*, III, 56–60; *TD*, IV, 172–3; *HAB*, 150–60; *NK*, 144–57; and especially *Pneuma*, 401–9.

82 See also *HNB*, 189–90. Punishment would describe a situation in which 'strict' justice was being administered, whereas even in the OT it is clear that it is God's 'saving' justice that is involved, in which God's anger at sin is a real but subordinate element in his effective saving will. For Balthasar's further reflections on the notion of substitution without punishment, see *TD*, III, 263–76, 295–6, 310–11, 314–15; *TD*, IV, 251–2; 'Crucifixus', 33–5.

83 See *MP*, 90–2 for the sacrifial aspect of the Eucharist.

84 *Au Coeur*, 14. For a more sustained treatment of Anselm's position and Balthasar's correction of it, see *TD*, III, 235–41. See also *TD*, III, 458–61, 465; *TD*, II/2, 218–25; 'Crucifixus', 33; *HC*, 121–33; Jöhri, *Descensus*, 396–7 (note 25); de Schrijver, *Le Merveilleux Accord*, 220–1; G. O'Collins, *Interpreting Jesus* (London, 1983), 149–50; G. Greshake, 'Der Wandel der Erlösungvorstellungen in der Theologiegeshcichte', in *Erlösung und Emanzipation*, L. Scheffczyk, ed., *QD*, (Herder, 1973), 69–101; Glenn W. Olsen, 'Hans Urs von Balthasar and the Rehabilitation of St Anselm's Doctrine of the Atonement', *SJT*, 34 (1981), 49–61. See also *TD*, II/2, 220, note 13 for a list of contemporary critics and defenders of Anselm's position.

85 *TD*, III, 238–9, 465–6; *TD*, II/2, 221–2. For a similar trinitarian account of the incarnation, see *TL*, II, 270–2.

86 See *MP*, 112 for the effect of sin on God's heart; also *TD*, II/1, 371–2; see *H*, II/1, 356 which also refers to the wound of love in God's vulnerable heart.

87 *Pneuma*, 401–9. Also *TD*, III, 326–95. For the quite opposed position of Rahner on this question and Balthasar's reply, see *TD*, III, 257–60; 'Crucifixus', 32–5. For the interesting development of Balthasar's views on this theme as expressed in the theology of N. Hoffman, see E. Salmann, 'Urverbundenheit und Stellvertretung', *Münchner Theol. Zeit.*, 35 (1984), 17–31.

88 *HNB*, 192–3; *TL*, II, 204–13, 221, 274, 280.

89 *Pneuma*, 402.

90 *TD*, III, 11. This work was published in 1980 after the christological accounts of Balthasar's theology by Heinz, Marchesi and Jöhri (see Jöhri, *Descensus*, 364).

91 See *TD*, III, 15–63, especially 49–53.

92 See also *TD*, III, 236–7 for a discussion of Anselm.

93 *Ibid.*, 67–186.

94 *Ibid.*, 212–94.

95 *Ibid.*, 241–5.

96 *Ibid.*, 253–62, 298–9.

97 See also *ibid.*, 290–1 in his concluding remarks on R. Girard and R. Schwager; R. North, 'Violence and the Bible: The Girard Connection', *The Catholic Biblical Quarterly*, 47 (1985), 1–27.

98 See *M. Buber*, 117; *TL*, II, 257–60; *TD*, II/1, 253, note 18; 'Hoffnung', 96.

99 *TD*, III, 295–395, especially 295–327 for the relationship between soteriology and divine immutability. See also *TD*, III, 461–5 and *TL*, II, 294–8, 314–29.

100 For a fuller account of the relationship between the immanent and economic Trinity in Balthasar's theology, see Jöhri, *Descensus*, 271–84, 359–62. And for similar treatment of this topic see the report of the International Theological Commission on Theology, Christology, Anthropology, *ITQ*, 49 (1982), 289–90; *TD*, II/2, 464–6.

101 *TD*, III, 298–9. On the charge of formalising the immanent Trinity, see J. H. P. Wong, Karl Rahner's 'Christology of Symbol', *The Heythrop Journal*, 27 (1986), 1–25 (especially 12–19).

102 *TD*, III, 299–301, 273–4, 333; *TD*, IV, 148–55; 'Hoffnung', 96. See also J. McDade, 'The Trinity and the Paschal Mystery', *The Heythrop Journal*, 29 (1988), 175–91 and J. J. O'Donnell, *Trinity and Temporality* (Oxford, 1983), chapter 4.

103 *TD*, III, 301–5; 'Der sich', 419; *TD*, II/2, 208; Heinz, *Der Gott*, 195–6. See also *TD*, II/2, 219 and *TD*, II/1, 112, where theories which propose that God is unaffected by the suffering and sin of the world are rejected, and instead the basic biblical truth of the inner effect on God of worldly events is asserted.

104 See *TD*, III, 273–4, especially 274, note 41; *Epilog*, 31–2, 72f; *HC*, 371, 373.

105 *TD*, III, 306; *TD*, IV, 165.

106 *TD*, III, 315f.

107 *Ibid.*, 290.

108 *Ibid.*, 319–27, and especially 322–3 for Balthasar's references to K. Barth's similar, if not identical, understanding of Christ's representative role.

109 *Ibid.*, 320–1. The reference is to Abraham J. Heschel, *The Prophets* (New York/Evanstown, 1955). See also de Schrijver, *Le Merveilleux Accord*, 279–81; John C. Merkle, 'Heschels' Theology of Divine Pathos', *Louvain Studies*, 10 (1984), 151–65.

110 See also *TD*, III, 324–5.

111 See *ibid.*, 294 for A. Feuillet's formulation that in God 'quelque chose . . . correspond à la souffrance'.

112 There is no such definitive study and assessment of Balthasar's soteriology yet available. The existing secondary material which is related to this topic all predates Balthasar's own major soteriological study in *TD*, III. For useful pointers in the direction of such an assessment see Jöhri, *Descensus*, 392–406; O'Donnell, *The Mystery*, chapter 2; Salmann, 'Urverbundenheit', 28–31.

113 See John P. Galvin, 'The Death of Jesus in the Theology of Edward Schillebeeckx', *ITQ*, 50 (1983–4), 168–80.

114 For Rahner's own presentation of his soteriology, see K. Rahner, *Schriften zur Theologie*, 15 (Einsiedeln, 1983), 236–64 'Versöhnung und Stellvertretung', *Geist und Leben*, 56 (1983), 98–110, 'Vom Geheimnis menschlichen Schuld und gottlicher Vergebung', *Geist und Leben*, 55 (1982), 39–54.

115 See O'Collins, *Interpreting*, 152, 155; also the defence of Balthasar by Jöhri against a similar charge by L. Boff-Jöhri, *Descensus*, 394, note 9.

116 See R. Schwager, 'Der Sohn Gottes und die Weltsünde, zur Erlösungslehre von Hans Urs v. Balthasar', *ZfKT*, 108 (1986) 5–44 (especially 41–44).

117 See G. O'Hanlon, 'Devotion to the Heart of Christ: A Theological Reappraisal', *Milltown Studies*, 24 (1989), 46–63.

118 For a justification of a similar methodological procedure in his work on Balthasar's christology, see Heinz, *Der Gott*, 296–7.

119 See Salmann, 'Urverbundenheit', 17; Maas, *Unveränderlichkeit*, 16–19, 166–89.

120 Nonetheless we have already indicated that the main lines of Balthasar's soteriology are rooted in the tradition, while for an indication of the considerable contemporary support he receives see Salmann, 'Urverbundenheit' 17–31, and the references in O'Collins, *Interpreting*, 151 to the statement in 1980 on this topic by the International Theological commission (of which, of course, as O'Collins points out, Balthasar was a member). See also G. Daly, *Creation and Redemption* (Dublin, 1988), chapters 9 and 10 for an interesting discussion of this whole area.

121 For a presentation of this traditional approach in the context of the contemporary discussion concerning the immutability and impassibility of God, see H. McCabe, 'The Involvement of God', *New Blackfriars*, 66 (1985), 464–76 (especially 471–3).

122 See *MP*, 78–9; *TD*, III, 300, 310.

123 Heinz, *Der Gott*, 261–2. For Balthasar's own account of the Chalcedonian dogma and, in particular, its development in the centuries after Chalcedon, see *TD*, II/2, 191–202.

124 See *TD*, II/2, 141–5, especially 143–5. For this whole discussion see also *TD*, II/2, 197–210; *Kosmische*, 238–57 and *passim*; Heinz, *Der Gott*, 254–76.

125 See *TL*, II, 265–70.

126 See also H. Mühlen, 'Christologie im Horizont der Traditionellen Seinsfrage? Auf dem Wege zu einer Kreuzestheologie in Auseinandersetzung mit der altchristlichen Christologie', *Catholica*, 23 (1969), 205–239 (especially 218–19).

127 See *TD*, III, 300–5.

128 *Ibid.*, 260; *TD*, IV, 11. For Rahner's own account, see K. Rahner, *Die Gabe der Weihnacht* (Herder, 1980), 29–33, *Schriften zur Theologie*, 15 (Einsiedeln, 1983), 193, 210–13.

129 *TD*, II/2, 144–5, 207; *H*, I, 609–18; *H*, II/1, 295–303; *MP*, 10; *TD*, II/1, 234; *TL*, II, 119–38, 284–8; Mühlen, 'Christologie', *passim*, especially 225–7; O'Collins, *Interpreting*, 178–83; Heinz, *Der Gott*, 168, 254–76.

130 For a fuller account of the notion of '*Hinterlegung*' in Balthasar, what it means and how it functions, see *TD*, IV, 232f, 369, 469–70, 472–3; *TD*, II/2, 209; 'Du Krönst', 287–8; Heinz, *Der Gott*, 185, note 91, 197, 226, 257; Marchesi, *La Cristologia*, 346; R. Schwager, review of Kasper, *Der Gott Jesu Christi*, *ZfKT*, 105 (1983), 337–40 (in a review of W. Kasper, *Der Gott Jesu Christi*).

131 Heinz, *Der Gott*, 194–9; *TD*, II/2, 219–20.

132 *TD*, II/1, 64–5; *TD*, II/2, 144–5; *GF*, 210–12; *CS*, 59–65; *Kosmische*, 255–7; *TL*, II, 61–76.

133 *TD*, II/2, 189–90, 202–10. See also *TL*, II, 284–8; *Epilog*, 69f; *MP*, 32; O'Hanlon, *Metaphysics*, 96–138.

134 See *Epilog*, 77–8; *HC*, 268–9.

135 See *CS*, 56–65, especially 58–63. In general for the positive sense in which Jesus may be said anthropomorphically to express God, see *TL*, II, 61–76.

136 See Mühlen, 'Christologie', *passim*; Heinz, *Der Gott*, 263–7; *TD*, II/2, 198–200.

137 *CS*, 58–9.

138 This is so despite the many other considerations concerning this whole area, several of them philosophical, which Balthasar advances – see de Schrijver, *Le Merveilleux Accord* for an account of Balthasar's position on analogy, including a differentiation of his own stance from that of Karl Barth or Erick Przywara. For an account of Balthasar's understanding of the person/nature distinction with reference to the philosophical distinction between existence and essence, see Heinz, *Der Gott*, 260–1, 266–76; *TD*, II/2, 210; O'Hanlon, *Metaphysics*, 96–158.

139 *CS*, 61. *H*, I, 614–15 actually describes 'the Son's form of humiliation and obedience as an authentic expression of the divine nature', but still refrains from attributing obedience even analogously to this divine nature.

140 *CS*, 59–65; *H*, I, 605; *TD*, III, 420–1; *SC*, 95–7; p. 10 above.

141 *H*, II/1, 303–11.

142 See *H*, II/1, 267–361, especially 277–311, 353–61; *SC*, 97; *H*, I, 609–18, which has an extended treatment of the notion of expression, with references (610) to the earlier philosophical work *Wahrheit der Welt* (1947), recently reissued as the first volume of *Theologik* (1985); *TL*, II, 151–5.

143 Heinz, *Der Gott*, 267–76, especially 269; *SC*, 95; *H*, I, 612.

144 See *H*, I, 605–18, especially 610–13; *H*, II/1, 303; *TD*, II/2, 141–5, where Balthasar argues the interpersonal nature of the Trinity from the economic mission of Christ (also, *H*, II/1, 360–1); *CS*, 64–5.

145 Rahner denies this reality, according to Balthasar – see *TD*, III, 298–300; *TD*, II/2, 481 note 15. For Balthasar's affirmation of a real I/Thou within God, see also *SC*, 95–7; *Die Wahrheit*, 28–9; *H*, I, 609–15; *Pneuma*, 420–1.

146 *H*, II/1, 285, 355, 361; *CS*, 59–65; *TG*, 18–19.

147 *SC*, 97; *TD*, II/2, 143; *CS*, 51–3, 61–2; *H*, I, 324–8, 617–18; *H*, II/1, 295–303; *TD*, II/1, 289–305; *Présence*, 81f.

148 *CS*, 51–3, 59–65; *H*, II/1, 288–311, 358; *Kosmische*, 238–257 and *passim*; *TL*, II, 171–4; *Epilog*, 77–8; *HC*, 268–9.

149 *Kosmische*, 249.

2 Creation and God's immutability

1 *TD*, II/2, 483–4.

2 *TD*, IV, 79, 469; *TD*, II/2, 479.

3 *TD*, II/1, 175.

4 *TD*, III, 304; *TD*, II/1, 233, 236, 238.

5 See *TD*, IV, 200–1, where it is recognised however that the axiom of Aquinas may indeed, despite appearances, be understood in a correct way. For a nuanced and positive presentation of the position of Aquinas, see Thomas G. Weinandy, *Does God Change?* (Massachusetts, 1985), 71–100.

6 *TD*, II/2, 479.

7 See p. 47 above, also *MP*, 9–11, 24–40, 198f, 249; *GF*, 71; *H*, II/1, 288–311; *TD*, II/2, 463–6; *TD*, IV, 53–7; also O'Donnell, *The Mystery*, chapter 10.

8 *TD*, III, 308. See also *H*, II/1, 295–6 for Bonaventure's departure from Augustine on this issue.

9 *TD*, II/1, 237–8, 242–5; *TD*, IV, 87–122.

10 *TD*, II/1, 126–7, 183–5, 220–3, 237, 363–4; *TD*, II/2, 264, 463–89; *TD*, III, 135; *TD*, IV, 53, 464, 483–6; *Pneuma*, 26–37; *SC*, 30; *SV*, 361–4; M. Buber, 111–17; *HRM*, 788–927; *Kosmische*, 110–14; De Schrijver, *Le Merveilleux Accord*, 71, note 47.

11 *TD*, II/1, 237. In *Kosmische*, 121 Balthasar speaks in the same sense of a 'hiatus' between the divine idea to create and the actual existence in itself of created reality.

12 *TD*, III, 305–6; *TD*, II/1, 246; *TD*, IV, 165; *HW*, 193–5.

13 *TD*, III, 305–8; also *MP*, 9–11.

14 A kenosis of this kind in God is rejected by Balthasar – see *TD*, II/1, 238–42.

15 See *TD*, II/1, 170–6; P. Knauer, 'Die Chalkedonische Christologie als Kriterium für jedes christliche Glaubensvertständis', *Theologie und Philosophie*, 60 (1985), 1–15 (especially 4).

16 See *Kosmische*, 111; Knauer, 'Die Chalkedonische', 1; *TD*, I, 512–53 for an overview of some of the principal contributions of Western thinkers to this whole question. See also *Pneuma*, 31.

17 *TD*, I, 15–22, 31–2; *TD*, II/1, 173–5, 207–8, 260–5; *SC*, 22–3, 26–50; *SV*, 367–9; *HRM*, 354–66; *Cordula*, 40, 40–8; *GF*, 78–9; Knauer, 'Die Chalkedonische', 1–5; see also H. McCabe, 'The Involvement of God', *New Blackfriars*, 66 (1985), 464–76; de Schrijver, *Le Merveilleux Accord*, 58–60.

18 For Balthasar's treatment of the fourfold difference between God and creatures, which ultimately finds its basis in the real distinction between existence and essence by which we are composed in contrast to the identity between existence and essence in God, who simply is, see *HRM*, 354–66, 943–63; *TD*, I, 456–8; *TD*, II/1, 38, 216–19, 263–4, 366; *TD*, II/2, 419–424; *VC²*, 27; *SC*, 13–20; O'Hanlon, *Metaphysics*, *passim*.

19 See Knauer, 'Die Chalkedonische', 1–15 for a very interesting development of this notion along lines which are remarkably consistent with Balthasar's approach.

20 For a fuller treatment in Balthasar of the theme of God's transcendence and immanence, see *TD*, I, 235–6; *TD*, II/1, 157–8; *TD*, II/2, 362–3, 483–6; *TD*, III, 347–8.

21 *TD*, IV, 464–5; *TD*, II/1, 173–6, 236–8, 262; *TD*, I, 512–24; *SC*, 13–50 (especially 20–42), 330–1, 342–3; *Pneuma*, 26–37, 321–3, 410–31; *HRM*, 943–67.

22 See especially *TD*, II/1, 232–59, in particular 232–5; also *GF*, 68–72; *Pneuma*, 31–4, 416–31; *SC*, 39–42, 330–1; *TL*, II, 165–70, 178–9; *TD*, IV, 71–4; *Epilog*, 23f; *HC*, 19–22; and W. Löser, 'Das Sein, ausgelegt als Liebe', *IkaZ*, 4 (1975), 417–24; Knauer, 'Die Chalkedonische', 9–10.

23 For a presentation of the relationship in Balthasar between humankind and God from the thematic viewpoint of the analogy of Being, see de Schrijver, *Le Merveilleux Accord, passim*; also *SC*, 36–7.

24 *TD*, II/1, 236, 242–6; *TD*, II/2, 481–3; *H*, II/1, 295–307; *Kosmische*, 112–17, 126–8.

25 See Knauer, 'Die Chalkedonische', 5–15, also *H*, I, 609–18, 679; *TD*, III, 354–5; *Kosmische*, 121, 129–30; *GF*, 204–17; *SV*, 22–3; *H*, II/1, 290–307; *TD*, II/2, 260–2; *TD*, IV, 48, 464; *KT*, 31–2; *Prayer*, 61–2; *CS*, 319–27.

26 *TD*, II/1, 232–3, 238f; *TD*, II/2, 474–5.

27 *TD*, II/1, 233–5; *TD*, IV, 465–6; *SC*, 39–40.

28 *TD*, II/1, 238–42; *TD*, IV, 463–6; *Pneuma*, 30–1; Knauer, 'Die Chalkedonische', 2–5, 12.

29 See Knauer, 'Die Chalkedonische', 4, 8, also *Pneuma*, 418–19; *TD*, II/1, 173–4.

30 For Balthasar's presentation of Bonaventure's argument on this issue, see *H*, II/1, 299–300; *H*, I, 506–7. See also *TD*, IV, 57; *TL*, 40.

31 *TL*, I, 301–10; *H*, I, 609–18; see also his 'Gottes Allmacht', *IKaZ*, 13 (1984), 195–6 ('Allmacht').

32 *TD*, IV, 92–5, 464–5; *TD*, II/1, 237, 260–5; *H*, I, 506–7; *TL*, I, 301–10; *H*, II/2, 503–4; *SC*, 41.

33 See *TD*, I, 521f; *TD*, II/1, 230–5; *Kosmische*, 112–16, 121; *HAB*, 138; *TD*, II/2, 479–83; *TD*, III, 306; *TD*, IV, 465; *CS*, 318–29.

34 *TD*, II/1, 246–59, especially 251–5, which is part of a more sustained treatment of the drama between infinite and finite freedom (*ibid.*,170–305). See also *TL*, II, 134–6.

35 See *TD*, II/1, 255, note 20, where Balthasar gives qualified approval to the rejection by Mühlen and Maas of a divine immutability understood within the horizon of Greek metaphysics, but refuses to accept that because of this one might correctly speak of God's mutability. He also asserts in this note that we cannot retreat behind what is said about the divine immutability towards the end of *The Republic*, Book 2 (see chapters

19 to the end): here Plato states, *inter alia*, that God can change neither for the better nor for the worse, so that it is impossible even for a God to wish to alter himself (*Republic*, chapters 19, 21). Balthasar refers to K. Rahner, *Schriften*, IV, 137–55 for a fuller treatment of the whole issue of divine immutability – see *TD*, II/1, 253, note 18; *TL*, II, 259–60.

36 See *TD*, II/1, 246, 265–75; *TD*, III, 240–5, 253–7.

37 *TD*, II/1, 252–3, 264–9, 271–2; *SC*, 20–42. For the quite different position of Kant, see *HRM*, 836–8.

38 See also *HAB*, 175–7 for the analogously representative role, involving prayer of petition, within the covenant relationship between God and Israel of such OT figures as Abraham and especially Moses. See also *HNB*, 436–7.

39 See *TD*, III, 245, 253–7 (including note 24), 272; *H*, II/2, 865–7; and *TD*, II/1 274–5, where Balthasar speaks of 'der Realismus einer "einwirkung" der endlichen auf die unendliche Freiheit'.

40 *TD*, II/1, 273: 'ist es immer Gott, der zu Gott fleht, auch mit der endlichen Freiheit zusammen'.

41 See *HNB*, 174–86 (especially 185–6), 288–90, 436–7; *AC*, 333–6; *HW*, 202–4; *TD*, II/2, 482–3; *TD*, IV, 157, 380, 455–63 (especially 458–9); *K*, 198–9; *NK*, 164; 'Du Krönst', 71–2; de Schrijver, *Le Merveilleux Accord*, 71–2, 310–11.

42 For what follows see *TD*, II/1, 170–305 (especially 170–6), 230–6, 245–6, 483–9; *TD*, II/1, 64–5; *TD*, III, 295–6, 305–6, 347–8; *TD*, IV, 87, 445–6; *HAB*, 138–47; *GF*, 200–17, 223, 233; *CS*, 319–27; *Pneuma*, 417–18, 426–43; *H*, II/2, 831.

43 For a treatment of this development in Balthasar, see Peelman, *Hans Urs von Balthasar et la théologie de l'histoire* (Bern/Frankfurt, 1978), 411–13; M. Kehl and W. Löser, 'Situation de la théologie systématique en Allemagne', *Revue de Théologie et Philosophie*, 113 (1981), 25–38 (30–2); M. Lochbrunner, *Analogia*, *passim*; and especially de Schrijver, *Le Merveilleux Accord*, 43–4, 47–8, 57–60 and *passim*. For the similarities and differences between Balthasar and Barth on this point, see de Schrijver, 70–1, 141–84, 288–96.

44 *GF*, 212.

45 'Du Krönst', 199.

46 *GF*, 204.

47 See Heinz, *Der Gott*, 258–9.

48 *SC*, 142; *TL*, I, 207.

49 See *TD*, II/1, 171, note 2; *TG*, 58–9.

50 *TG*, 33.

51 Peelman, *Théologie de l'histoire*, 484. See also O'Donnell, *The Mystery*, chapter 10.

52 See *Kosmische*, 176–7, 187, 300 for the tendency in Greek Patristic thought, with the exception in some respects of Irenaeus, to downgrade the value of human history.

53 Peelman, *Théologie de l'histoire*, 538–55; de Schrijver, *Le Merveilleux*

Accord, 337–8; Jöhri, *Descensus*, 385–9, 395–6, 403–6; and especially Balthasar's contribution to this theme in *TD*, IV, 133–54, 447–50, published in 1983 after the remarks of his critics.

54 For Balthasar's thought on this whole area, see *TD* (especially 130–40) and *GF* (especially 103–77). For Balthasar's own stance vis-à-vis Liberation and Political Theology in particular, and the role of the Church in the world, see *TD*, III, 399–413, 444–53; *TD*, I, 23–46; *TD*, II/1, 56–69; *TD*, IV, 122–67; *Engagement with God* (London, 1975), *passim*; 'Heilsgeschichtliche Überlegungen zur Befreiungstheologie', in K. Lehmann (ed.), *Theologie der Befreiung* (Einsiedeln, 1977), 155–71. For my criticism of Balthasar's position as it is outlined in his theology of hope, see G. O'Hanlon, 'May Christians Hope for a Better World?', *ITQ*, 54 (1988), 175–89. See also O'Hanlon, 'von Balthasar and Ecclesial States of Life', *Milltown Studies*, 22 (1988), 111–17.

55 See *TD*, III, 347–8. If one allows for the enormous difference, however, Balthasar is prepared to concede an analogy between the relationship of freedom involving God and us and that involving a merely human I/Thou. See *Pneuma*, 417–18.

56 It should be noted that this volume of *TD* contains many quotations from and much agreement with the theology of Adrienne von Speyr, the medical doctor and woman of prayer whom Balthasar directed for so many years (see *TD*, IV, 11). There are several accounts of von Speyr's influence on Balthasar – see Balthasar, *Erster Blick auf Adrienne von Speyr* (Einsiedeln, 1968); *In Retrospect*, 204, 208, 218–19; *Il filo*, 58–60; Jöhri, *Descensus*, 191–7; Peelman, *Théologie de l'histoire*, 82–3; de Schrijver, *Le Merveilleux Accord*, 38–46, 311–33; Marchesi, *La Cristologia*, 339–40; Heinz, *Der Gott*, 61–2; M. Kehl in his Introduction to *In der Fülle des Glaubens*, ed. M. Kehl and W. Löser (Freiburg, 1980), 49–52. However cautiously one might approach the assessment of that influence in all its particularity it is certainly true that in a general sense it is compatible with Balthasar's own understanding of the relationship between theology and prayer; see *MP*, 40–6; *VC*², 49–86; de Schrijver, *Le Merveilleux Accord*, 29–48, 52–322 and *passim*; Heinz, *Der Gott* 57–66. And clearly also the positions which he adopts in his theology, whatever their inspiration, must satisfy the normal criteria of theological truth and be innerly consistent.

57 See *TD*, IV, 173, 463–4; *TD*, II/1, 247.

58 *TD*, IV, 17, 47–9, 171, 174–82, 189–91, 463–4; 'Hoffnung', 88.

59 *TD*, IV, 171–3. One notes of course the distinction between proposing apocatastasis as a thesis and as an object of hope; see also *Encyclopaedia of Theology, A Concise Sacramentum Mundi*, ed K. Rahner (London, 1975), the articles by Rahner on Eschatology and Hell.

60 *TD*, IV, 87, 463.

61 *TD*, IV, 122–222. For the discussion with Moltmann in particular, see *ibid*., 148–54 and 'Zu einer christlichen Theologie der Hoffnung', *Münchner Theol. Zeit.*, 32 (1981), 81–101 ('Hoffnung').

62 *TD*, IV, 148–55; 'Hoffnung', 86–95.

63 In what precedes and follows we are outlining positions which Balthasar either rejects or accepts: the exact provenance of these positions is of secondary importance. Balthasar is well aware that Moltmann's own position is nuanced – see *TD*, IV, 152–3; 'Hoffnung', 96–8.

64 For a description of the difference between Moltmann and Balthasar on this issue, see *TD*, IV, 148–50; 'Hoffnung', 82–95. For a further presentation of Balthasar's own position, see also *TD*, IV, 14–46, 155–67; *K*, 192–9; *GF*, 103–77, especially 136–40; P. Escobar, 'Das Universale Concretum Jesu Christi und die "Eschatologische Reduktion" bei Hans Urs von Balthasar', *ZfKT*, 100 (1978), 560–95 (especially 591–5). For a critique of Balthasar's position see O'Hanlon, 'May Christians Hope?'

65 'Hoffnung', 99.

66 For the reality of something like prayer within God, see *H*, II/2, 870–1; *H*, I, 616–18; *TD*, IV, 83–6; Olsen, 'Hans Urs von Balthasar', 58–61. For the reality of something like faith in God, see *TD*, IV, 83–6, 160; *La Foi du Christ* (Paris, 1968); 'Die Einheit der theologischen Tugenden', *IKaZ*, 4 (1984), 306–14. ('Einheit').

67 'Hoffnung', 98–100; *TD*, IV, 153, 459–61; *HC*, 333.

68 For a discussion of how this differs from Moltmann's 'certain hope' on the basis of the cross, which Balthasar criticises on the grounds that its inherent tendency is towards a triumphalistic denial of hell, see 'Hoffnung', 91–5; *TD*, IV, 134–5, 151–2, 126–7.

69 For what follows, see *TD*, IV, 154, 160–7. For a more detailed account of the theological significance of Péguy, see *H*, II/2, 769–880, and especially 858–73 for the notion of hope in the heart of God.

70 See Einheit, 307–14.

71 See pp. 42–6 above for an earlier, related consideration of this theme. For what follows *re* the theology of God's pain, see *TD*, IV, 191–222.

72 *TD*, IV, 191–2.

73 *TD*, IV, 196–9. See also *Kosmische*, 182, note 4; *Présence*, 45–7; Maas, *Unveränderlichkeit*, 42–53.

74 *TD*, IV, 202–4, 221, 446, 465; 'Hoffnung', 96–8; *TL*, II, 42–5, 292–4; *Pneuma*, 421; *Epilog*, 77–8; *HC*, 268–9. For other interpretations of Hegel's views see Maas, *Unveränderlichkeit*, 178–83.

75 *TD*, IV, 211–13.'

76 *TD*, IV, 211–16, 194, note 9, 197, 202, 205, 207.

77 *TD*, IV, 216–18; Maritain argues against the position of Aquinas on this issue. See 'Quelques réflexions sur le savoir théologique', *Revue Thomiste*, 77 (1969), 5–27.

78 Maritain calls the divine suffering metaphorical; see Maritain, 'Quelques réflexions', 16–23.

79 *TD*, IV, 218, 371–3; *TD*, II/12; *TL*, II, 60–4, 137–8; see also Weinandy, *Does God change?*, 174–86.

80 See *TD*, IV, 218–19; Maritain, 'Quelques réflexions', especially 10–24, also *TD*, IV, 240–2 for a somewhat similar treatment under the heading of *Das Reservat der Finsternis* and drawn from Adrienne von Speyr. See also J. Macquarrie, *The Humility of God* (London, 1978), 59–71 and J. Ratzinger, *Behold The Pierced One* (San Francisco, 1986), 56–60.

81 *TD*, IV, 219.

82 *Ibid.*, 219–20.

83 For what follows see *TD*, IV, 221–2, 226–8; 'Hoffnung', 99–102.

84 See *TD*, IV, 221–2.

85 For what follows see especially *TD*, IV, 223–93 (and in particular *ibid.*, 243–93), 14–49, 171–91, 220–1, 341–3, 447–55, 463–6; *HNB*, 211–17; *Pneuma*, 410–55; *VC²*, 147–75; *GF*, 207–8; P. Escobar, 'Das Universale', *passim*; our sections in chapter 1 above on the cross and soteriology (pp. 25–42). For an early treatment by Balthasar of the eschatological question, in dialogue with the position of German Idealism, see *Apokalypse der deutschen Seele*, I (1937), II and III (1939) (*Apokalypse*).

86 *Pneuma*, 443–4; *TD*, III, 326.

87 *TD*, IV, 266.

88 *TD*, IV, 272–3. For what follows see *ibid.*, 171–3, 220–2, 232–60, 273–88, 441–2, 459–61, 465–76; *Pneuma*, 443–4; *H*, II/2, 862–3; 'Allmacht', 196–8; *TD*, III, 300–9; *TL*, II, 294–8, 314–29, *HNB*, 216; *MP*, 74–7, 165–7; Jöhri, *Descensus*, 88–9, note 19; de Schrijver, *Le Merveilleux Accord*, 326–30.

89 *TD*, IV, 270, 273–7.

90 *TD*, IV, 47, 245, 291–3, 341–3, 447–55, 464; *VC²*, 160–5; *Pneuma*, 436–7, 443–4; *TD*, III, 18; *HC*, 314–15; Jöhri, *Descensus*, 258–71; Escobar, 'Das Universale', 561–2, 573.

91 *TD*, IV, 291–2; see also *Thérèse*, *passim*; *VC²*, 163–5.

92 Balthasar is prepared to use the phrase the 'certainty of hope' only if it is clearly rooted in God's mercy; see *TD*, IV, 154–5, 272–3, note 13; *Einheit*, 307.

93 See *Encyclopaedia of Theology* article by K. Rahner on *Eschatology*, p. 437: 'It must be made clear in theology and preaching that in basic principle what is said about heaven and what is said about hell are not on the same plane. The Church eschatologically proclaims as a *fact* already realised in Jesus and the saints that saving history (in its totality) ends victoriously as the triumph of the grace of God. It only proclaims as a serious *possibility* that the freedom of each individual may operate to his eternal ruin.' And see *VC²*, 163–5 (especially 165 note 2 for the same approach in Balthasar).

94 *TD*, IV, 476. And, for what follows, see *ibid.*, 432–64, especially 463–76 (the final pages of *TD*, IV), 218–22, 228–32; *HRM*, 604–5; *HNB*, 389–404; *HC*, 135; *Einfaltungen*, 124–7; Heinz, *Der Gott*, 106.

95 *TD*, IV, 222. For God's joy see also *Die Wahrheit*, 131–2.

96 *GF*, 105; *TD*, IV, 245.

97 *TD*, IV, 68, note 50, 452–3; *SC*, 36–9; *TL*, II, 61–113, 137–8; *Pneuma*, 321; de Schrijver, *Le Merveilleux Accord*, 255–9.

98 See Knauer, 'Die Chalkedonische', 7, 12–15; *TG*, 100–4.

99 See *TL*, II, 306, note 5 and complete discussion in *ibid.*, 298–329.

100 For what follows see *TD*, IV, 447–64; *GF*, 105.

101 *TD*, IV, 11–12.

102 For what follows see *Einheit*, 306–14; 'Allmacht', 193–200; *TD*, IV, 84–6; *TL*, III, 26; *HAB*, 207–8; *K*, 52; *H*, II/1, 353–61; *Der Christ und die Angst* (Einsiedeln, 1951), 89; *Engagement with God*, 49–53.

103 *TD*, IV, 226–32, which offers an illuminating account of the difference between creaturely death as end and that death in God which has to do with the giving up of life.

104 *NK*, 144–57 (an essay entitled 'Fragment über Leiden und Heil'); *GF*, 275–85; *Pneuma*, 154–5; *TL*, II, 321, notes 57, 61; Jöhri, *Descensus*, 148–52, 358.

105 *Pneuma*, 328–30; *SC*, 103–5, 111–13; *GF*, 212–13; Jöhri, *Descensus*, 276; Maas, *Die Hölle*, 248–51.

106 *Triple Couronne*, (Paris, 1978), translated from *Der dreifache Kranz* (Einsiedeln, 1977), 35–6.

107 *TD*, IV, 57–8; *TL*, II, 119–38; O'Hanlon, 'H. U. von Balthasar and De Deo Uno – New Tract?', *Milltown Studies*, 5 (1980), 115–30.

108 See 'Allmacht', 194; *TL*, II, 134–8; Maritain, 'Quelques réflexions', 11–12.

109 It has been usual, of course, to associate receptivity with deficiency and need, thus traditionally ruling out its attribution to God; see H. McCabe, 'The Involvement', 469–71.

110 See *Einheit*, 306–14; *H*, II/2, 858–73.

111 *TD*, IV, 243. All economic attributes are modalities of immanent ones and ultimately of the central divine attribute of love; see *TL*, II, 128–38.

112 'Allmacht', 195–200; *NK*, 153–7.

113 *H*, II/2, 870–1.

114 *TD*, IV, 240–3.

115 For what follows see Knauer, 'Die Chalkedonische', 1–5; de Schrijver, *Le Merveilleux Accord*, 255–9; Maritain, 'Quelques réflexions', 8–14; Aquinas, *Summa Theologica*, Prima Pars, B.A.C. ed. (Salamanca, 1955), q. 13; *TL*, II, 80–113; *H*, I, 244–6; *H*, II/2, 871–3; *Kosmische*, 83.

116 *MP*, 40–6; *TD*, II/1, 48, 55; *VC*², 49–86; *H*, II/1, 297–8; *H*, II/2, 871–3; *SC*, 36–9; *Pneuma*, 321; de Schrijver, *Le Merveilleux Accord*, *passim*, especially 47–72, 255–9, 266–71, 278–81, 322–9; Heinz, *Der Gott*, 53–62; Jöhri, *Descensus*, 179–97, 407–19; Marchesi, *La Cristologia*, 56–76, 348–51; *Encyclopaedia of Theology*, 569–75; O'Hanlon, *Metaphysics*, 135–40.

117 For an account of one such traditional way of speaking about God, see Aquinas, *Summa Theologica*, qq 1, 9; 3, 1, ad 1; 3, 2, ad 2; 4, 2; 4, 3, 6; 9; 13; 19, 7, ad 1; 20; 21, 3; 24, 1. See also *TL*, II, 68–73, 284–8.

118 *SC*, 36–9; *Pneuma*, 321; *VC*², 49–86 (especially 82–6).

119 *TD*, IV, 221; *H*, II/2, 858–73; *H*, II/1, 353–61; *NK*, 153–4.

120 See Aquinas, *Summa Theologica*, especially q 13. For the hermeneutical principles of Philo with regard to Scripture – so influential in early Christian circles – see Maas, *Unveränderlichkeit*, 116–18. And for those of the Fathers of the Church, see *ibid.*, 125–62.

121 *TL*, II, 225, 245–50; see also *ibid.*, 69–73; *TD*, II/2, 130–5.

122 Maritain, 'Quelques réflexions', 15–16; see also *Encyclopaedia of Theology*, 557–60.

123 *TD*, III, 320; *GF*, 275–8; *HAB*, 207–8; 'Hoffnung', 99 (as applied to hope in God); *Epilog*, 78; *HC*, 265–7. This goes beyond the position of Jöhri, *Descensus*, 393–8, who speaks of the very realistic and anthropomorphic way (394) in which Balthasar describes the sufferings of the cross.

124 For what follows see *TD*, IV, 218–22, 240–3, 466–7, 471–6; *TD*, III, 299–327; also *GF*, 210–13, 275–85; *H*, I, 614–16; 'Hoffnung', 99–100; 'Allmacht', 195–200; *H*, II/2, 861–2; *HAB*, 207–8; *NK*, 153–7.

125 See 'Der sich', 419.

126 See also 'Allmacht', 193–4.

127 For what follows see *TD*, IV, 221–2, 236–43, 458–9, 472–6; *TD*, III, 175–6, 183–6, 302, 337–42; *GF*, 275–7; *Die Wahrheit*, 131–46; 'Hoffnung', 98–102; *NK*, 144–57; Maritain, 'Quelques réflexions', 221–2; Baillie, *God was in Christ* (London, 1948), 198–9; de Schrijver, *Le Merveilleux Accord*, 322–9.

128 *H*, II/2, 858f; *H*, II/1, 181–7; 'Allmacht', 195–6; *Einheit*, 314; *HRM*, *passim*; Maritain, 'Quelques réflexions', 8, 11–13, 15, 24–6; Marchesi, *La Cristologia*, 344–53. For a thematic consideration of the notion of symbolic consciousness in a way which is *ad rem* in assessing Balthasar's approach, see B.J.F. Lonergan, *De Verbo Incarnato* (Rome, 1961), 484–6, also Lonergan, *Method in Theology* (New York, 1972), 57–99 (especially 64–9, 81–5), 120–4, 302–20, 338–53; Lonergan, *Insight* (London, 1958), 314–47, 526–47.

129 See Aquinas, *Summa Theologica*, Prima pars, q 2, 1; Aquinas, *In Librum Boetii de Trinitate Exposito*, (Fribourg, 1948), 1, 2; *HRM*, 354–5; *TL*, II, 91–8; O'Hanlon, *Metaphysics*, 137–8.

130 *TD*, III, 310, 400–1, note 3; *TD*, IV, 427–8; 'Hoffnung', 99.

131 Aquinas, *Summa Theologica*, Prima Pars, q 4, 2; q 6; q 13, 1, ad 2; 20; 25, 1.

132 See Maas, *Unveränderlichkeit*, 171–2, with a reference to Barth, *Kirchliche Dogmatik*, II/1, 55–7.

3 Time, eternity and God's immutability

1 See *TL*, I, 219–20; *TD*, III, 88–96.

2 For what follows see *GF*, in particular 1–42, on Augustine's notion of time, drawn largely from his autobiographical account in the *Confessions*. For a helpful treatment of Augustine's own account of time in

Book 11 of the *Confessions*, see J. McEvoy, 'St Augustine's Account of Time and Wittgenstein's Criticisms', *Review of Metaphysics*, 37 (1984), 549–77.

3 *TL*, I, 216–21; *GF*, 20–3; *TD*, II/1, 231–5; *Présence*, 1–2; *Kosmische*, 132–4.

4 *GF*, 5–9, 22, 27–31; *TD*, IV, 10; *TG*, 33–5.

5 See *TD*, I, 237–8, also McEvoy, 'St Augustine's Account', 574–6 for his conclusions about the disputed position of Augustine on this issue.

6 *GF*, 19–25, 29, 54–6, 62–3, 75, 143–4; *TG*, 29–30, 58–9; *TD*, I, 26–7; *H*, I, 643–7; *K*, 56; *KT*, 22; *TD*, IV, 27–8, 43–5.

7 *GF*, 14–15, 23–25, 39–40, 63, 105–6. See also *TD*, IV, 80–3, 361–2; *TG*, 119–20.

8 *GF*, 33–6, 63–5, 169–70, 239–74; *TD*, IV, 24–5, 43–5, 110–11; *TG*, 28–45, 69–70, 82–3, 119; *MP*, 86–8; *Au Cœur*, 17–20; *HNB*, 150–61. See also Heinz, *Der Gott*, 176–80 and P. Escobar, 'Das Universale', 576.

9 *GF*, 15–16, 24–6, 33–5; *TD*, IV, 88–102.

10 *TG*, 24–5; *TD*, II/2, 145; *TD*, IV, 81, 102–13, 223–6; *HNB*, 150–61; *HC1*, 38–51; also Marchesi, *La Cristologia*, 236–45; Peelman, *Théologie de l'histoire*, 332–92; McCabe, 'The Involvement', 473.

11 *TG*, 29. See also *ibid.*, 24–5; *TD*, IV, 80–3, 104–9, 223–6; Marchesi, *La Cristologia*, 236–46.

12 For what follows see *TD*, II/2, 141–5; *TD*, IV, 24–6, 48–9, 57–9, 66–70, 79–84, 88–90, 109–13, 367, 467–71; *TG*, III, 300–5.

13 *TD*, IV, 26, 57–60, 63; *TD*, III, 302–5; *GF*, 243–9; *VC*[1], 51; *HC*, 38–51; *K*, 121–2; *CS*, 149–57; see also W. Hill, 'The Historicity of God', *TS*, 45 (1984), 320–33 (330–1).

14 *TD*, IV, 25–6, 47–9, 58, 67–70, 79–84 (especially 81, note 2), 349, 467–71; *TL*, I, 219–24; *TD*, II/2, 144–5; *TD*, III, 301–3; *HAB*, 380; *La Foi*, 218–19; 'Hoffnung', 96.

15 See especially *TD*, II/2, 143–5 with particular reference to E. Jüngel, H. Schlier and B. Welte, also *TD*, IV, 24, 66–70; *TL*, I, 216–33.

16 *TD*, IV, 21, note 7, 24–5, 48–9, 72, 80–3, 88–90, 101–4, 109–10, 225, 365, 367; *TD*, III, 91; *TD*, II/1, 254; *GF*, 63; *Présence*, 144–9; *Einfaltungen*, 114.

17 See *TD*, IV, 80–1; *TG*, 83; *TG*, 83; *K*, 56; Escobar, 'Das Universale', 576–7. Balthasar does ascribe a form of duration which is exclusive, a negation of time, and in this sense a *nunc stans*, to the eternity of hell; see *TD*, IV, 277–86; *TD*, III, 313; *HNB*, 158–9; *H*, II/2, 812; *MP*, 74; *TL*, I, 223–4; *TL*, II, 314–20. The eternity of heaven – which is our created participation in God's eternity – must somehow also include the transformed *semper fluens* of time; see *TD*, IV, 96–103, 279, 341–3, 442; *GF*, 9–12, 15, 26, 31–2, 75; *MP*, 185–6.

18 *TD*, IV, 380, 456. See also McEvoy, 'St Augustine's Account', 554; L. Scheffczyk, 'Prozeßtheismus und christlicher Gottesglaube', *Münchner Theol. Zeit.*, 35 (1984), 81–104, especially 96–8. For an account of this

position in the context of a discussion with O. Cullman on the issue, see J. Marsh, *The Fullness of Time* (London, 1952), 174–81 and H. Küng, *Justification* (trans., London, 1964), 273–5.

19 *GF*, 34–5; *TD*, IV, 80–3, 88–9, 109–10, 380, 470, note 25; *TD*, III, 26.

20 *TD*, IV, 24–5, 68, 81–2, 109–13; *TD*, III, 30, 304; *TD*, II/I, 233; *TL*, I, 223–4; *HC*, 292.

21 *TD*, III, 301–4; *GF*, 25; *TD*, IV, 227.

22 See *TD*, IV, 280–3, 361; *GF*, 6–8, 21, 61, 110; *TL*, I, 219–22, 226–7, 231–2, 276–8; *HAB*, 289–91; *Présence*, 144–9; *TD*, III, 27–8, 91–2.

23 *Présence*, 144–9. It is worth noting that in the historical discussion concerning the notion of eternal life Balthasar prefers the position of Gregory to that of either Origen or Maximus. Gregory advances a paradoxical synthesis of repose and movement in his notion of eternal life; Origen and Maximus in different ways opt for a more static notion. See *Présence*, 123–32; *Parole*, 113–16; *Kosmiche*, 132–6, 346–55; *TD*, IV, 67, note 16, 362–5, 373–5, 460; *H*, II/I, 192; *TD*, II/I, 212–16, 233–5.

24 See *Présence*, 144–9; *GF*, 110–11, 146–7; *MP*, 122–3.

25 *TD*, IV, 112–13, 343–7, 359–60, 367; *TL*, I, 223–4; *TD*, III, 46–7; *CS*, 151–2. For a different image see N. Frye's distinction between a sequential and unified reading of a literary text in J. McDade, *The Trinity*, 179–81.

26 *TD*, IV, 363–5, 380, 456, 459; *Pneuma*, 433; *GF*, 248.

27 McEvoy, 'St Augustine's Account', 554.

28 For an example see Marsh, *The Fullness of Time*, 29f, 139–54, 174–81; Küng, *Justification*, 272–88, especially 272–5; D. Baillie, *God Was In Christ*, 190–7; E. Jüngel, *The Doctrine of the Trinity: God's Being is in Becoming* (trans., Edinburgh and London, 1976), 17, 70, 75–6, 95–7, 100; W. Hill, 'The Historicity of God', 320–33; W. Maas, *Unveränderlichkeit*, 30–2; J. Thompson, 'The Humanity of God in the Theology of Karl Barth', *SJT*, 29 (1976), 249–69.

29 *TD*, IV, 53, 278–9; Küng, *Justification*, 274–5; Hill, 'The Historicity of God', 327–31; T. J. Kondoleon, 'The Immutability of God: Some Recent Challenges', *The New Scholasticism*, 58 (1984), 293–315, especially 301–2.

30 For what follows see especially *GF*, 239–74; *HNB*, 150–62; *TD*, IV, 80–3, 109–13; *HC*, 38–51; *TG*, 68–9; *HAB*, 381.

31 See also *TD*, IV, 24, 80–1, 105, 367.

32 *GF*, 239–74; *TG*, 66–7, 88–9; Peelman, *Théologie de l'histoire*, 348–59; Escobar, 'Das Universale', 577.

33 *GF*, 249–67. See *ibid.*, 257, where in the course of a meditative argument the childlikeness of the Son is seen ultimately as 'the reflection of the eternal newness of the whole trinitarian life: of the eternally young, potent richness of the Father and the "youngest one" in God, the Spirit'. See also Hans Urs von Balthasar, 'Die Jugendlichkeit Jesu', *IKaZ*, 12 (1983), 301–5; *HC*, 165–74.

34 This would apply to created time both as natural and as graced, albeit in a differentiated way: *gratia non destruit, elevat, perficit naturam.* See *TD,* IV, 366–7, 278; *VC¹,* 92.

35 *TD,* IV, 80–2, 88–90, 109–10, 467–8.

36 *TD,* III, 72, 75–80, 88–124; *VC¹,* 91–2; *TL,* I, 221–4, 275–8; *TD,* I, 26–7; *GF,* 15–16; and, against Origen, *Parole,* 13–16.

37 *TD,* IV, 377–8, 464.

38 For what follows see especially *TD,* IV, 48–9, 80–3, 88–122, 153, 278–86, 341–88, 458, 463–76; *TG,* 25–45; *TL,* I, 268f; *TD,* III, 300–5; *GF,* 24–6, 34–5, 63–5; *KT,* 22; *K. Barth,* 274–7, 282–4. For the related discussion concerning the mutual ordering to one another of heaven and earth, see *TD,* IV, 96f, 343–52, 377–88; *TD,* II/1, 155–69; *TD,* II/2, 239–50; *TD,* III, 15–63.

39 See *TD,* IV, 227–8, where it is made clear that in calling time a shadow of eternity Balthasar does not mean to deny the reality of time but rather to stress its derivative and secondary nature. See also *GF,* 29.

40 See *La Foi,* 216–21; *TD,* IV, 475.

41 See *TD,* III, 39, 301–5; *Parole,* 106–7; *TD,* IV, 132, 344, 459; *Présence,* 145.

42 *GF,* 64.

43 *TD,* IV, 24, 88–90, 109–13, 343–4, 377, 467–8; *TG, passim; CS,* 145–54; *HC,* 38–51.

44 *TD,* IV, 25, 42, 102–13, 223–6; *GF,* 36–7; *TG,* 42; *HAB,* 380.

45 *TL,* 221–6; *VC¹,* 91; *HRM,* 540; *TD,* III, 96–124; *Warum,* 19–23.

46 *TD,* IV, 100. See also *GF,* 18–19, 22, 26–42; *TD,* III, 103; *TD,* IV, 100–1, 309f.

47 For what follows see especially *TG,* 79–107; *GF,* 245–73, 285–302; *TD,* IV, 341–88, also Peelmann, *Théologie de l'histoire,* 310–15; Escobar, 'Das Universale', 577. The special place given to the resurrection accounts in this discussion is already a feature of Barth's approach – see J. Thompson, 'The Humanity of God', 258–9.

48 *TG,* 83.

49 *HAB,* 380–1; *Parole,* 106–7, 113–16; *TD,* IV, 132, 341–88, 438–9; *TD,* III, 313, 338–9, 364–6; *Pneuma,* 221; *GF,* 285–302, 319.

50 See especially *GF,* 245–73.

51 *GF,* 33, 297–8; *HRM,* 473–6; *TG,* 84–5; *TD,* III, 28–40, 123, 366; *TD,* IV, 231, 358–60, 377–88, 456–63.

52 *TG,* 90–7; *TD,* IV, 109–11, 116, 223–6, 348–50, 438–44, 466–7; *GF,* 298–9; *TD,* III, 338–9; *Parole,* 106–7; *TD,* II/1, 66.

53 'Warum', 27–29, 37–42; *GF,* 33; *TG,* 20, 49–75; *TD,* III, 41–3; *TD,* IV, 462–3; Escobar, 'Das Universale', 565.

54 'Warum', 38–42; *TD,* IV, 227–8, 352–60, 380; and for similar terminology in Barth, see Thompson, 'The Humanity of God', 260 (this article also has a very helpful account of the more general discussion of the relationship between time and eternity).

55 *TD,* IV, 470, note 25. One must distinguish carefully here: while it is true

that one may speak of eternity being temporalised in the life of Christ (see Escobar, 'Das Universale', 575–6), nonetheless this is to be taken in a sense analogous to the differentiation within unity of the Hypostatic Union, whereby, in this instance, the very real insertion of eternity into time does not, mysteriously, entail the cessation of the eternal form of being.

56 *TD*, IV, 345, 455–63, 467–70; *TD*, III, 121–3.

57 *TD*, IV, 21–3, 80–3, 112–13, 341–2; see also Escobar, 'Das Universale', 589.

58 See Peelman, *Théologie de l'histoire*, 538–55; de Schrijver, *Le Merveilleux Accord*, 337–8; Jöhri, *Descensus*, 385–9, 395–6, 403–6. W. Hill, 'The Historicity of God', 331–2 attributes such a 'jettisoning' of a concern for history to Barth and the neo-orthodox movement in general. J. Thompson, in 'The Humanity of God', 264, defends Barth against this charge.

59 For a very succinct statement of the traditional Christian position on how the omniscience of God is not (*pace* A. Kenny) to be conceived of as God's foreknowledge, see G. Barden, 'An Incoherent God?' *Doctrine and Life*, 34 (1985), 541–2; see also chapter 5 above for a fuller discussion of this topic.

60 *TG*, 32, 52.

61 For the notion of a 'theological note' (rather like a grade on a certainty scale) see B. J. F. Lonergan, *The Way to Nicea* (London, 1976), trans. Conn O'Donnovan, p. xxv (translator's introduction). See also *New Catholic Encyclopaedia*, x (Washington, D.C., 1967), 523–4, E. J. Fortman on Notes, theological.

62 *TD*, IV, 153–4, note 50, 365.

63 For a detailed elucidation of this distinction see B. J. F. Lonergan, *Insight* (London, 1958), especially chapters 10 and 11, also Lonergan, 'Cognitional Structure', *Continuum*, 2 (1964), 530–42, reprinted in Lonergan, *Collection* (London, 1967).

64 For this interplay between incomplete understanding and yet real truth, see Escobar, 'Das Universale', 578; with reference to Augustine, McEvoy, 'St Augustine's Account', 576–7; and with reference to Barth, Thompson, 'The Humanity of God', 264.

65 See the Dogmatic Constitution '*Dei Filius*' of the First Vatican Council, chapter 4, *De fide et ratione*, in *Enchiridion Symbolorum*, ed. Henricus Denzinger and Adolfus Schönmetzer, 32nd ed. (Freiburg, 1963), 590–2 (nos. 3015–3020, especially 3016).

66 See P. McShane, 'The Hypothesis of Intelligible Emanations in God', *TS*, 23 (1962), 545–68.

67 For Balthasar's recognition of the general failure of European theology to dialogue sufficiently with the natural sciences, see *TL*, III, 387–8.

68 See G. Hanratty, 'The Early Gnostics', *ITQ*, 51 (1985), 208–24, who reports that the third-century system of Mani claimed to dissolve the mysteries of time and eternity 221.

4 Is the trinitarian God immutable?

1 For what follows see *H*, I, 609–12; *TL*, II, 117–55; *TD*, II/1, 170–5, 253–5; *TD*, II/2, 141–5, 207–8, 463–89; *TD*, III, 303–4; *CS*, 146–8.

2 See *Enchiridion Symbolorum*, ed. Henricus Denzinger and Adolfus Schönmetzer (Freiburg, 1963), nos. 125 (Nicea), 150 (Constantinople), 75 ('Quicumque' creed), 800 (Fourth Lateran) and 1330 (Florence).

3 *TD*, II/2, 480–1. Balthasar refers to the psychological analogy of Augustine and Aquinas in all its forms, the social analogy of Richard of St Victor in all its forms, or any combination of these two basic forms.

4 *TD*, II/2, 483–6; *TD*, IV, 230–1, 267, 275, 286, 392, 442–4, 450–1; *H*, I, 609–16; *MP*, 32, 38–9, *CS*, 147–8; *SC*, 132; *Einheit*, 309.

5 For a trenchant criticism of the isolated role of the teaching on the Trinity in the history of Christian theology, see K. Rahner, *The Trinity* (London, 1970), 9–15.

6 See the discussion in Theodore J. Kondoleon, The Immutability of God, 296–9.

7 See *Wahrheit*, I: *Wahrheit der Welt* (Einsiedeln, 1947), which appeared as the first volume of *Theologik* (1985), 16–19, 32–3, 79–141, 221–4 and *passim* (page references are to the 1985 ed.). For a further account of Balthasar's philosophising in this area, see Kleiner Lageplan, 215–16; *HRM*, *passim*; *TD*, II/1, 11, 17–19; and O'Hanlon, *Metaphysics*, *passim*.

8 *TD*, I, 24–46, especially 23–6.

9 *H*, I, 123–48; *HRM*, 958f; *SC*, 13–50, 264–79; *VC*[1] 57–86, 87–119; *VC*[2], 49–86; K. Barth, 263–82; *MP*, 54–63; *TD*, II/1, 172–3; *TL*, I, vii–xxii; *TL*, II, 88–90, 107, 159, 179–80; *Romano Guardini* (Munich, 1970), 100–1; 'Evangelium und Philosophie', *Freiburger Zeitschrift für Philosophie und Theologie*, 23 (1976), 3–12; 'Thomas von Aquin im kirchlichen Denken von heute', *Gloria die*, 8 (1953), 65–76; O'Hanlon, *Metaphysics*, 169–86.

10 *TD*, III, 184–5; *TD*, IV, 84–6, 367, 471; *TL*, II, 78; *HC*, 308; 'Allmacht', 193–5.

11 *TD*, III, 49–53, 300–1, 308; *TD*, II/1, 243; *TD*, II/2, 463–76, 480–3; *TD*, IV, 24–5; *H*, I, 616–17; *CS*, 147–9.

12 For what follows see especially *TD*, II/1, 231–55; *TD*, III, 300–10; *TD*, IV, 57–8, 65–6, 84–6, 463–76; *TL*, II, 117–55; *MP*, 9–11, 26–40; *CS*, 145–54, 379–80; *Epilog*, 69f; 'Hoffnung', 99–101.

13 *SC*, 95–7, 131–2; *CS*, 59–65; *Pneuma*, 223–7; *TD*, IV, 56–7, 435. See also note 23 below.

14 *TD*, II/2, 476–9, 468, 167–75; *TD*, III, 301; *TD*, IV, 300–1; *TL*, II, 130–1; *Pneuma*, 223–7; *TL*, III, 145f, 208–9; *TD*, II/1, 231–2.

15 *TD*, II/1, 231–5, 251–5; *Présence*, 125–7, 131–2; *TL*, I, 219–28, 253–4; *TL*, II, 117–64; *TD*, IV, 84–6, 470–1; *Einheit*, 313–14; *SC*, 132, 151–5; *Pneuma*, 225–7.

16 *TD*, II/2, 476–9, 167–75; *CS*, 151–2; *Pneuma*, 223–7; *TL*, III, 28f, 166f; Jöhri, *Descensus*, 275–8, 363–5.

17 *TD*, II/1, 234–5; *TD*, II/2, 485–6; *TD*, IV, 450–1; *Pneuma*, 224–5.

18 *TD*, III, 49–53; *TD*, II/2, 464–86; *SC*, 95–100.

19 *TD*, II/2, 466–9; *H*, I, 609–12; *TD*, IV, 65–6, 71–3, 57–8, 90; *TL*, II, 119–27; *Einheit*, 309; *HC*, 314–15.

20 *TD*, III, 49–53.

21 *TD*, II/2, 466–9; *H*, I, 609–12. For the monism of Eckhart, with its neo-Platonic background, see *TD*, IV, 398–415, especially 405–6.

22 *TL*, II, 124–8. For Balthasar's criticisms of Rahner in this regard see *TD*, III, 298–300; *TD*, II/2, 481, note 15.

23 *TD*, II/2, 480–2; *TD*, IV, 71; *TL*, II, 35–9; 72, 119–25, 148–9, 163–4, 298. Indeed in *TL*, II, 54–7, 79, 149–51, 154, note 37, Balthasar argues that the human analogate of parents–child is a better instance of Richard's trinitarian inter-subjective analogy in being able to show the inner faithfullness of divine love as well as its differentiated unity.

24 *TL*, II, 40–57, 117–28, 162–3; *Pneuma*, 31–4; *TD*, IV, 71–4.

25 *TL*, II, 39; *TD*, II/2, 464–7, 481–4; *SC*, 95–7; *Pneuma*, 420–1; *TD*, IV, 65–6, 71–2, 83–4, 442–5. Allowing for differences in terminological usage it would still seem that the position of Balthasar on the divine consciousness and subjectivity is closer to that of Lonergan than to that of Rahner. Lonergan defends the thesis that the one divine consciousness is shared by 'three subjects' in different ways, whereas Rahner denies the existence of three 'active subjects' – see J. Wong, 'Karl Rahner's Christology of Symbol', *The Heythrop Journal*, 27 (1986), 1–25 (especially 12, 9–19).

26 *TD*, IV, 445–6, 77–80; *Pneuma*, 327–30; *SC*, 95–7; *TL*, II, 54–7.

27 *TD*, II/2, 483–4, 167–76; *TD*, IV, 77–9, 83–4, 232–40, 297–9; *CS*, 149–51.

28 *CS*, 150–2.

29 For what follows see *TD*, IV, 148–54, 71–4, 83–6, 106–7, 202–43, 281–3, 297–301, 455, 463, 472–3; *TL*, II, 40, 76–9, 130–1, 213–14, 294–98, 314–29; *HNB*, 229–31; *TD*, II/1, 174–5, 234–46; *TD*, II/2, 469; *TD*, III, 300–10; *MP*, 26–40, 77–80; *CS*, 318–27, 345–54; Jöhri, *Descensus*, 395.

30 *TD*, IV, 80–3, 345, 458–9; *TD*, II/1, 233, 237–42; *TD*, II/2, 206–10; *TD*, III, 21–5; *TL*, II, 77–8; *HNB*, 229–31.

31 *TD*, IV, 82–3, 232–40; *CS*, 63–4.

32 *Pneuma*, 226–7.

33 *TD*, IV, 466–7. See also *ibid.*, 221–2 for a statement of the very real earnestness of this aspect of inner-trinitarian love.

34 *MP*, 32.

35 *TL*, II, 36–8, 163–4.

36 Balthasar cautions that this supra-suffering in particular needs to be distinguished carefully before it may be seen as part of God's positive receptivity – *TD*, IV, 191–2.

37 *TD*, IV, 472–3, 82–6, 106–7; *TD*, II/1, 242–3.

38 For what follows see especially 'Hoffnung', 99–101; *TD*, II/1, 231–43; *TD*, IV, 74–86, 106–7, 221–2; *H*, II/1, 348–9; *Pneuma*, 327–31.
39 For what follows see especially *TD*, II/1, 231–43; *TD*, IV, 74–86; *TL*, II, 77–9, 321, note 57.
40 *Wahrheit* (TL, I). For what follows see especially *TL*, I, 36–57, 80–107, 113–28, 139, 239, 259. Once again activity and passivity, in the relationship between subject and object, are likened to what occurs in the man/woman relationship – *TL*, I, 46–57, 80–107.
41 *HC*, 138–40; 'Du Krönst', 199.
42 'Hoffnung', 100: *Weizenkorn*, 57.
43 *TD*, IV, 58–9.
44 *TD*, IV, 90.
45 For what follows see *TD*, IV, 67, note 46, 361–76, 442, 460–1; *TD*, II/1, 212/16, 233–5, 249; *Présence*, 123–32; *Kosmische*, 121–6, 132–8; *Parole*, 113–16; *SC*, 95–7; see also W. Löser, *Origenes*, 100–18; K. Barth, *Church Dogmatics* (trans., Edinburgh, 1958), IV/2, 338–46.
46 *Kosmische*, 138.
47 *HNB*, 389–404, especially 396–9.
48 *H*, II/1, 349–53.
49 For what follows see *TD*, IV, 57–71, 239–40; *TD*, II/1, 231–6; *H*, I, 244–6; *TL*, II, 159–70; *Apocalypse*, III, 436–8; 'Allmacht', 195; Heinz, *Der Gott*, 267–76; Löser, 'Trinitätstheologie heute', 39–44 (especially 39–40).
50 See W. Löser, 'Das Sein', 410–24.
51 For what follows see especially *TD*, IV, 57–86, 361–76; also *TD*, II/1, 231–59; *TL*, II, 40–57, 63–4, 159–70; Heinz, *Der Gott*, 267–76, 289–92.
52 *TL*, I, 112, 221–6, 235–55, *TL*, II, 40–57, 63–4.
53 *TD*, II/1, 233.
54 *TD*, IV, 66–9, 80–6, 463–7; *Einheit*, 311–14; *SC*, 151–5; *Prayer*, 20, 151; *TL*, I, 233–55, 290–312; *VC*[1], 13, 20, 51.
55 Faith is used analogously to refer to something like a trust that accompanies inter-personal exchange; it does not refer to any intellectual deficiency in God. See *Einheit*, *passim*; *La Foi*, 13–79.
56 *TD*, IV, 445; *TL*, II, 27–57, 159–80; *TL*, I, 80–107, 113–28, 143–4, 152–5, 214, 233–55, 297–312; *TL*, III, 208–9, 408.
57 *TD*, IV, 26; *MP*, 203–8; *TD*, II/2, 141–5; *TL*, II, 96–8, *H*, I, 611–12, 615–18; *TD*, II/1, 115–16; *TL*, II, 96–8.
58 See also Heinz, *Der Gott*, *passim*, for this whole point.
59 *CS*, 59–65; *SC*, 151–5; *Pneuma*, 222–6, 327–30; *TD*, IV, 66–9; *TL*, II, 143; *TL*, III, *passim*, especially 145f; Heinz, *Der Gott*, 290–1.
60 *SC*, 132.
61 *Pneuma*, 222–6; *Weihnacht*, 13–14.
62 *TD*, IV, 63.
63 *TD*, IV, 234.

64 *TL*, II, 131–55; *TD*, IV, 77; *HNB*, 397–9; *TL*, I, xxii, 14–15, 31–2, 107–13, 143–4, 253–5.

65 *TD*, IV, 67, 365.

66 In what follows we concentrate mainly on the immutability of God, although the application to the divine impassibility is clear from the preceding context. For a thematic treatment of divine impassibility see especially pp. 69–73, 81–7 above.

67 See especially *MP*, 9–11, 26–40; *TD*, II/1, 252–9; *TD*, II/2, 141–5, 479; *TD*, III, 256–7; *TD*, IV, 62–7, 191–222, 467–76; *TL*, II, 133–6, 257–64, 321–9. See also Marchesi, *La Cristologia*, 345–53; Heinz, *Der Gott*, 13–14, 96–101, 222–30, 254–9; Jöhri, *Descensus*, 361–5, 342–3, 384.

68 For a good summary account, see *TD*, IV, 467–71.

69 Contemporary representations of the traditional approach would include McCabe, 'The Involvement'; Kondoleon, 'The Immutability of God'; B. Davies, *Thinking about God* (London, 1985), especially 148–72; E. L. Mascall, *Whatever Happened to the Human Mind?* (London, 1980), chapter 4; and Weinandy, *Does God Change?*, passim.

70 *TD*, II/1, 255, note 20; also Maas, *Unveränderlichkeit*, 42–53.

71 See W. J. Hill, 'The Historicity of God', 320–33, 331–2, also Kondoleon, 'The Immutability of God', 312–15; McCabe, 'The Involvement', 470.

72 See *M. Buber*, 117; *TD*, III, 253–62, especially 256–7; *TD*, II/1, 253, note 18; 'Hoffnung', 96; *TL*, II, 257–60; *TL*, III, 38.

73 See K. Rahner, *Schriften*, (Einsiedeln, 1954), 202; *IV* (Einsiedeln, 1960), 137–55 (especially 147–9); IX (Einsiedeln, 1970), 231; *Sacramentum Mundi*, 2 (1968), 951. See also H. Küng, *Justification*, 286–8; E. L. Mascall, *Whatever Happened?*, 76–8; Maas, *Unveränderlichkeit*, 187–8; Weinandy, *Does God Change?*, 163–74.

74 Löser, 'Trinitätstheologie heute', 24–31, 44. Even allowing for the difference between their two positions it would seem that in suspecting the 'neo-Chalcedonian' school of monophysitism Rahner does not in fact catch the distinctiveness of Balthasar's position. Balthasar does not attribute created mutability or suffering to the divine nature but rather attributes a supra-mutability, analogous to change in us, to the trinitarian God.

75 Maas, *Unveränderlichkeit*, 187; K. Rahner, *Die Gabe der Weihnacht* (Herder, 1980, 32, *Schriften*, xv (Einsiedeln, 1983), 190–3; H. Küng, *Justification*, 287; Weinandy, *Does God Change?*, 163–74; Mascall, *Whatever Happened?*, chapter 3.

76 Balthasar is of course at one with Rahner in allowing that the person of the Logos, and thus God, is affected by the incarnation and death of Christ, and that this is mysterious. It is his understanding of the mutuality of the relationship between nature and person, and of the analogy between the divine and human natures, that leads him to go beyond Rahner to posit a supra-mutability in God's own being – see pp. 42–6 above, and *TD*, II/2, 202–10.

77 *TD*, IV, 218–22, especially 219.

78 For a more detailed account of Balthasar's nuanced reception of traditional versions of the Western metaphysics of Being, and his rejection of the more modern metaphysics of Spirit intended to replace it, see O'Hanlon, *Metaphysics*, 42–158; Löser, 'Trinitätstheologie heute', 39–44.

79 *TD*, IV, 64–5; K. Hemmerle, *Thesen zu einer trinitarischen Ontologie* (Einsiedeln, 1976), 38.

80 *HRM*, 958–83.

81 *TD*, II/1, 243: 'es nicht angeht, das sogennante "theo-ontologische" Denken der Philosophie einfach durch ein "personologisches" zu ersetzen, das heißt, das Sein in reine Relation aufzulösen'; and *TD*, II/1, 287: 'auch das Personale ist ontisch: und nach der Aussage Plotins (die unreduzierbar bleibt) ist Gott, was er sein will, und er will sein, was er ist'. See also *TD*, IV, 64–5; *TL*, III, 136–139; Löser, 'Trinitätstheologie heute', 39–40; Hemmerle, *Thesen*, 46–8; W. Kasper, *The God of Jesus Christ* (trans., London, 1982, 308–13.

82 See pp. 81–3 above; also J. McDade, 'The Trinity', for a similar distinction between a narrative and an ontological approach in theology, and the reference to Frye's distinction between a 'sequential' and a 'unified' sense in reading a literary text.

83 *TD*, II/1, 254–5; Jöhri, *Descensus*, 364–5.

84 *Epilog*, 77–8; *HC*, 268–9; Jöhri, *Descensus*, 394, note 9.

85 *TL*, II, 321, note 57.

86 For a full account of Balthasar's notion of theological discourse the primary source would be his own *Theologik*. Much of the material for such an account is contained in de Schrijver, *Le Merveilleux Accord*, *passim*.

87 For Balthasar's distinction between correct and incorrect anthropomorphic speech about God, see pp. 44–5, 81–5 above; also *HAB*, 207–8; *HNB*, 187–90; *H*, I, 314–16; *Kosmische*, 115; *TD*, II/1, 172–3, 240, 267; *TD*, II/2, 481; *TD*, IV, 200, 380, 469.

88 See p. 10 above; also *TL*, II, 61–7, 129; *TD*, IV, 447–55.

89 *TL*, II, 254–6, 286.

90 *TL*, II, 330–2; *TL*, I, vii–xxii, 107–13, 143–255; *GF*, 210–11; *TD*, III, 54–5; *TD*, IV, 65–6, 77.

91 *TL*, II, 42–5, 136–7, 216, 292–3; *TD*, III, 427–8; *MP*, 59–60.

92 *TL*, II, 42–5, 292–3, 298, 310; *TL*, III, 144f. Balthasar does also use the term dialectic in the specifically theological sense of sin as a contradiction of God's word to us: once again this is a dialectic which is overcome by Christ's cross in a way which does not threaten God's freedom. See *TL*, II, 289–329; *TD*, IV, 451.

93 *TL*, II, 298–305; *MP*, 244–7; *TD*, II/1, 254–5.

94 *Pneuma*, 33–4.

95 *TL*, II, 222–5, 289–332 (especially 314–29); *MP*, 40–80; *TD*, IV, 273–88; *CS*, 60–2; Marchesi, *La Cristologia*, 329–84; Jöhri, *Descensus*, 36–96.

96 For Balthasar's reservations concerning what he judges to be Luther's excessively formal interpretation of the 'sub contrario', which then issues logically in a philosophical dialectic of the Hegelian type, see *TL*, II, 305–14; *TD*, III, 263–9, 299; *MP*, 47–63, 136; *TD*, IV, 451–3; *Die Wahrheit*, 32–41; Jöhri, *Descensus*, 408–22.

97 *MP*, 51, 136; *TD*, IV, 238.

98 *TD*, III, 297; *HNB*, 245–95 (especially 247–9); *Die Wahrheit*, 32–41; *TL*, II, 330–2; *TD*, IV, 447–55; *MP*, 194.

99 *MP*, 77–80; *TL*, II, 27–57, 139–43; *TD*, IV, 452–5.

100 *TL*, II, 298–332, 61–7, 159–64; *GF*, 210–11; *Kosmische*, 57–66, 74–84; *Die Wahrheit*, 32–41; Jöhri, *Descensus*, 408–22. It should be noted that Balthasar distances himself from E. Przywara's notion of analogy because he judges that Przywara so emphasises the aspect of 'greater dissimilarity' that it is difficult to see how there remains the possibility of speaking positively about God. See *TL*, II, 87–8, note 16; *TD*, II/2, 202, note 1; de Schrijver, *Le Merveilleux Accord*, 255–88.

101 For what follows see *TL*, II, 80–113, 251–5, 294–8; *H*, I, 314–16; *MP*, 77–80; *HNB*, 189–90. See also S. Tugwell, 'Spirituality and Negative Theology', *New Blackfriars*, 68 (1987), 257–63.

102 See Mühlen, 'Christologie', 230–2; Maas, *Unveränderlichkeit*, 180–1; Hill, 'The Historicity of God', 328–9.

103 For what follows see *TL*, II, 27–57, 110–11, 225–7, 284–8, 321–2, 330–2; *TD*, IV, 57; *TD*, II/2, 130–5. For the plurality of viewpoints within the NT itself see in particular *TD*, II/2, 130–5.

104 For what follows see *TL*, II, 225–55 (especially 245–50); *HNB*, 247–9; *MP*, 244–7; *TD*, IV, 447–55, 372–3; *TD*, III, 427–33; *TD*, II/2, 130–5, 471; *VC²*, 64–5; Heinz, *Der Gott*, 51–62; Marchesi, *La Cristologia*, 346–7, 351–2; de Schrijver, *Le Merveilleux Accord*, 47–72. See also D. Burrell, *Aquinas, God and Action* (London, 1979), chapters 2 and 4; R. Haughton, *The Passionate God* (London, 1981), 14 and *passim*.

105 *TL*, I, 152–5.

106 *TL*, II, 248, note 3. See also *ibid.*, 284–8 and *TD*, II/2, 131, note 1.

107 *TL*, I, xxii.

108 *TL*, II, 68–75, 225, 245–50, 284–8; *TD*, II/2, 130–5. For the sense in which all human language is metaphorical, see *TL*, II, 247–9, where the position of E. Jüngel is presented very briefly.

109 For Balthasar's differentiated stance towards the presuppositions and findings of exegetes, in particular with reference to the historical–critical method, see *H*, I, *passim*, *TD*, III, 427–33; 'Exegese und Dogmatik', *IKaZ*, 5 (1976), 385–92; Heinz, *Der Gott*, 57–66, 209–11; Marchesi, *La Cristologia*, 383; Jöhri, *Descensus*, 71, 335, 352–4; Maas, *Die Hölle*,

254–6. With Barth he calls for a constant critical dialogue between historical analysis and theological understanding. In this context the limited contribution of exegetes is made within a framework which takes account of the wider horizon of theology, including the experience of the saints as well as Church teaching. Only in this framework of explicit faith may the whole of revelation be contemplated, and not be reduced by a scientific method whose rationalistic presuppositions preclude the realm of mystery.

110 *TL*, ii, 249–50, 253–7, 331–2; *H*, i, 870–1; *TD*, iii, 427–33; *TD*, ii/2, 130–5.

111 *VC²*, 83–6.

112 See Jöhri, *Descensus*, 421–2; de Schrijver, *Le Merveilleux Accord*, 326–7. It should be noted that these criticisms were made prior to the publication of *TL*, ii in 1985 and of *TL*, iii in 1987.

113 *MP*, 77, 194; *TL*, ii, 94, 255; *Pneuma*, 33–4; *HNB*, 198; *Kosmische*, 81.

114 *MP*, 244–7.

115 *TD*, iv, 424. Here, with reference to Ruusbroeck's speech about God in such terms, Balthasar notes: 'Man sollte hier nicht voreilig von Anthropomorphismen sprechen; es geht um die unvermeidbaren Auffassungsweisen der innergöttlichen Lebendigkeit, wie wir sie zu Beginn dieses Buches geschildert haben.' For a pertinent illustration of the language of von Speyr in this respect see *TD*, iv, 66–9, 467–76.

116 *TD*, iv, 272, in which Balthasar refers to the position of Aquinas in *Summa Theologica*, i, 12, 7, ad 3: 'sicut aliquia probabiliter scire potest aliquam propositionem esse demonstrabilem, licet ipse eam demonstrative non cognoscat'.

117 See the remark by D. M. Baillie, *God Was In Christ* (London, 1948), 65: 'It is a commonplace to say that most of the great heresies arose from an undue desire for simplification, and undue impatience with mystery and paradox, and an endeavour after a common-sense theology.'

5 Balthasar and other approaches

1 See O'Donnell, *Trinity*; also his *The Mystery*, (especially chapter 10); and his 'The Trinity as Divine Community', *Gregorianum*, 69. 1 (1988), 5–34; Weinandy, *Does God Change?*; D. Burrell, *Aquinas*, (especially chapter 6); E.L. Mascall, *Whatever Happened?*, (chapter 3); W. Norris Clarke, *The Philosophical Approach to God* (North Carolina, 1979); J.J. Mueller, 'Process Theology and the Catholic Theological Community', *TS*, 47 (1986), 412–27.

2 Brian Davies, *Thinking about God*. See especially chapters 5, 6, 7, 10 and 11.

3 *Ibid.*, 148.

4. *Ibid.*, 304.

5 See Kondoleon, 'The Immutability of God', 296–301; McCabe, 'The Involvement', *passim*; Weinandy, *Does God Change?*, 67–100; Michael J. Dodds, 'St Thomas Aquinas and the Motion of the Motionless God', *New Blackfriars*, 68 (1987), 233–42.

6 For what follows see Dodds, 'St Thomas Aquinas', 238–41. Norris Clarke, *The Philosophical Approach*, chapter 3 is even closer to Balthasar's overall position, while also lacking the required trinitarian dimension.

7 See A. Kenny, *The God of the Philosophers* (Oxford, 1979), 'Divine Foreknowledge and Human Freedom', in *Aquinas*, ed. A. Kenny (London, 1969), 255–70.

8 See W.E. Mann, 'Simplicity and Immutability in God', in *The Concept of God*, ed. Thomas V. Morris (Oxford, 1987), 253–67.

9 See Kenny, 'Divine Foreknowledge', 261.

10 See Kenny, *The God of the Philosophers*, chapter 4, especially 39 ff. See also D. H. Mellor, *Real Time* (Cambridge, 1981), 47–57; J. L. Kvanvig, *The Possibility of an All-Knowing God* (London, 1986), 152–3.

11 See W. Hasker, 'Yes, God has Beliefs!', *Religious Studies*, 24 (1988), 385–94 for a similar conclusion that to know temporal matters directly God must himself be temporal.

12 Kenny, 'Divine Foreknowledge', 264.

13 Kenny, *The God of the Philosophers*, 81–2.

14 See G. Barden, 'An Incoherent God?', *Doctrine and Life*, 39 (1985), 541–2.

15 See B. Davies, *Thinking About God*, 165ff.

16 See E. Stump and N. Kretzmann, 'Eternity', in *The Concept of God*, 219–52.

17 *Ibid.*, 228.

18 *Ibid.*, 230–32 for these details.

19 *Ibid.*, 235.

20 *Ibid.*, 237.

21 See N. Kretzmann, 'Omniscience and Immutability', *Journal of Philosophy*, 63 (1966), 409–21, referred to in Kenny, *The God of the Philosophers*, 38–48 and in Davies, *Thinking About God*, 182–8.

22 See Davies, *Thinking About God*, 182–9, where Davies in fact is agreeing with some of the difficulties expressed by Kretzmann in his 1966 article (see note 21 above).

23 See Kenny, *The God of the Philosophers*, 58–9 and p. 157 above. This is very different from Geach's understanding, referred to by Kenny, of the relationship between God and us in terms of God as Supreme Grand Master engaged in a game of chess with us.

24 See P. T. Geach, *Providence and Evil* (Cambridge, 1977) (the Stanton Lectures of 1971–2; see especially chapter 3, 'Omniscience and the Future'); see also his 'The Future', *New Blackfriars*, 54 (1973), 208–18. Kenny agrees with Geach that eternity does not mean timelessness, but

otherwise rejects Geach's position – see Kenny, *The God of the Philosophers*, 53–9. Kvanvig, *The Possibility*, challenges Geach's view that knowledge of the future is knowledge about merely the present tendencies of things – see 5–13 for an outline and critique of Geach's position. For a revision of the position of Aquinas, in dialogue with Geach among others, and in a way which resonates with Balthasar's notion of the mutuality of the relationship between us and God but arguably at the expense of an ultimately unsatisfactory distinction between God's actual and intentional being, see W. J. Hill, 'Does God Know the Future? Aquinas and Some Moderns', *TS*, 36 (1975), 3–18, and 'The Historicity of God', *TS*, 45 (1984), 320–33.

25 Geach, 'The Future', 209.
26 Geach, *Providence*, 58.
27 See Davies, *Thinking About God*, 216–29 for a less agnostic treatment of the difficulty to which Geach adverts.
28 Kenny, *The God of the Philosophers*, 53–9.
29 Kenny, *The God of the Philosophers*, 41; Geach, 'The Future', 214.
30 Geach, *Providence*, 24ff; Stump and Kretzmann, 'Eternity', 243–6.
31 See also Davies, *Thinking About God*, 184–93.
32 See Jonathan L. Kvanvig, *The Possibility*
33 *Ibid.*, 164.
34 See *ibid.*, 5–13 for a detailed discussion of Geach's position.
35 *Ibid.*, 119.
36 *Ibid.*, 121–49; 166–71.
37 *Ibid.*, 124ff.
38 *Ibid.*, 167.
39 See B.J.F. Lonergan, *Grace and Freedom* (London, 1971), 103–16, *Insight* (New York, 1958), *passim*, especially chapter 11 ff; W. Kasper, *The God of Jesus Christ* (trans., London, 1982), 87–99 (a presentation of the argument for a correspondence notion of truth).
40 See Kvanvig, *The Possibility*, 27f, 127f.
41 See Lonergan, *Grace and Freedom*, 103–9.
42 See Lonergan, *Grace and Freedom*, *passim*; also *Insight*, chapter 19.
43 See Kvanvig, *The Possibility*, 151–65.
44 *Ibid.*, 118–21.
45 *Ibid.*, 162–5.
46 *Ibid.*, 163.
47 *Ibid.*, 163.
48 Lonergan, *Grace and Freedom*, 105.
49 See p. 106 above.
50 See D.H. Mellor, *Real Time* (Cambridge, 1981).
51 *Ibid.*, 1–12.
52 *Ibid.*, 5.
53 *Ibid.*, 6.
54 *Ibid.*, 6.

55 *Ibid.*, 10.
56 *Ibid.*, 10.
57 *Ibid.*, 34.
58 *Ibid.*, 39–40.
59 For example P. Davies would seem to support Mellor's position, while R. Sorabji clearly does not: see P. Davies *God and the New Physics* (London, 1983), 119–35; W. Lane Craig, review of *Time, Creation and the Continuum*, by Richard Sorabji, *IPQ*, 25 (1985), 319–26. For a detailed refutation of Mellor's position see D. Braine, *The Reality of Time and the Existence of God* (Oxford, 1988), chapter 2 and *passim*. Braine uses the image of a furnace rather than a geometrical point to illustrate that God's activity and life are eternal in a way which admits of logically distinguishable aspects, with even certain kinds of priority between them, but with the absence of the distinction found in temporally causal and factual explanations (132ff; 349–53; 357ff). There is much support in Braine's approach to this and related issues for Balthasar's overall position. It does seem to me however – and regrettably this very interesting book came to my attention too late to offer a more detailed treatment or anything but a rather tentative assessment – that Braine's way of preserving human freedom and God's surprise *re* the future (within which the notion of the 'dramatic now' plays a pivotal part) depends too much on an understanding of God's knowledge as dependent on the existence of the world. That God knows us through self-knowledge, and that this still allows for our otherness and freedom, is the more coherent intelligibility outlined by Balthasar's trinitarian reading of the relationship between divine omniscience and love. In this latter approach the transcendence of God is maintained and Braine would better realise his own desire to eliminate any movement from potency to act in God, which J. Bracken sees as a logical conclusion of Braine's position. See J. Bracken, *TS*, 50 (1988), 175–6. For reference to Braine's position vis-à-vis Mellor see also H. Meynell, *Philosophy*, 64 (1989), 119–20.
60 See Mellor, *Real Time*, 2, 68.
61 See Dr Arthur H. Williams, 'The Trinity and Time', *SJT*, 39 (1986), 65–81.
62 See *ibid.*, 76 and p. 89 above on objective and subjective time in Augustine.
63 See also P. Davies, *God and the New Physics*, 100–18, especially 107.
64 For further discussion of the relevance of relativity theory for an understanding of time which is congruent with the basic position of Stump and Kretzmann, see P. Davies, *God and the New Physics*, chapter 9, and Lonergan, *Insight*, chapter 5.
65 For some indication of Balthasar's own views on linguistic analysis in particular as a philosophical movement, see *HC*, 248. See also Kasper, *The God of Jesus Christ*, 87–99 for a more detailed discussion of this issue.

6 Final assessment

1 It would seem that P. Sequeri's considered criticism of Balthasar's theology of the divine immutability in *MP* misses some of these nuances. Sequeri, 'Cristologie', 119–21 is correct in suggesting that if one applied a modified Hegelian model of the identity and immutability of the subject, in his movement of identification with the other, to the semantically different and pre-modern ontology of the immutability of the divine being then there would result a Modalistic interpretation of divine immutability. But Balthasar's approach is more subtle than this: he allows for a supra-mutability of the divine being (not simply the traditional ontology of no created change), and is careful to combine an intra-subjective with an inter-subjective approach. Furthermore he allows for the distinctions to be observed when moving from the notion of human love (between different beings) to the love between Persons who are one being in the Trinity. Similarly J. Macquarrie, *The Humility of God* (London, 1978), appears to attribute an almost univocal vulnerability to God which does not take sufficient account of the kind of nuanced adjustments that are necessary and are present in Balthasar's use of analogical discourse.

2 Despite the limited thematic treatment, Balthasar's theology of the divine immutability is considerably more nuanced and developed than the position proposed in the programmatic piece of H. Mühlen – see Mühlen, 'Cristologie', *passim*.

3 *TD*, IV, 214, note 11, 447; Jöhri, *Descensus*, 385–9, 395–8; de Schrijver, *Le Merveilleux Accord*, 332–3.

4 For a more detailed discussion of the meaning and role of hypothesis in theological method, see P. McShane, 'The Hypothesis of Intelligible Emanations in God', *TS*, 23 (1962), 545–68.

5 See the report of the International Theological Commission on Theology, Christology, Anthropology in *ITQ*, 49 (1982), 285–300. See also D. Carroll, *A Pilgrim God for a Pilgrim People* (Dublin, 1988), chapter 9, especially 163–74.

6 For what follows, see Heinz, *Der Gott*, 51–66 (especially 62–6), 209–11; Maas, *Die Hölle*, 254–6.

7 We note in particular the debate in North America along these lines, involving such scholars as J. Donceel, D. Burrell, W. J. Hill, J. Bracken and W. Norris Clarke; see Bibliography for references. See also S. Sia, 'The Doctrine of God's Immutability: Introducing the Modern Debate', *New Blackfriars*, 68 (1987), 220–32.

8 Heinz, *Der Gott*, 62–3; O'Hanlon, *Metaphysics*, 192–3.

9 Heinz, *Der Gott*, 209–11.

10 *TL*, I, viii.

11 See John M. McDermott, 'A New Voice for American Theology', *America*, 26 November 1977, 374–6 (375); O'Hanlon, *Metaphysics*, 8–11.

12 *VC*², 64–5.

13 See Maas, *Unveränderlichkeit, passim*, and especially 42–53.

14 See O'Hanlon, *May Christians Hope?, passim*.

Bibliography

Works by Hans Urs von Balthasar

This section of the Bibliography gives a list, in order of publication, of the works consulted: for a more comprehensive catalogue of Balthasar's works, including those available in translation, see B. Widmer, *Rechenschaft 1965*. *Balthasar-Bibliographie 1965* (Einsiedeln, 1965); C. Capol, *Hans Urs von Balthasar, Bibliographie, 1925–75* (Einsiedeln, 1975); C. Capol, *Hans Urs von Balthasar, Bibliographie, 1925–1980* (Einsiedeln, 1981). All the works of Balthasar are cited in the original version: where the translated version is also cited it is to this version that citations in the text and notes refer, except in the case of *Herrlichkeit*, II/1, II/2 and III/1, where citations always refer to the original version.

Books

Geschichte des eschatologischen Problems in der modernen deutschen Literatur (Zürich, 1930)

Apokalypse der deutschen Seele, I *Der deutsche Idealismus* (Salzburg, 1937)

Apokalypse der deutschen Seele, II *Im Zeichen Nietzsches* (Salzburg, 1939)

Apokalypse der deutschen Seele, III *Die Vergöttlichung des Todes* (Salzburg, 1939)

Présence et pensée, Essai sur la philosophie réligieuse de Grégoire de Nysse (Paris, 1942)

Das Weizenkorn (Luzern, 1944; 2nd ed., Einsiedeln, 1953).

Das Herz der Welt (Zürich, 1945), trans. as *Cœur du Monde*, 4th ed. (Paris, 1956)

Wahrheit, I: *Wahrheit der Welt* (Einsiedeln, 1947). Reissued, with a new introduction, as *Theologik*, I: *Wahrheit der Welt* (Einsiedeln, 1985)

Der Laie und der Ordensstand (Einsiedeln, 1948)

Thérèse von Lisieux (Cologne/Olten, 1950), trans. as *Thérèse of Lisieux* (London, 1953)

Karl Barth (Cologne/Olten, 1951), trans. as *The Theology of Karl Barth* (New York, 1971)

Der Christ und die Angst (Einsiedeln, 1952)

Elisabeth von Dijon und ihre geistliche Sendung (Cologne/Olten, 1952) trans. as *Elisabeth of Dijon* (London, 1956)

Schleifung der Bastionen (Einsiedeln, 1952)

Rheinhold Schneider. Sein Weg und sein Werk (Cologne/Olten, 1953)

Thomas von Aquin. Besondre Gnadengaben und die zwei Wege menschlichen Lebens (Heidelberg, Graz-Vienna-Salzburg, 1954)

Bernanos (Cologne/Olten, 1954); 2nd ed., *Gelebte Kirche. Bernanos* (Einsiedeln, 1971)

Das betrachtende Gebet (Einsiedeln, 1955), trans. as *Prayer* (London, 1961)

Thessalonicher-und Pastoralbriefe (Einsiedeln, 1955)

Die Gottesfrage des heutigen Menschen (Vienna, 1956), trans. as *Science, Religion and Christianity* (London, 1958)

Parole et Mystère chez Origène (Paris, 1957)

Einsame Zwiesprache. Martin Buber und das Christentum (Cologne/Olten, 1958), trans. as *Martin Buber and Christianity* (London, 1961)

Theologie der Geschichte (Einsiedeln, 1959), trans. as *A Theology of History* (New York and London, 1963)

Verbum Caro. Skizzen zur Theologie, I (Einsiedeln, 1960), trans. as *Essays in Theology I. Word and Revelation* (New York, 1964), *Essays in Theology II. Word and Redemption* (New York, 1965)

Sponsa Verbi. Skizzen zur Theologie, I (Einsiedeln, 1960), trans. as *Church and World* (New York, 1967) (contains four of the original fifteen essays)

Kosmische Liturgie. Das Weltbild Mazimus des Bekenners (Einsiedeln, 1961)

Herrlichkeit. Eine theologische Ästhetik, I: *Schau der Gestalt* (Einsiedeln, 1961), trans. as *The Glory of the Lord*, I: *Seeing the Form* (Edinburgh, 1982)

Herrlichkeit. Eine theologische Ästhetik, II: *Fächer der Stile* (Einsiedeln, 1962). A 2nd ed. appeared in two vols. in 1969: II/1, *Klerikale Stile* (Einsiedeln); II/2, *Laikale Stile* (Einsiedeln), trans. as *The Glory of the Lord, A Theological Aesthetics*, II: *Studies in Theological Style: Clerical Styles* (Edinburgh, 1984); III: *Lay Styles* (Edinburgh, 1986)

Das Ganze im Fragment (Einsiedeln, 1963), trans. as *Man in History* (London and Sydney, 1967)

Glaubhaft ist nur Liebe (Einsiedeln, 1963) trans. as *Love Alone: The Way of Revelation* (London, 1968)

Der Kreuzweg der St.-Hedwigs-Kathedrale in Berlin (Mainz, 1964), trans. as *The Way of the Cross* (New York and London, 1969)

Herrlichkeit. Eine theologische Ästhetik, III/1: *Im Raum der Metaphysik* (Eindiedeln, 1965), first vol. trans. as *The Glory of the Lord. IV: The Realm of Metaphysics in Antiquity* (Edinburgh, 1989)

Wer ist ein Christ? (Einsiedeln, 1965), trans. as *Who is a Christian?* (London, 1968)

Rechenschaft 1965 (Einsiedeln, 1965), trans. as 'In Retrospect', *Communio, International Catholic Review*, 2 (1975), 197–200

Cordula oder der Ernstfall (Einsiedeln, 1966), trans. as *The Moment of Christian Witness* (New York, 1968)

Herrlichkeit. Eine theologische Ästhetik, III/2, 1.Teil: *Alter bund* (Einsiedeln, 1967)

Spiritus Creator. Skizzen zur Theologie, III (Einsiedeln, 1967)

Erster Blick auf Adrienne von Speyr (Einsiedeln, 1967)

La Foi du Christ (Paris, 1968)

Theologie der drei Tage (Einsiedeln, 1969) (This work also appeared as *Mysterium Pascale*, in *Mysterium Salutis*, III/2, ed. J. Feiner and M. Löhrer (Einsiedeln/Cologne 1970), 133–326. Trans. as *Pâques le Mystère*, 2nd ed. (Paris, 1981)

Herrlichkeit. Eine theologische Ästhetik, III/2, 2.Teil: *Neuer Bund* (Einsiedeln, 1969)

Einfaltungen (München, 1969)

Romano Guardini. Reform aus dem Ursprung (München, 1970)

Klarstellungen (Freiburg, 1971), trans. as *Elucidations* (London, 1975)

In Gottes Einsatz leben (Einsiedeln, 1971), trans. *Engagement with God* (London, 1975)

Die Wahrheit ist symphonisch (Einsiedeln, 1972)

Theodramatik, I: *Prolegomena* (Einsiedeln, 1973)

Der antirömische Affekt (Freiburg, 1974)

Pneuma und Institution. Skizzen zur Theologie, IV (Einsiedeln, 1974)

Katholisch (Einsiedeln, 1975), trans. as *Catholique* (Paris, 1976)

Henri de Lubac (Einsiedeln, 1976)

Theodramatik, II: *Die Personen des Spiels*, 1.Teil: *Der Mensch in Gott* (Einsiedeln, 1976)

Der dreifache Kranz (Einsiedeln, 1977), trans. as *Triple couronne* (Paris, 1978)

Christlicher Stand (Einsiedeln, 1977)

Weihnacht und Anbetung (privately printed, 1977)

Theodramatik, II: *Die Personen des Spieles*, 2.Teil: *Die Personen in Christus* (Einsiedeln, 1978)

Neue Klarstellungen (Einsiedeln, 1979)

Die Stille des Wortes (privately printed, 1979)

Kennt uns Jesus – Kennen wir ihn? (Freiburg-Basel-Vienna, 1980)

Kleine Fibel für verunsicherte Laien (Einsiedeln, 1980), trans. as *Aux croyants incertains* (Paris, 1980)

Theodramatik, III: *Die Handlung* (Einsiedeln, 1980)

Au Cœur du Mystère rédempteur. (with text by Adrienne von Speyr) (Paris, 1980)

Il filo di Arianna attraverso la mia opera (Milan, 1980)

'Du Krönst das Jahr mit Deiner Huld', Psalm, 65, 12. Radiopredigten (Einsiedeln, 1982)

Theodramatik, IV: *Endspeil* (Einsiedeln, 1983)

Christen sind einfältig (Einsiedeln, 1983)

Theologik, I: *Wahrheit der Welt* (Einsiedeln, 1983)

Theologik, II: *Wahrheit Gottes* (Einsiedeln, 1985)

Skizzen zur Theologie, V: *Homo Creatus Est* (Einsiedeln, 1986)

Theologik, III: *Der Geist der Wahrheit* (Einsiedeln, 1987)

Epilog (Einsiedeln, 1987)

Articles/contributions to other works

'Thomas von Aquin im kirchlichen Denken von heute', *Gloria Dei*, 8 (1953), 65–76

'Warum ich noch ein Christ bin?', in *Zwei Plädoyers*, compiled with J. Ratzinger (Munich, 1971), 11–52, trans. as *Two Say Why* (London, 1973)

'Aktualität der Gnosis', in *Was heißt – 'Wiederkunft Christi'?*, ed. Paul Schütz (Freiburg, 1972), 42–7

'Das Katholische an der Kirche', *Kölner Beiträge*, 10 (1972), 1–19

'Neun Thesen zur christlichen Ethik', in *Prinzipien christlicher Moral*, compiled with J. Ratzinger (ed.) and Heinz Schürmann (Einsiedeln, 1975) 67–93

'Evangelium und Philosophie', *Freiburger Zeitschrift für Philosophie und Theologie*, 23 (1976), 3–12

'Exegese und Dogmatik', *IKaZ*, 5.5 (1976), 385–92

'Geist und Feuer. Ein Gespräch mit Hans Urs von Balthasar', *Herder Korrespondenz*, 30 February 1976, 72–82. (The interviewer is Michael Albus.)

'Zugänge zu Christus', in *Wer ist Jesus Christus?*, ed. J. Sauer (Freiburg, 1977)

'Crucifixus etiam pro nobis', *IKaZ*, 9.1 (1980), 26–35

'Die neue Theorie von Jesus als dem "Sündenbock"', *IKaZ*, 9.2 (1980), 184–5

'Gericht', *IKaZ*, 9.3 (1980), 227–35

'Alle Wege führen zum Kreuz, *IKaZ*, 9.4 (1980), 333–42

'Der sich für mich dahingegeben hat (Gal.2, 20)', *Geist und Leben*, 53.6 (1980), 416–19

'Plus loin que la mort', *Revue Internat. Cath. Communio*, 6 (1981), 2–4

'Adrienne von Speyr. Über das Geheimnis des Karsamstags', *IKaZ*, 10 (1981), 32–9

'Drei Formen der Gelassenheit', *Geist und Leben*, 54 (1981), 270–5

'Zu einer christlichen Theologie der Hoffnung', *Münchner Theol. Zeit.*, 32 (1981), 81–102

'Liebe steigt "von oben" ab', *Geist und Leben*, 55 (1982), 87–91

'Regagner une philosophie à partir de la théologie', in *Pour une philosophie chrétienne*, ed. P-Ph. Druet (Paris, 1982)

'Der Tod vom Leben verschlungen', *IKaZ*, 11.1 (1982), 1–5

'Maria und der Geist', *Geist und Leben*, 56 (1983), 173–7

'From the Theology of God to Theology in the Church', *The Clergy Review*, 68 (1983), 79–94

'Die Jugendlichkeit Jesu', *IKaZ*, 12 (1983), 301–5

'Gottes Allmacht', *IKaZ*, 13 (1984), 193–200

'Die Einheit der theologischen Tugenden', *IKaZ*, 13 (1984), 306–14

Works about Hans Urs von Balthasar

Once again this list is restricted to the works consulted: for a more comprehensive catalogue of the secondary literature on Balthasar, see M.

Lochbrunner, *Analogia Caritatis* (Freiburg, 1981); M. Jöhri, *Descensus Dei* (Rome, 1981)

Béguin, A., *Préface de théologie de l'histoire* (Paris, 1955), 1–14.

Escobar, P., 'Das Universale Concretum Jesu Christi und die "Eschatologische Reduktion" bei Hans Urs von Balthasar', *ZfKT*, 100 (1978), 560–95

Faux, J.M., 'Un Théologien: Hans Urs von Balthasar', *NRT*, 94 (1972), 1009–30

Heinz, H., *Der Gott des Je-Mehr. Der christologische Ansatz Hans Urs von Balthasar* (Bern/Frankfurt, 1975)

Hyde, J., 'A Dhia Mhóir – Seanliodán. Machnamh Diagaire', *Milltown Studies*, 3 (1979), 109–12

'Another Method in Theology', *Horizons*, 13 (1979), 14–16

Jöhri, M., *Descensus Dei. Teologia della Croce nell'opera di Hans Urs von Balthasar* (Rome, 1981)

Kay, J., 'H.U. von Balthasar, Post-Critical Theologian?', *Concilium*, 141–6 (1981), 84–9

Kehl, M., and Löser, W., eds., *In der Fülle des Glaubens, Hans Urs von Balthasar – Leserbuch* (Freiburg, 1980), with Introduction by Kehl, trans. as *The von Balthasar Reader* (Edinburgh, 1982)

Lochbrunner, M., 'Hans Urs von Balthasar. Ein Werkporträt zum 75. Geburtstag', *Die Welt der Bücher*, 6.4 (1980), 145–54

Analogia Caritatis. Darstellung und Deutung der Theologie Hans Urs von Balthasar (Freiburg, 1981)

Löser, W., 'Das Sein – ausgelegt als Liebe', *IKaZ*, 4 (1975), 410–24

Im Geiste des Origenes (Frankfurt, 1976)

Darstellung einiger repräsentativer christologischer Entwürfe des 20 Jahrhunderts (Frankfurt, 1979–80) (unpublished lecture notes)

'Trinitätsthelogie heute. Ansätze und Entwürfe, in W. Breunning, ed., *Trinität. Aktuelle Perspektiven der Theologie, OD*, 101 (Freiburg, 1984), 19–45

de Lubac, H., 'A Witness of Christ in the Church', in *The Church, Paradox and Mystery* (trans. Shannon, 1969), 103–21. Also in *Communio, International Catholic Review*, 2 (1975), 228–49

McDermott, J., 'A New Voice for American Theology', *America*, 26 November 1977, 374–6

McKinnon, D., 'A Master in Israel: Hans Urs von Balthasar', *The Clergy Review*, 54 (1969), 859–69. (For an extended version of this article, see the introduction to Balthasar's *Engagement with God*)

Marchesi, G., *La Cristologia di Hans Urs von Balthasar* (Rome, 1977)

'Hans Urs von Balthasar e la Sinfonia della Verita cristiana', *La Civilta Cattolica*, 135 (1984), 119–33

Nichols, A., 'Balthasar and his Christology', *New Blackfriars*, 66 (1985), 317–24

O'Donnel, J.J., 'The Trinity in Recent German Theology', *Heythrop Journal*, 23 (1982), 153–67

'Man and Woman as *Imago Dei* in the Theology of Hans Urs von Balthasar', *The Clergy Review*, 68 (1983), 117–28

O'Donoghue, N.D., 'A Theology of Beauty', *ITQ*, 50 (1983–4), 250–6

O'Hanlon, G', 'H.U. von Balthasar and *De Deo Uno* – New Tract?' *Milltown Studies*, 5 (1980), 115–30

'The Theological Metaphysics of Hans Urs von Balthasar', unpublished S.T.L. dissertation (Dublin, 1980)

'Does God Change? H. U. von Balthasar and the Immutability of God', *ITQ*, 53 (1987), 161–83

'Von Balthasar and Ecclesial States of Life', *Milltown Studies*, 22 (1988), 111–17

Olsen, G.W., 'Hans Urs von Balthasar and the Rehabilitation of St Anselm's Doctrine of the Atonement', *SJT*, 34 (1981), 49–61

Palaccio, C., 'L'Obéissance chrétienne. Etude comparative de quelques christologies actuelles en relation à l'obéissance de Jésus', *Concilium*, 159 (1980), 105–117

Peelman, A., *Hans Urs von Balthasar et la théologie de l'histoire* (Bern/Frankfurt, 1978)

Rahner, K., 'Hans Urs von Balthasar', *Civitas*, 20 (1964–5), 601–4

Riches, J., 'The Theology of Hans Urs von Balthasar', *Theology*, 45 (1972), 562–70, 647–55

(ed.) *The Analogy of Beauty* (Edinburgh, 1986)

de Schrijver, G., *Le Merveilleux Accord de l'homme et de Dieu, Etude de l'analogie de l'être chez Hans Urs von Balthasar* (Louvain, 1983)

Schwager, R., 'Der Sohn Gottes und die Weltsünde. Zur Erlösungslehre von H. Urs von Balthasar', *ZfKT*, 108 (1986), 5–44

Sequeri, P., 'Cristologie nel quadro della problematica della mutabilità e passibilità di Dio: Balthasar, Küng, Mühlen, Moltmann, Galot', *La Scuola Cattolica*, 105 (1977), 114–51

Vorgrimler, H., 'Hans Urs von Balthasar', in *Bilanz der Theologie im 20 Jahrhundert*, IV (Freiburg, 1970), 122–42

Other works consulted

Baillie, D.M., *God Was in Christ, an Essay on Incarnation and Atonement* (London, 1948)

Barden, G., 'An Incoherent God?', *Doctrine and Life*, 34 (1985), 541–2

Barth, K., *Church Dogmatics*, IV, 2 (trans., Edinburgh, 1958)

Bracken, J., 'The Two Process Theologies: A Reappraisal', *TS*, 46 (1985), 115–28

review of D. Braine, *The Reality of Time and the Existence of God, TS*, 50 (1989), 175–6

Braine, D., *The Reality of Time and the Existence of God* (Oxford, 1988)

Brantschen, J.B., 'Die Macht und Ohnmacht der Liebe', Randglossen zum dogmatischen Satz: Gott ist unveränderlich, *Freiburger Zeitschrift für Philosophie und Theologie*, 27 (1980), 224–46

Brown, R., *The Community of the Beloved Disciple* (London, 1979)

Burrell, D., *Aquinas, God and Action* (London, 1979)
  'Does Process Theology rest on a mistake?', *TS*, 43 (1982), 125–35
Carroll, D., *A Pilgrim God for a Pilgrim People* (Dublin, 1988)
Norris Clarke, W., *The Philosophical Approach to God* (North Carolina, 1979)
Craig, W.L., review of Richard Sorabji, *Time, Creation and the Continuum*, *International Philosophical Quarterly*, 25 (1985), 319–26
Daly, G., *Creation and Redemption* (Dublin, 1988)
Davies, B., *Thinking about God* (London, 1985)
Davies, P., *God and the New Physics* (London, 1983)
Dodds, M.J., 'St Thomas Aquinas and the Motion of the Motionless God', *New Blackfriars*, 68 (1987), 233–42
Donceel, J., 'Can our God never Change?', *Theology Digest*, 20 (1972), 207–12
Dunne, T., 'Trinity and History', *TS*, 45 (1984), 139–52
Galvin, J.P., 'The Death of Jesus in the Theology of Edward Schillebeeckx', *ITQ*, 50 (1983–4), 168–80
Geach, P.T., *New Blackfriars*, 54 (1973), 208–18
  Providence and Evil (Cambridge, 1977)
Hanratty, G., 'The Early Gnostics', *ITQ*, 51 (1985), 208–24
Hasker, W., 'Yes, God has Beliefs!', *Religious Studies*, 24 (1988), 385–94
Haughton, R., *The Passionate God* (London, 1981)
Hemmerle, K., *Thesen zu einer trinitarischen Ontologie* (Einsiedeln, 1976)
Hengel, M., *Crucifixion* (trans., Philadelphia, 1978)
Hill, W.J., 'Does God Know the Future? Aquinas and Some Moderns', *TS*, 36 (1975), 3–18
  'The Historicity of God', *TS*, 45 (1984), 320–33
'International Theological Commission: Theology, Christology, Anthropology', *ITQ*, 49 (1982), 285–300
Jüngel, E., *The Doctrine of the Trinity' God's Being is in Becoming* (trans., Edinburgh and London, 1976)
Kasper, W., *The God of Jesus Christ* (trans., London, 1982)
Kehl, M. and Löser, W., 'Situation de la théologie systematique en Allemagne', *Revue de Theologie et Philosophie*, 113 (1981), 25–38
Keller, J., 'Basic Differences between Classical and Process Metaphysics and their Implications for the Concept of God', *International Philosophical Quarterly*, 22 (1982), 3–20
Kenny, 'Divine Foreknowledge and Human Freedom', in *Aquinas*, ed. A. Kenny (London 1969), 255–70
  The God of the Philosophers (Oxford, 1979)
Knauer, P., 'Die chalzedonensische Christologie als Kriterium für jedes christliche Glaubensverständnis', *Theologie und Philosophie*, 60 (1985), 1–15
Kondoleon, T.J., 'The Immutability of God: Some Recent Challenges', *The New Scholasticism*, 58 (1984), 293–315
Kretzmann, N., 'Omniscience and Immutability', *Journal of Philosophy*, 63 (1966), 409–21

Küng, H., *Justification: The Doctrine of Karl Barth and a Catholic Reflection*, (trans., London, 1964)

Kvanvig, J. L., *The Possibility of an All-Knowing God* (London, 1986)

Lee, B.J., 'The Two Process Theologies', *TS*, 45 (1984), 307–19

Lonergan, B.J.F., *Insight* (New York, 1958)

   De Verbo Incarnato (Rome, 1961)

   Collection (London, 1967)

   Grace and Freedom (London, 1971)

   Method in Theology (New York, 1972)

Maas, W., *Unveränderlichkeit Gottes, Zum Verhältnis von griechisch-philosophischer und christlicher Gotteslehre* (Munich-Padeborn-Vienna, 1974)

   Gott und die Hölle. Studien zum Descensus Christi (Einsiedeln, 1979)

   'Jusq'où est descendu le Fils', *Revue Internat. Cath. Communio*, 6 (1981), 5–19

McCabe, H., 'The Involvement of God', *New Blackfriars*, 66 (1985), 464–76

McDade, J., 'The Trinity and the Paschal Mystery', *The Heythrop Journal*, 29 (1980), 175–91

McEvoy, J., 'St Augustine's Account of Time and Wittgenstein's Criticisms', *Review of Metaphysics*, 37 (1984), 549–77

Macken, J., *The Autonomy Theme in Karl Barth's Church Dogmatics and in Current Barth Criticism* (Inaugural dissertation, Tübingen, 1984)

Macquarrie, J., *The Humility of God* (London, 1978)

Mann, W. E., 'Simplicity and Immutability in God', in *The Concept of God*, ed. T. V. Morris (Oxford, 1987), 253–67

Maritain, J., 'Quelques réflexions sur le savoir théologique', *Revue Thomiste*, 77 (1969), 5–27

Marsh, J., *The Fullness of Time* (London, 1952)

Mascall, E.L., *Whatever Happened to the Human Mind?* (London, 1980)

Mellow, D. H., *Real Time* (Cambridge, 1981)

Merkle, J.C., 'Heschel's Theology of Divine Pathos', *Louvain Studies*, 10 (1984), 151–65

Meynell, H., review of D. Braine, *The Reality of Time and the Existence of God*, *Philosophy*, 64 (1989), 119–20

Moltmann, J., *The Crucified God* (trans., London, 1974)

   The Trinity and the Kingdom of God (trans., London, 1981)

Moore, S., *The Inner Loneliness* (London, 1982)

Mühlen, H., 'Christologie im Horizont der Traditionellen Seinsfrage? Auf dem Wege zu einer Kreuzestheologie in Auseinandersetzung mit der altchristlichen Christologie', *Catholica*, 23 (1969), 205–39

Mueller, J.J., 'Process Theology and the Catholic Theological Community', *TS*, 47 (1986), 412–27

New Blackfriars, 58 (1987), 212–67: issue on God and change

North, R., 'Violence and the Bible: The Girard Connection', *The Catholic Biblical Quarterly*, 47 (1985), 1–27

O'Collins, G., *Interpreting Jesus* (London, 1983)

O'Donnell, J., *Trinity and Temporality* (Oxford, 1983)

The Mystery of the Triune God (London, 1988)

The Trinity as Divine Community, *Gregorianum*, 69 (1988), 5–36

O'Donovan, L., 'The Mystery of God as History of Love: Eberhard Jungel's Doctrine of God', *TS*, 42 (1981), 251–71

O'Hanlon, G., 'An Image of God for Ireland To-day', *Milltown Studies*, 21 (1988), 13–27

'May Christians Hope for a Better World?', *ITQ*, 54 (1988), 175–89

'Devotion to the Heart of Christ, a Theological Reappraisal', *Milltown Studies*, 24 (1989), 48–65

Pedersen, O., 'The God of Space and Time', *Concilium*, 166–70 (1983), 14–20

Rahner, K., *Schriften zur Theologie*, IV (Einsiedeln, 1964); XV (Einsiedeln, 1983)

Die Gabe der Weihnacht (Herder, 1980)

'Vom Geheimnis menschlicher Schuld und göttlicher Vergebung', *Geist und Leben*, 55 (1982), 39–54

'Versöhnung und Stellvertretung', *Geist und Leben*, 56 (1983), 98–110

Rattigan, M.T., 'The Concept of God in Process Thought', *ITQ*, 49 (1982), 206–15

Ratzinger, J., *Behold The Pierced One* (trans., San Fransisco, 1986)

Salmann, E., 'Unverbundenheit und Stellvertretung', *Münchner Theol. Zeit'.* 35 (1984), 17–31

'Gnade und Leid. Zur Leidensmystik bei Anna Katharina Emmerick', *Geist und Leben*, 57 (1984), 322–36

'Offenbarung und Neuzeit (christologische Überlegungen zur geistesgeschichtlichen Situation', *Freiburger Zeitschrift für Philosophie und Theologie*, 31 (1984), 109–54

Scheffczyk, L., 'Prozeßtheismus und christlicher Grottesglaube', *Munchner Theol. Zeit.*, 35 (1984), 81–104

Schwager, R., review of W. Kasper, 'Der Gott Jesu Christ', *ZfKT*, 105 (1983), 337–40

Segundo, J., *Our Idea of God* (trans., New York, 1974)

Sia, S., 'On God, Time and Change', *The Clergy Review*, 63 (1978), 378–86

'An Interview with Charles Hartshorne', *Milltown Studies*, 4 (1979), 1–23

'The Doctrine of God's Immutability: Introducing the Modern Debate', *New Blackfriars*, 68 (1987), 220–32

von Speyr, A., *Kreuz und Hölle*, I (privately printed, Einsiedeln, 1966)

Stump, E. and Kretzmann, N., 'Eternity', in *The Concept of God*, ed. T. V. Morris (Oxford, 1987), 219–52

Thomas Aquinas, *Summa Theologica*, Prima Pars, B.A.C. ed. (Salamanca, 1955)

In Librum Boetii de Trinitate Exposito, ed. Paul Wyser, O.P. (Fribourg, 1948)

Thompson, J., 'The Humanity of God in the Theology of Karl Barth', *SJT*, 29 (1976), 249–69

Christ in Perspective, Christological Perspectives in the Theology of Karl Barth (Edinburgh, 1978)

Trethowen, I., *Mysticism and Theology* (London, 1975)

Weinandy, T.G., *Does God Change?* (Massachusetts, 1985)

Wild, R., *Who I Will Be: Is there Joy and Suffering in God?* (New Jersey, 1976)

Williams, A. H., 'The Trinity and Time', *SJT*, 39 (1986), 65–81

Wong, J.H.P., 'Karl Rahner's Christology of Symbol', *The Heythrop Journal*, 27 (1986), 1–25

Index of names

Index of subjects